THE COMPLETE IDIOT'S GUIDE® TO

Songwriting

by Joel Hirschhorn

ALPHA

A Pearson Education Company

To Jennifer, with appreciation for her love, her support, and her creative brilliance.

Copyright © 2001 by Joel Hirschhorn

International Standard Book Number: 0-02-864144-2
Library of Congress Catalog Card Number: 200188754

03   02   01   8   7   6   5   4   3   2   1

Interpretation of the printing code: The rightmost number of the first series of numbers is the year of the book's printing; the rightmost number of the second series of numbers is the number of the book's printing. For example, a printing code of 01-1 shows that the first printing occurred in 2001.

Printed in the United States of America

Note: This publication contains the opinions and ideas of its author. It is intended to provide helpful and informative material on the subject matter covered. It is sold with the understanding that the author and publisher are not engaged in rendering professional services in the book. If the reader requires personal assistance or advice, a competent professional should be consulted.

The author and publisher specifically disclaim any responsibility for any liability, loss, or risk, personal or otherwise, which is incurred as a consequence, directly or indirectly, of the use and application of any of the contents of this book.

Publisher
Marie Butler-Knight

Product Manager
Phil Kitchel

Managing Editor
Jennifer Chisholm

Acquisitions Editor
Amy Zavatto

Development Editor
Doris Cross

Senior Production Editor
Christy Wagner

Copy Editor
Heather Stith

Illustrator
Chris Sabatino

Cover Designers
Mike Freeland
Kevin Spear

Book Designers
Scott Cook and Amy Adams of DesignLab

Indexer
Angie Bess

Layout/Proofreading
Svetlana Dominguez
Cheryl Lynch
Lizbeth Patterson

Contents at a Glance

Part 1: How to Write a Hit   **1**

1 Music Training: Is It a Must?   3
Make the most of your musical education.

2 A Century of Songwriting   13
A look at some of the factors that make a song a hit, from the era of vaudeville to the age of videos.

3 The Idea Is King   25
Absorb every influence for inspiration and stop suffering from writer's block.

4 What Comes First, Words or Music?   37
Well-known songwriters weigh in on this chicken-and-the-egg debate.

5 Finding and Keeping Collaborators   47
Communication is the name of the game in establishing a successful musical marriage.

6 Title Power!   59
A good title helps to tell the song's story and hook the audience.

Part 2: Dressing Up the Song   **69**

7 The Visual Songwriter   71
Develop your visual sense, use all your senses in your songwriting, and you might see a hit record.

8 Cooking Up Your Hit Ingredients   79
With a savory song structure and a rich rhyme scheme (add a dash of alliteration), you can create a tasty tune.

9 Repetition and Hooks   89
You can say that again!

10 The Secrets of Hit Melody Writing   101
Get the best grooves and killer chords, and you'll be on your way to success.

11 Rewriting   111
Fight to make it right.

Part 3: Genre Gold   **123**

12 Crossing Into Country   125
Let simple chords and honest heartache lead you to the Grand Ole Opry.

13 R&B and Rap 135
Rhythm plus passion equals chart success.

14 Commercials and Children's Music 147
The joy of jingles and the charm of children.

15 Movie Scoring and Songwriting 159
From Hammerstein to Horner: how composers match their music to the movies.

16 Live and Animated Musicals 171
Capturing movie characters with words and music.

17 Musicals for the Stage 181
How to write tunes that win Tonys.

Part 4: Showing It Off **197**

18 The Power of a Hit Demo 199
Making a model of a hit song.

19 Becoming a Great Song Salesman 211
Networking your way to your next hit.

20 The Singer/Songwriter 223
Creating an image as an artist and a writer.

21 Home Studio 233
Have the convenience of recording whenever the mood strikes you.

22 Producing Your Own Hit Songs 243
Writing, recording, arranging, mixing—it's all you.

Part 5: Finishing Touches **255**

23 Royalties and Guilds 257
How BMI and ASCAP help you get what you have coming to you.

24 What's Happening in Songwriting? 271
The effects of the Internet on the songwriting industry, and how the Grammys signal musical trends.

Appendixes

A Glossary 287

B Resources 291

C Contests and Competitions 297

Index 299

Contents

Part 1: How to Write a Hit   **1**

1   Music Training: Is It a Must?   **3**

Looking at the Hit-Makers...3
  Is There Success Without Counterpoint? 5
  Prestige vs. Poverty 5
Don't Delay Your Dreams 6
  From the Harbor Club to Elvis 6
  Make It Big Through a Local Gig 7
  Accompany Your Way to a Hit 7
  Play Sessions 7
  Join an Orchestra 8
  Say Yes! 8
Put Your Musical Knowledge to Work 8
  Teach Me Tonight 8
  Write What You Know 9
  Spin Some Tunes 9
  Let the Music Keep You Going 9
Preserving and Submitting Your Songs 9
  Keep the Cassette Player Running 10
  Lead Sheet vs. Lyric Sheet 11
  Preparing a Lead Sheet 11

2   A Century of Songwriting   **13**

Hey Mr. Ziegfeld, Here I Am!.......................................13
  The Rise of Ragtime 14
  Beyond Blackface 14
"Give My Regards to Broadway" 15
  George M. Cohan 15
  Jerome Kern 15
  George Gershwin 16
  Irving Berlin, a Man of the People 16
  The Elite Cole Porter 16
  Songs of the Great Depression and World War II 16
  Rodgers, Hart, and Hammerstein 17
Crosby, Sinatra, and the Pop Singers 17
The Role of Rock 17

Rocking the Clock Forward 18
Bob Dylan 18
Sex in a Red Jumpsuit 19
The Beach Boys 19
The Beatles' Artistic Fearlessness 19
The Rolling Stones 20
Motown Magic 20
Independent Women...20
Bruce Springsteen 21
The Rap Revolution 21
Michael Jackson and the MTV Explosion 21
Quick Cuts..21
Videos Come of Age 22
A Rock Genre Mini Guide 22

3 The Idea Is King   25

Banish Writer's Block 26
Dig Deeper 26
Keep Your Eye on the Idea 26
Satisfy Yourself..27
Inspiring Characters 27
The People on the Street 28
Loved Ones 29
Your Own Life 29
Universal Themes 29
The Blues...29
The Tragedy Trigger 29
Cheating Hearts 30
Breaking Up 30
Endless Love 30
Pride in Your Parents 30
Traveling Back in Time 31
All Apologies 31
Mining the Media 31
Chance Encounters Lead to Hits 31
I Am Woman..32
Simple Starting Points 32
Devil or Angel 32
"Barbara Ann" to "A Boy Named Sue" 32
Location, Location, Location 33
The Songwriter's Paintbrush 33
Animal Magic 33

Good Days and Bad Days *33*
Questions and Answers *34*
Holiday Songs *34*
The Four-Minute Screenplay 34
Priming the Idea Pump 35
Travel the Highway to Hits 35

4 What Comes First, Words or Music?   37

Working Styles 37
Preparing to Create Songs for Artists 39
As a Composer *39*
As a Lyricist..*39*
Major Songwriters Weigh In 40
Was Richard Rodgers Wrong?.....................................*40*
Tim Rice *40*
Hal David *40*
Randy Newman *41*
The Rhythm in Your Mind 41
Practice Wearing Both Hats *41*
No Borders *42*
Take This Song and Shove It...*42*
Don't Stick to Your Own Area..*43*
Positive Disaster..*43*
Hooked on a Feeling...*44*
Feel Your Way to Creativity...45

5 Finding and Keeping Collaborators   47

A Roller Coaster Worth Riding 47
Work Habits 49
How Important Is the Job? *49*
Punctuality Problems *49*
Last-Minute Blues *49*
Deferring to the Larger Ego..*50*
It's the Song, Stupid *50*
"Let's Try It Another Way"..*50*
Stick to Your Guns *51*
I Do (but Sometimes I Don't) *51*
Part-Time Collaboration...*51*

How to Find Your Partner 52
  Start Locally..52
  Advertise 53
  Establish Industry Contacts 53
  Be in the Right Place at the Right Time 53
  Contact ASCAP, BMI, and SESAC.............................54
  Go for a Lucky Long Shot 54
  Work an Artist's Muscle 54
Cold, Hard Business..55
Inspiration from Across the Sea 55
  Long-Distance Gold 56
  Traveling in Your Mind 56
  Starting Out with a Hit 57
  Gaining a Worldwide Reputation 57

6 Title Power!   **59**

Titles That Tell the Story 59
  Simple and Straightforward 59
  Title Characters 60
Titles That Set the Tone 61
  Built-In Drama 61
  The Message in the Music 62
  Pleading, Hoping, Begging 62
  Hot-Blooded...62
  For All the Victims of the World..................................63
Title Triggers..64
  Go from Text to Title 64
  Find the Right Word..64
  Dance to the Music 64
  Cover the Country 65
  Keep Your Titles in the Trunk 65
Words That Work..65
  "Come On, Baby, Light My Fire" 66
  Letters 66
  Cry Your Way to the Charts 66
  A Taste of Sugar...66
  One Is the Magic Number..67
  Only 67
  Kiss 67
First-Line Fever...67

Part 2: Dressing Up the Song   69

7 The Visual Songwriter   71

A Unique Visual Personality 71
The Visual Lifestyle 72
  Start with Cereal 72
  Live in the Visual Landscape 72
  Twain and Conroy 73
  The Drama in the Details 73
  Brides and Brothers 74
  Analyze Nonvisual Lyrics 74
  Look for Consistently Visual Writers 74
  Describe Everyday Experiences Visually 75
  Visual, but Not Verbose 76
The Other Four Senses 76
  Sound 76
  Smell 76
  Taste 76
  Touch 76
Writing with the Five Senses 77
  Look at Who's Talking 77
  Write It All Down 77
  Music and Colors 78

8 Cooking Up Your Hit Ingredients   79

Rhyming Time 79
  Types of Rhymes 80
  A Hit Mixture 80
  Endings That Set You Free 81
  Inner Rhymes 81
Wayward Rhymes 81
  Rhymes Without Reason 82
  Rhymes That Box You In 82
In Search of Colorful Rhyme Words 82
  Rhyming Dictionaries 83
  Rhyme Schemes 84
Other Hit Ingredients 85
  Structure 85
  Alliteration 86
  Vibrant Vowels 87
Act Out Your Lyrics 87

9 Repetition and Hooks   89

Styles of Musical Repetition 89
The Strength of Simplicity 91
Repeat Hits 92
Repetition and Tempo..92
Hooking the Audience..92
Hooking the Emotions 92
Developing Your Hook Consciousness 94
Creating and Testing Your Hooks 94
Verse vs. Hook 95
Instrumental Breaks 95
Sleep on It 95
What Hooks Your Friends? 95
Tell Yourself the Truth 96
Instrumental Icing: Figures and Riffs 96
Figure on Catchy Figures 96
Write Cool Riffs...97

10 The Secrets of Hit Melody Writing   101

What Makes a Tune Singable?..................................102
Reliable Rhythms...103
Prosody...107
You Gotta Shop Around 108
Do a Prosody Search...108

11 Rewriting   111

Bad Reasons to Avoid Rewriting 111
The Best Things Will Be Thrown Away 112
The Rhyme Is Fine 112
Second Verses Aren't That Important 113
The Bridge Is No Big Deal 113
It's Just a Little Like Britney 113
But the Rhythm Fits the Words! 113
I'll Fix It in the Studio 114
My First Draft Is Always the Best 114
I Just Want It Done 114
The Title Is Strong Enough 114
The Ending Is Okay 115
It's Not Worth Bothering About 116
You're a Genius 116
You *Do It!* 117

Starting the Process 117
Take It from the Top *118*
It's His Song, Not Mine *118*
Tell Yourself It's Fun...*118*
Create Your Own Time Patterns *118*
Choose the Right Environment *118*
Staying with It 119
The Record Lost Its Bullet..*119*
This Is Show Business *119*
Try a Different Instrument *120*
Let the Song Breathe..*120*
Going in Reverse *121*

Part 3: Genre Gold   **123**

12 Crossing Into Country   **125**

Nashville News...125
A Little Background *126*
The Currents of Country...*127*
Musical Elements of Country 130
Chord Patterns of Country *131*
Keeping the Nashville Flavor *132*
Recommended Listening..133

13 R&B and Rap   **135**

Birth of the Blues 136
Minstrel to Motown 136
The Johnson Influence *137*
Jordan's Jump..*137*
The Gospel Truth *137*
Doo Wop *138*
Early R&B Hits *138*
The Motown Sound *139*
The Many Faces of R&B...139
The Sound of Young America *139*
Chicago Soul *140*
Southern Soul..*141*
Funk: Forerunner of Rap..*141*
Disco and Dance *141*

Rap and Hip-Hop 142
  Hip-Hop to the Top 143
  Going to Extremes 143
  Regan on Rap..143
  Rapturous Albums 144
Rhythm and Rap 145

14 Commercials and Children's Music   147

Composing Commercials 148
  Getting Engaged..148
  Pressing the Right Buttons 149
Ready to Write 150
  Analyze the Objective 150
  Give Me "Yesterday" 150
  Don't Be Obscure 150
  Personality 151
  Play with Words 151
  Think Showtime! 151
  Don't Bury the Singer 151
  Offer a Choice 152
  Don't Wing It 152
What's the Deal? 152
  Publishing 152
  Getting Paid..152
  Package Deals and Their Drawbacks 153
The Market for Children's Songs....................153
  Do Your Research 153
  Educational Productions 153
Respecting the Minds of Children 154
  Make It Modern 154
  Keep It Moving...155
  Create Characters, Not Caricatures..............155
  Thou Shalt Not Preach 155
  Frame Your Story 155
  Match the Songs to the Story 156
  Don't Be Afraid to Be Dark 156
  Free Your Mind..157

15 Movie Scoring and Songwriting   159

Scorers as Songwriters 159
Make It Happen 160
Read the Hollywood Bibles 161
The Fat Spy—No Jurassic Park.................................161
Respect Your Material.......................................162
A Successful Disaster—on Spec............................162
Have a Strategy 163
Underscoring 163
In the Scoring Game 164
Follow the Right Leader 164
Provide Reassurance 164
Ask Questions and Do Your Research 165
Work Closely with the Music Supervisor 165
Talking About Titles...166
Spotting the Picture..166
Practical Scoring Tips...168
Get Into It 169

16 Live and Animated Musicals   171

Not Eliza Doolittle, but a Dragon 172
Keeping Up with Current Styles 172
Television Musicals 172
Music Behind the Scenes....................................173
Dialogue vs. Music...173
The Song's the Thing...174
Nailing the Characters 174
Where Songs Belong..174
Easy Does It..175
Stand Up to Stars 175
The Performers and the Song 176
Bring Out the Actor's Best Qualities 177
Vocal Ranges That Match...................................177
Every Job Is Your Job 177
Arranger and Best Friend 177
Think Like a Choreographer 178
I Just Want This Small Change 178
Monetary Rewards from a Musical 179

17 Musicals for the Stage   **181**

Creating an Illusion of Reality 181
  Belting to the Balcony 182
  Songs on Stage and Screen 183
Important Musical Categories 183
  Adult Fairy Tales: Love Heals 183
  The Revue 184
  The Historical Musical 185
  The Musical Fantasy 186
  The Musical Biography 186
  Novel Adaptations 187
  Play Adaptations 188
  Movie Adaptations 188
  Offbeat Adaptations 189
  Shakespeare and the Bible 189
  Originals 189
Get It on the Stage 189
  Show Me the Money 190
  Do a Local Production 190
  Be a Talent Scout 191
  Hold a Workshop 191
  Take It on the Road 192
  Cut a CD 192
  Find Available Theaters 192
  The Producer's Viewpoint 193
Hits from Shows 193
Special Material 194

Part 4: Showing It Off   **197**

18 The Power of a Hit Demo   **199**

Choosing Your Musical Approach 200
  Piano-Voice Demos 200
  Guitar-Voice Demos 201
  Voice with Piano, Guitar, Bass, and Drums 201
  Cover Your Bases 201
Finding the Singer and Musicians 201
  Choosing the Singer 201
  Picking the Right Musicians 202

Locating the Best Players 202
When You're the Artist..203
Figuring Costs 204
Royalties: Targeting Elvis 204
Prepare Now or Pay Later 204
Making the Demo 205
Choosing a Studio 205
Enlisting Creative Support 205
Staying Creatively Focused 206
Holding Your Ground on Tempo 206
Handling Studio Disasters 206
Demos at Home 207
Upgrade Slowly 207
Who Uses What 207
Be a Maniac About the Mix 208
Demo Presentation 208

19 Becoming a Great Song Salesman   211

Casting Your Songs 212
Ricky Martin Is on Tour 212
Listen to the Artists' Records 213
Personal Casting That Worked 213
Selling to a Publisher 215
The Right Publisher 215
Publishers with Production Companies 216
What Good Publishers Do for You 216
Working for a Publisher 218
Sign with a Publisher or Freelance? 218
Signing Up 218
Doing Your Own Publishing 220
Creative Selling 220

20 The Singer/Songwriter   223

What Makes a Good Agent? 224
Small Agencies..224
The Big Enchiladas 225
Managers 225
Mutual Obsession 225
I Just Want to Be Your Everything..................................225
A Lawyer You Can Trust 226

You Gotta Shop Around 226
Don't Be Frightened by Fees 226
Do You Have What It Takes? 226
Who Are Your Future Fans? 226
What Do You Look Like? 227
Russ Regan's Rules 227
Feed the Media Monster 228
Signing with a Label 229
The Majors 229
The Minors 230
Come to the Cabaret 230

21 Home Studio   **233**

Embracing the Technology 234
Equipment Choices 234
Roger LaRocque's Experience 234
Ease into the Manual 235
Equipment Terms 235
Where to Buy 237
Computer Software 237
Equipment Recommendations 237
Roger's Picks 237
Memory 238
Workstation 238
Other Inexpensive Approaches 238
Making Music 239
Live vs. Synthesizers: No Conflict! 239
Keep It Short 240
Mixing 240
Old vs. New Arranging 241
Engineering a Session 241

22 Producing Your Own Hit Songs   **243**

How Do You Learn to Produce? 243
A Producer's Job 245
Techno or No? 245
How Involved Will You Be? 246
Be a Director 246
Planning a Recording Date 246
What Are the Songs? 246
Try Different Studios 247

The Engineer 247
Up-Front Budgeting 247
Earnings 248
Rehearsal 248
In the Studio 249
One Hundred Ways to Confuse Yourself 249
Artists Are Only Human 249
Musical Approaches 249
Soul Power 249
Potent Performances 250
Good Goofs 250
Experiment 250
Be Weird If It Works 250
Play with the Atmosphere 251
Vary Your Themes 251
Voice First 251
You Have to Love It, Too 252
Top Producers 252

Part 5: Finishing Touches   **255**

23 Royalties and Guilds   **257**

The Big Three: ASCAP, BMI, and SESAC 258
Basic Functions 258
Distribution of Royalties 259
ASCAP 259
Membership 260
Showcases and Awards 260
Payment Procedure 261
Payment System 261
ASCAP Locations 262
BMI 262
Membership 263
Seminars, Workshops, and Showcases 263
Payment Procedure 264
Payment System 266
BMI Locations 266

SESAC 267
Copyright Basics 267
  Copyright Registration 268
  Watch Out! 268
The Songwriter's Guild of America 269
  The Guild's Creed...269
  The Popular Songwriter's Contract 269
  Copyright Act of 1976 270

24 What's Happening in Songwriting?   271

The Good New Days 272
Steve Schalchlin's Internet Miracle 272
  The AIDS Crisis and the Internet 273
  More Online Miracles 274
Napster 274
  Fund-Raising 275
  The Future of Music Downloading 275
Working the Internet.......................................276
  But He's Too Important! 277
  Tonos...277
  Record Labels 278
  Workshops 278
  Publishers 279
The Importance of History 279
  The Simon Syndrome 280
  Other Opinions 280
Looking Ahead...280
Reading the Grammy Tea Leaves 280
  Song of the Year 281
  The Freelance Writer's Heroine 281
  Best Rock Song 282
  Best R&B Song 282
  Best Country Song 283
  Best Song Written for a Motion Picture, Television,
    or Other Visual Media 283
  Other Categories..284
  Grammys 2001 284
Common Denominators 284

Appendixes

A Glossary   287

B Resources   291

C Contests and Competitions   297

Index   299

Foreword

The majority of books about songwriting are written by individuals who have never had a hit. Contrast that with Joel Hirschhorn, who has won two Oscars (four nominations), five BMI Awards, a People's Choice Award, and four Angel Awards. He is also a two-time Tony nominee for Best Broadway musical score and the recipient of four Golden Globe nominations. Joel is the only composer/lyricist I know who has triumphed in every medium: pop, R&B, country, theater, and movie musicals—and he has sold over 93 million records!

Joel and I met under the most auspicious of circumstances. He co-wrote two Oscar-winning songs, "The Morning After" from *The Poseidon Adventure* and "We May Never Love Like This Again" from *The Towering Inferno*. Both became million sellers worldwide and launched my career as a singer when I recorded them.

Aside from being a singer and an actor, one of my greatest loves is songwriting. I've recorded and performed many of my compositions in regional children's theater and concert halls, on television around the world, and with symphony orchestras, including the National Symphony and the Hartford Symphony Orchestra.

As a composer and a singer, I so deeply appreciate Joel's clear, practical approach to the composing craft. When he talks about "hooks," it's because he learned through trial and error (in the form of publishers, artists, and producers) that a song without a hook will be a song without a chart position. When he stresses the importance of ideas, titles, visual action, and structure, it's because he learned firsthand that including those elements almost always guaranteed acceptance.

His chapters on rewriting and demo production are valuable lessons in how to polish a song and show it to its best advantage. The advice Joel gives on casting and promoting your material offers indispensable shortcuts to success for the novice as well as the seasoned songwriter. You'll also see "what works" for Diane Warren, Stephen Sondheim, Billy Joel, Marvin Hamlisch, and other classic songwriters such as Johnny Mercer, Richard Rodgers, Oscar Hammerstein, Jule Styne, and Sammy Cahn.

I've always called "The Morning After" the "generic hope anthem" because it was generally specific for the movie, but also specifically general enough for the public to embrace it outside of the film and apply it to their own lives. Some 28 years later, I still receive letters from people telling me how "The Morning After" has changed or saved their lives or has seen them through difficult times with its life-affirming message, and that kind of reaction is the true test of a timeless song.

Any person who has had recording hits by such diverse artists as Elvis Presley, Sheena Easton, Julian Lennon, Taj Mahal, Charlie Rich, Roy Orbison, Charles Aznavour, and yours truly has insights that no other book writer on contemporary songwriting can duplicate.

If you want a career in composing or lyric writing, one that covers every conceivable area, you will find that in this gracious and insightful book; Joel Hirschhorn has dozens and dozens of great ideas, and our creative road is easier to travel for his sharing them with us. Thank you, Joel!

Maureen McGovern
Los Angeles
December 2000

Maureen McGovern's 28-year career spans recordings, concerts, theater, films, television, and radio. Her children's musical, *The Bengal Tiger's Ball,* had its East Coast premiere in 1999; Maureen wrote the music, co-created, and starred in the show. Her films include *Airplane, Airplane II: The Sequel, The Towering Inferno, The Cure for Boredom,* and the voice of Rachel in DreamWorks' animated video/DVD *Joseph: King of Dreams!* Her recording career began with being nominated for a Grammy for the Oscar-winning gold record, "The Morning After," from *The Poseidon Adventure,* followed by the Oscar-winning gold record "We May Never Love Like This Again" from *The Towering Inferno.* Maureen made history in 1975 as the first singer to record two Oscar-nominated songs in the same year, "We May Never Love Like This Again" and "Wherever Love Takes Me" from *Gold.*

Introduction

When I first began writing songs, Manhattan's Brill Building was the magnet that drew every hungry, starry-eyed songwriter. Music publishers waited in their dark, tiny offices while eager hopefuls like me knocked on their doors, ventured timidly inside, and said, "I've got a song. I think it's a hit."

In those days, kids off the street could wander in and be assured of an audience. The first person to hear my masterpiece, "I'm Going to Peggy's Party," was named Sal Giancarlo. He was six feet four and 300 pounds and resembled a wrestler more than a man of musical taste. The needle went on the vinyl, and he listened, legs sprawled over his desk. After three or four bars, he abruptly yanked off the needle and said, "Buddy, this song doesn't have enough fire. Passion. And remember," he continued, delivering the worst possible advice any newcomer could receive, "craft doesn't matter in pop music. You have to feel it, and it'll come out right."

Minutes later, I was out on the street. My bleak mood wasn't helped by a sudden, drenching rain that soaked my sheet music. There's nothing more depressing than feeling like an 18-year-old has-been, and I walked down Broadway, replaying his words.

Over 30 years later, I now realize that Mr. Giancarlo was half right: passion matters intensely. But passion without craft is a shortcut to oblivion. Even the successful songwriters who can't articulate all their composing methods have an instinctive understanding of certain rules. When a writer has no grasp of structure, his or her songs wander aimlessly. The music doesn't build, the rhythms are static, and the rhymes are clichéd.

This talk of craft is not to exclude emotion: Without it, songwriting is meaningless. But no architect would build a house, however beautiful, without a foundation. This book will teach you how to build that foundation and incorporate all the necessary elements so that your songs will be recorded and reach an international audience.

As a two-time Oscar winner and composer/lyricist of songs that have sold over 93 million copies, I've been fortunate. En route to those achievements, however, I fell into every trap and made every mistake. My goal is to provide you with the knowledge you need to avoid most of the pitfalls.

This book deals with the vital need for repetition, the ingredients required for a hit hook, and the importance of a colorful title. I also talk about the elements that make a melody unforgettable and analyze chord progressions to illustrate which ones draw the strongest response.

Through examination of various rhythms, you'll see which ones stimulate listener excitement. By studying lyrics from all genres (pop, country, R&B, hip-hop, theater, and motion pictures), you'll become aware of why certain words touch the heart and stir the senses. After I cover basic rules for hit melodies, lyrics, and rhythms, you'll learn how to cut the kind of demo that excites producers and artists.

Finally, this book will teach you how to sell the hit song you've just written. The outlets for selling your material are greater than ever, but you have to know who to approach and how. Let me show you what those rules are and spell out the steps of the game, so you can play it and crash the Top 10.

The late Curtis Mayfield, legendary lead singer of the Impressions and writer of such classics as "Amen," "Keep on Pushing," and "It's All Right," once told me, "People listen to songs on the radio, then do the opposite. The rules are there—why do so few composers bother to learn them?"

The first thing this book asks you to do is absorb every influence around you and be willing to learn your craft. Writing hits is amazingly easy if you keep an open mind. You may have talent, but in this book, you'll find the tools for success that all major songwriters use.

How to Use This Book

This book is divided into five parts:

Part 1, "How to Write a Hit," deals with the many ways you can support yourself in musical fields while working to get your first break. It examines the issue of formal training and how to educate yourself musically even if you've never had a lesson. You can discover what influence the various eras of the twentieth century had on the hit songs of the day and learn about the most important element of successful songwriting: a great idea! The best writers don't just wait for ideas to magically show up; they have numerous ways to locate them, and you'll find out what these ways are in this part.

Words or music: What comes first? This question is explored through the work of classic and contemporary songwriters. Finding and keeping collaborators is another matter of tremendous concern to songwriters. I discuss all those unwritten rules that ensure a harmonious, long-lasting, and successful collaboration.

You'll also need dynamite titles for your songs. I point out the difference between an ordinary title and one that takes you to the top of the charts and what route the legendary songwriters took to find their best titles. This road is available to every composer and lyricist.

Part 2, "Dressing Up the Song," gives you vital tips about writing once your idea is hatched. We live in a visual age, and you'll learn how to sharpen your sense of sight, as well as smell, hearing, taste, and touch. I cover all kinds of rhyme and go over the basic rhythmic grooves that producers and artists look for. I also explain the foundation of popular songwriting: the hook. Once you get the hang of writing a hit hook, you're home free, and this part will show you how to do it.

No one wants to rewrite, but it's often inescapable. You'll see how to ease into it by accepting the fact that it will make you a better songwriter.

Part 3, "Genre Gold," points out the elements that make great country, R&B, and hip-hop songs. I also cover how to write and sell commercials as well as children's music. As a two-time Best Score Tony nominee for Best Broadway musical (*Copperfield* and *Seven Brides for Seven Brothers*) and two-time Oscar nominee for best movie musical (*Pete's Dragon*), I lived through the process of creating shows from the ground up. I also had the benefit of a brilliant mentor, Irwin Kostal (who scored *The Sound of Music, Mary Poppins,* and *West Side Story* for films). The information that you'll find here on movie and theater musicals explains everything you need to know about writing a show and getting it produced. You'll also learn how to write the kind of motion picture song that works within the film and has the ingredients to become a hit outside of it.

Part 4, "Showing It Off," moves beyond writing into the commercially crucial phase: getting your song sold. I talk about the secrets of cutting a demo that matches any record on the air for quality, a demo so realized and exciting that artists and producers can't resist it.

As a songwriter today, it pays to think of yourself as a producer, and the chapter on record production will help you to build and polish your producing skills, whether you work in a rented studio or your own home setup.

Part 5, "Finishing Touches," educates you about protecting your material. Royalties are a songwriter's lifeblood, and such organizations as BMI, ASCAP, SESAC, and the Songwriter's Guild of America exist to help you hold on to the money you earn and negotiate the best contracts.

I discuss the miraculous new ways the Internet can aid your career, as an invaluable research tool and a link to other writers, producers, and artists. I also look at the dynamics of popular music today and why opportunities for songwriters will continue to increase as traditional genre lines break down and recombine.

Finally, this book provides you with a glossary of key musical terms; a list of helpful Web sites; the names of influential publishers, organizations, and trade papers; and a guide to songwriting contests and competitions you can enter.

Extras

In addition to the information in the chapters and appendixes, the sidebars throughout the book contain fascinating quotes from songwriters and others in the music business, cautionary tales, helpful advice, and translations of terms you may not be familiar with. Here's what to look for:

Trouble Clef

You can avoid 95 percent of the pitfalls if you're aware of what they are. These sidebars give you every warning you need to know.

Backstage Banter

Read these sidebars for colorful, informative quotes and stories about your favorite performers and songwriters.

Lyrical Lingo

These basic terms will equip you for dealing with the professional songwriting world.

Hirschhorn's Hints

These tips make the path to composing, producing, and selling songs easier.

Acknowledgments

My deepest thanks to Amy Zavatto and Doris Cross for their guidance, friendship, and enormous skill in helping me put together this manuscript. I'd also like to express gratitude to Maureen McGovern, Marvin Hamlisch, Jerry Herman, Lee Holdridge, Peter Bart, Phil Gallo, Ramin Zahed, Roger LaRocque, Mark Wyckoff, Lisa McKinnon, James Brochu, Steve Schalchlin, Russ Regan, Frances Preston, Del Bryant, Paige Sober, Michael Kerker, Rodney Mencia, Rob O'Neill, Madeleine and Richard Desjardins, Evelyn Hirschhorn, Kevin Carter, Brent Carter, Derek Carter Jr., Arthur Seidelman, Dimitri Logothetis, Aaron Meza, Emily Carter, Doreen Ringer Ross, Will Jennings, Fred Karlin, Carole Bayer Sager, Alan Menken, Michael Gore, Paul Williams, and Justin Tseng.

Special Thanks to the Technical Reviewer

The Complete Idiot's Guide to Songwriting was reviewed by an expert who double-checked the accuracy of what you'll learn here to help us ensure that this book gives you everything you need to know about songwriting. Special thanks and my gratitude are extended to technical reviewer Jennifer Carter, a meticulous perfectionist who checked all my facts and never settled for anything but complete accuracy. Jennifer has been a researcher, technical adviser, and producer for *National Geographic,* Walt Disney's Educational Division, *The New York Times* Science Show, Stephen Low Productions, and WQED. Jennifer, who won an Emmy in 1978, was the researcher, technical adviser, and field producer of a television special, *Return to the Titanic,* that spotlighted her role as expedition leader of the voyage that brought up 1,500 artifacts. In 1987, she became the first woman in history to dive down to the legendary ocean liner.

Trademarks

All terms mentioned in this book that are known to be or are suspected of being trademarks or service marks have been appropriately capitalized. Alpha Books and Pearson Education cannot attest to the accuracy of this information. Use of a term in this book should not be regarded as affecting the validity of any trademark or service mark.

Songwriters Sing the Praises of Joel Hirschhorn and His *Complete Idiot's Guide to Songwriting*

"Joel Hirschhorn has won two Best Song Oscars and has been nominated for two Tony Awards and four Golden Globes. The writing principles he used and the secrets of his amazing success are contained in these remarkable pages. Joel covers it all in absorbing detail—from first demos to gold records—with practical, instructive chapters on finding collaborators, writing Top 10 lyrics and melodies, and developing the knack of selling your material. If you want to know how to write million sellers and award-winning songs, this is the book for you."

—Marvin Hamlisch, "The Way We Were," "Nobody Does It Better," *A Chorus Line*

"Anyone who has sold 93 million records, won two Oscars for Best Song, and been nominated for two Tony Awards for Best Broadway Score has seen and done it all. In this practical and fascinating book, Joel reveals all the secrets that brought him fame and recognition. These invaluable tips will benefit every songwriter and give him the keys he needs for success."

—Jerry Herman, *Hello, Dolly!, Mame, La Cages Aux Folles*

"Here's a book that offers realistic, practical advice on how to tap your hit potential, from a two-time Oscar winner who's traveled every road—from the Brill Building to Broadway."

—Carole Bayer Sager: *Arthur,* "Nobody Does It Better," *They're Playing Our Song*

"Here's a great collection of tips for anyone interested in writing songs, film scores, and stage musicals."

—Paul Williams, "Evergreen," "We've Only Just Begun"

Part 1

How to Write a Hit

If you love music and you're determined to succeed as a songwriter, you have the potential to do it, even if you have no musical training. The first and most important step is to learn everything you can about songwriting and what makes a song a hit. Part 1 begins with ways to go about getting this education by finding work that can finance some musical training while also increasing your knowledge of the music business.

Understanding how historical events and social attitudes influenced which songs became hits during the twentieth century sets the stage for exploring what hits are made of.

Yip (E. Y.) Harburg, who wrote the lyrics for The Wizard of Oz, *once said, "It doesn't matter what else you have if you don't have the idea." You'll discover how to find and tap into all the great ideas around you. You'll learn about the many ways that words and music can come together and find out how to meet the right partner, establish a successful working routine, and keep the partnership going no matter what pressures arise.*

Most of the major songwriters feel that their work is half done if they come up with an exciting title. Why do some titles instantly grab the public's imagination? I analyze hit titles, past and present, and determine which ones have built-in hit potential.

Chapter 1

Music Training: Is It a Must?

In This Chapter

➤ How training helps

➤ Ways to learn while you earn

➤ How to preserve and submit what you write

I remember my mother standing over me, urging me to practice the Beethoven piece my teacher had assigned me for that week. I was bored and rebellious, and finally I shouted, "I want to be a songwriter. How can studying Beethoven help?" She shrugged her shoulders and said, "How can it hurt?"

Years later, I'm grateful for my mother's advice. Admittedly, formal knowledge of music isn't necessary to become a hit songwriter. Songwriting, as multimillion-selling composer Barry Mann has said, is an inborn ability. You may hit *Billboard*'s top spot without a single lesson of any kind. But a musical background can make songwriting success easier.

Looking at the Hit–Makers

Songwriters can be trained by teachers or be entirely self-taught. The question is: If you want to make a career of songwriting, how much training do you need? Let's look at some chart-topping writers for an overview.

These songwriters studied music from the time they were young:

➤ Sheryl Crow received a degree in classical music from the University of Missouri and taught music at a St. Louis elementary school.

➤ Bo Diddley studied violin as a child at the Ebeneezer Baptist Church in Mississippi.

➤ Ray Charles learned classical piano at St. Augustine's School for the Deaf and Blind in Orlando.

➤ Marvin Gaye was taught piano and drums at an early age.

➤ Quincy Jones, who scored the Oscar-nominated Steven Spielberg film *The Color Purple,* was a master on trumpet by age 13. At 17, he won a scholarship to the Berklee School of Music in Boston.

➤ Janis Ian, writer of the groundbreaking "Society's Child," started her classical training at the tender age of 2, and Billy Joel began piano lessons at 4 and continued them until he was 14.

Hirschhorn's Hints

More important than training and hard work is to believe in yourself and never give up. Martika, who wrote and recorded the number-one hit "Toy Soldiers," was two years old when she begged to go to dance and ballet class. At age 11, she was combing the telephone directory for agents, and by 12, she landed a role in the film version of *Annie.*

Lyrical Lingo

Counterpoint is note against note. This type of polyphonic music weaves and fits two or more together, or it weaves the same melody around itself.

On the other hand, many successful songwriters took a different road:

➤ Pete Townshend of The Who admits to being a self-taught guitarist, motivated by his desire to "get girls.

➤ Felice Bryant, who had numerous country hits with her husband Boudleaux Bryant, couldn't play an instrument or read music. She sang all her songs into a tape recorder or to her husband/collaborator, who then wrote them down.

➤ Barry White, whose melodies are now a recurring plot device on the hit series Ally McBeal, claims he has a "fantastic rhythm ability" although he's never had music lessons.

Is There Success Without Counterpoint?

You don't have to be a walking textbook on theory, harmony, and *counterpoint* to be a successful song-writer; any amount of musical training you pick up will help. Carol Hall, composer/lyricist of *Best Little Whorehouse in Texas,* was told by her music instructor at Sarah Lawrence that she would never be able to write a Broadway musical because she didn't do her work in counterpoint. Carol later said, with satisfaction, "I went to New York and had a big Broadway hit without counterpoint."

Producer/songwriter Chris Barbosa followed the success of his first hit song with music lessons and admits that they helped him to write faster. But he also feels, as do many other instinctive writers, that too many rules can get in the way of creativity. When that happens, he drops them and composes with spontaneous feeling.

As Marvin Hamlisch says, talent can't be taught. Still, geniuses such as Paul McCartney, who have all the talent in the world, have expressed regret that they didn't receive more formal training. (McCartney is the only one of the four Beatles able to read music.)

Suppose a fantastic tune comes to you. Without the ability to write music, you can't notate either the melody or the chords. By the time you get to a studio or reach a tape recorder, you might forget the tune altogether.

Prestige vs. Poverty

Some songwriters are able to enroll in a conservatory and gain their education at a prestigious music academy. Burt Bacharach, son of syndicated columnist Bert Bacharach, was one of these fortunate few. He took piano lessons in elementary school; studied at McGill University in Montreal, Canada; and acquired his training in the classics from such distinguished teachers as Darius Milhaud, Boguslav Martinu, and Henry Cowell.

Hirschhorn's Hints

It's never too late to learn music. Jerry Herman, composer of *Mame, Hello, Dolly!,* and *La Cage Aux Folles,* disliked his piano teacher and gave up lessons. It wasn't until after he wrote his first Broadway hit, *Milk and Honey,* that he decided to learn how to read and write music.

Hirschhorn's Hints

Whether you're formally trained or not, persistence and believing in your product are essential. As Diane Warren puts it, "Don't give up if you believe in your heart that you're meant to be a song-writer." Diane admits that she knocked on doors, ran after people trying to give them tapes, and even followed people down the street in her car.

Most aspiring songwriters lack Bacharach's advantages. They have to struggle for recognition without financial aid and cope with parental objections to "such an insecure business." Starting out, composers can't spend 24 hours a day expressing themselves creatively; they have to earn money in order to eat and pay the rent. But just because you need to work doesn't mean your musical education has to stop. Working with music in any capacity will teach you about the craft and business of songwriting.

Don't Delay Your Dreams

I once had a girlfriend who said, "You'll never make it in this business. It's too hard. If you love me, you'll give it up and find a better job." Her mother supported this bleak view. The message was "Stop in the Name of Love." Fortunately, I found the strength to tune it out. Sweet satisfaction came when I won my first Oscar, and my former girlfriend called to congratulate me.

The trick is not to panic and latch on to a tedious but necessary job from which you might never escape. If your job seems like a dead end, remind yourself that it's *only temporary.* You can't become so tired and discouraged by hours invested in uncreative pursuits that you drop out, vowing to get back to songwriting "eventually." Eventually never comes. The only defense against this thinking is blind, persistent tenacity and a reminder to yourself, no matter how much tension you feel, to keep writing!

Backstage Banter

Arnold Lanni, writer of the number-one song "When I'm with You" for Sheriff, shocked his Italian family when he announced in 1979 he was dropping out of York University in Toronto to join a rock-and-roll band. Parents, friends, and lovers (well-meaning and otherwise) often tell writers to give up their dreams. Ignore them; keep your eye trained on your goal and go for it!

From the Harbor Club to Elvis

A person with solid background in music has dozens of exciting employment options to embrace. When I realized that Elvis wasn't going to record my songs immediately, I decided to take a gig in a nightclub. It was far from paradise. I lived in Manhattan, and the joint that hired me, the Harbor Club in Staten Island, could be reached only by driving to a ferry and then driving another hour from the dock. The Harbor Club was dingy and run-down and featured an over-the-hill stripper named Desiree.

My responsibility was to play standards (mostly Sinatra songs) until four in the morning. It wasn't the setting my mother had envisioned for me. I was groomed from earliest childhood to be a concert pianist, and my parents never considered the possibility that I would be playing "Someone to Watch Over Me" for an overweight stripper and three drunks. Nevertheless, I was a skilled pianist, thanks to having studied my craft and later attending Manhattan's High School of Performing Arts.

The Harbor Club allowed me to pay my bills and, with careful money management, eat cheeseburgers and tuna salads at a local dive called The Pink Cloud. I was able to write songs and survive until my hit record, "Your Time Hasn't Come Yet, Baby" by Elvis Presley, made it possible for me to compose all day and get some sleep at night.

Make It Big Through a Local Gig

You can be formally trained like Burt Bacharach or self-taught like Pete Townshend, but if you can perform—and particularly if you can perform your own material—you'll eventually be noticed by someone who can advance your career.

Where you play or how much you're being paid is not the most important thing. The head of Columbia Records might just possibly be a guest at a bar mitzvah you've been hired for. If you're playing at a wedding, you might find out that a Top 40 singing star is a cousin of the bride or groom. The point is to get out there and gain exposure!

Accompany Your Way to a Hit

If you're a pianist, you can become an accompanist for shows. Marvin Hamlisch was the dance arranger for *Funny Girl.* The job gave him a chance to strike up a lifelong friendship and working association with Barbra Streisand. Just as important, he worked with dancers and got to know them. Marvin makes light of it by saying that this experience made him "perverted every time he sees a leotard." What the experience did, even more powerfully, was give him an understanding of how dancers talked, danced, sang, and *thought.* When he wrote *A Chorus Line,* he had that wealth of understanding and experience behind him. Dance arranging was the first step toward the Tony and Pulitzer Prize he won for that groundbreaking show.

John Kander, composer of *Cabaret, Zorba,* and *Chicago* recalls that he started playing piano at age four. When he moved to New York from Kansas City, everything he did to support himself was music-related. As John puts it, "The jobs I had were either accompanying, or coaching, or arranging; or later on, in summer stock, [I worked as a] choral director and a director. I don't think I skipped any stops."

Play Sessions

Guitar players who read proficiently and have a creative grasp of country, blues, and rock will eventually be noticed and hired for record sessions. The same is true if you're a percussionist. In addition to overall skill on every type of percussion instrument, sight-reading counts for a lot in session playing. If you're an excellent player but a poor reader, you can easily remedy that with practice. Playing by ear is something you're born with; reading is a skill any student can master. Give it an hour a day, and within a few months you'll be astonished at what an outstanding reader you've become.

Join an Orchestra

Not everything is rock. If you played oboe or flute in a high school or college orchestra, you might be good enough to play on motion picture dates or orchestral record sessions. Did you study violin, viola, or cello? Even if you're a little rusty, you might be able, with practice, to polish your technique and do orchestra work.

Say Yes!

Sometimes, even with formal training, you're not specifically trained for a particular job when it comes along. If at all possible, if the offer comes, say yes. When the chance to do dance arrangements presented itself, Marvin admits, "I had never done a dance arrangement in my life. But I said, 'Of course I have.' You must seize the opportunity and know when it's a break. You must recognize that a given situation is important and then deliver!"

Put Your Musical Knowledge to Work

When I started working, I had two choices: become a typist at a law firm or work as a typist at a music publisher's office for half the money! I took the job with the lower salary because the office was in New York's Brill Building, home of countless music publishers. While I was typing letters, I watched songwriters as they came up and presented their material. I studied how my boss took these songs and promoted them to different artists. I went to the studio with him and observed how he made demos and worked with demo singers and musicians.

My musical background came in handy at that time, because he wanted me to write neat, correct lead sheets of songs he had in his musical catalogue. Between the typing (always a valuable skill) and song arrangements I supplied, I was in the right position to interest him in one of my songs: "I'll Get You (If I Only Play Hard to Get)," by Jay Bentley and the Jet Set. It didn't set the charts on fire, but it gave me the impetus to go on.

As this experience shows, you don't have to be a performer to work in the music field. You can use whatever skills you have to help you move that much closer to your goal of being a songwriter.

Teach Me Tonight

If you have a vocal background, consider becoming a voice coach. Pianists and guitarists can usually find a host of eager pupils. The best aspect of teaching is that it can be organized to give you mobility. You have no boss to answer to, so you can allow yourself enough time to write songs and take them around.

Write What You Know

Do you have music background and a keen eye for the music scene? Do you have a sense of contemporary trends and an instinctive understanding of the record business? If so, you might want to consider a sideline as a music critic or commentator.

When I needed money, I became a columnist for *Songwriter* magazine, analyzing songs and interviewing artists and groups. Not only did it supplement my income during lean days, it also gave me the opportunity to meet industry people and raise my profile.

Spin Some Tunes

Being a deejay sharpens your instinct for what's current and what people respond most enthusiastically to. Chris Barbosa started out as a deejay spinning records at clubs and parties. With the money he earned, Chris bought a drum machine, a Roland Bass Line, and later a synthesizer. This new technology brought forth a tune, "Let the Music Play," which went to the top of the charts.

Backstage Banter

A young and rising songwriter named Neil Dorval found a creative way to earn money and continue his songwriting career. He became a music therapist, working in hospitals and motivating mentally troubled individuals with a combination of therapy and music. This growing field offers valuable insight into human emotions.

Let the Music Keep You Going

Sometimes finding work in the music world seems impossible. Kris Kristofferson was a janitor at a Nashville studio, and no one paid much attention to him at first. But he internalized everything he saw, and this education led to "Sunday Mornin' Comin' Down," "Me and Bobby McGee," and "Help Me Make It Through the Night."

Country legend Tammy Wynette ("Stand by Your Man") toiled in a shoe factory, a hair salon, a doctor's office, and the cotton fields. Allan Rich, who composed the number-one hit, "I Don't Have the Heart" for James Ingram, waited tables in Beverly Hills and sold shoes in Venice Beach. Mariah Carey also waited tables and checked coats, but said, "The music kept me going."

Preserving and Submitting Your Songs

Whatever the extent of your musical training, you must have the right supplies handy to preserve your ideas and ready your songs for submission. If a great idea comes to you, you don't want to have to start a hysterical search for paper and pencil.

Always have the following within easy reach:

Writing paper

A package of eight-stave music paper

Three sharpened #2 pencils

Cassette recorder

Two or three 120-minute audiocassettes

Dictionary

Rhyming dictionary

Thesaurus

Keep the Cassette Player Running

If you play an instrument, chances are you know basic chords. Some composers scribble down music without using the piano or guitar, but it's perfectly fine to sit at a keyboard and peck away before making note of the tunes you hear. You'll be amazed, as you write out your ideas, how quickly you become proficient at it. The added plus is that writing down melodies and chords stimulates your mind and gives you a flock of fresh ideas. You see what you have and are tempted to embellish on it.

Lyrical Lingo

A **copyright** is registration of your work with the U.S. Government Copyright Office to establish legal ownership and prevent your songs from being stolen. For information and forms, write to Register of Copyrights, Copyright Office, Library of Congress, Washington, DC 20559; or go to www.loc.gov/copyright.html.

Whether you're writing music down or just noodling idly, turn on the cassette recorder and let it play. I can't tell you how many times I've just been playing piano for relaxation and a great idea has popped into my head, prompting hasty, frantic efforts to turn the recorder on before the idea disappeared. Consider every second you spend at your instrument composing time. If you wear out a few batteries by letting it run, so be it. The best tunes and concepts may sneak up unexpectedly. Spontaneous ideas don't stick unless they're caught the second they occur to you.

When you're ready to write out your song on the music paper, follow these guidelines:

➤ Write your name clearly, along with your address, phone number, fax number, and e-mail.

➤ Never write in ink. Use a #2 pencil.

➤ Use a ruler when writing out the song's title. Don't try for fancy lettering; keep the letters plain, with even spacing between each one.

➤ Include a *copyright* notice.

Lead Sheet vs. Lyric Sheet

When submitting a song, many people feel that sending a lyric sheet (typewritten lyrics with contact information and a copyright notice) and a recording of the song is enough. This attitude assumes that most producers and artists evaluating your work can't read music. My feeling is that the more information you can send, the better off you'll be. Therefore, I recommend sending a *lead sheet* (handwritten sheet music with melody, chords, and lyric) whenever you submit a song. For all those who can't read music, dozens can, and if they like the song, they'll probably want to follow the music as they listen in order to familiarize themselves with every aspect of it.

Preparing a Lead Sheet

To prepare a lead sheet, go through these steps:

➤ Define the style. Here are some examples:

Moderate gospel rock

With a heavy beat

Moderately bright

Slowly

Swing feel

Lighthearted rock

Folk-ballad style

Moderately slow with a double-time feel

Medium rock beat

Heavy backbeat

Trouble Clef

Above everything, be neat. Many composers labor to make their songs perfect and then present them in a sloppy fashion. Nothing screams "amateur" more than messy lead sheets.

➤ Put in the treble clef.

➤ Don't forget the key signature, whether it's G, D, F-sharp, B-flat, or any other key you choose. If you don't specify the number of sharps and flats your key contains, the person who plays the music will hear only a senseless cacophony.

➤ Specify the time signature: Is it 3/4, 4/4, 2/4?

➤ No crooked bar lines. Again, use a ruler.

➤ Don't cram notes unevenly into each measure. Keep the spacing even.

➤ Write lyrics under the correct notes. Many beginners (and even those who should know better) dash off words and don't align them exactly with the proper notes. When artists, producers, or publishers see this kind of sloppiness, they usually throw the song into the discard pile.

➤ Use chord symbols properly. Like lyrics, they should be placed over the notes they belong to. These are the correct chord symbols:

C major = C

C minor = Cm

C augmented = C+

C diminished = Co

C major 6th = C6

C major 7th = Cmaj7

C major 9th = Cmaj9

C minor 6th = Cm6

C minor 7th = Cm7

C minor 9th = Cm9

Dominant 7th = C7

Dominant 9th = C9

Dominant 11th = C11

Dominant 13th = C13

Diminished 7th = Co7

Hirschhorn's Hints

A songwriter doesn't have to be an arranger. When you notate music, it's best to keep it simple. A complicated, chord-packed lead sheet will frighten off artists and producers, most of whom can't read music. The melody line and chord symbols are usually enough.

➤ When you've completed the lead sheet, play it as written and check for mistakes. Go over it two or three times, because the eye frequently misses errors the first time.

➤ Don't send out your only copy. Always keep one for yourself.

Remember, even if you never become an expert at music notation, it's enough if you capture the basic chords and melody for your own convenience, so each idea is preserved.

The Least You Need to Know

➤ Musical training is helpful, but many songwriters have written hits without it.

➤ Don't let anyone or anything stop you from pursuing your dreams.

➤ Perform your music at clubs, weddings, bar mitzvahs, industrial shows—wherever industry people might hear your material.

➤ Investigate off-beat avenues such as teaching music or being a deejay to keep you going while you write.

➤ Have the supplies you need to keep track of your ideas on hand, and make sure your lead sheets are neat, clear, and carefully organized.

Chapter 2

A Century of Songwriting

In This Chapter

➤ From Jolson to Joplin

➤ Broadway's golden age of songwriting

➤ Crosby, Sinatra, and the crooners

➤ Rock and roll takes center stage

➤ MTV changes the face of songwriting

Music has traveled a long way, from the ragtime of a hundred years ago to today's rap. But no matter how it changes, it never loses the power to bind people together in times of crisis, to speak for dreamers who can't speak for themselves, and to express heartache in a way that allows a rejected lover the catharsis of a good cry. More than newspapers, television, or movies, music reflects cultural change and represents society's feelings.

Hey Mr. Ziegfeld, Here I Am!

To look at the popular songs of the twentieth century we have to reach back a little way into the nineteenth. In 1865, Tony Pastor became one of the fathers of vaudeville when he opened an opera house in New York City's Bowery. But the figure from the vaudeville era who is best remembered today is Florenz Ziegfeld. Ziegfeld spotlighted such enduring stars as Fanny Brice, Eddie Cantor, and Marilyn Miller. He also produced George White's *Scandals* and Earl Carroll's *Vanities*.

Vaudeville was the first important venue for promoting hit songs. Unlike many music forums to follow, it was pure escapism. It didn't preach about social ills; instead, it served mindless, opulent entertainment in the form of trained dogs, jugglers, and dancing girls.

From the 1890s on, music publishers were centered in New York. *Tin Pan Alley* was born, and a host of standards sprang from it: "Take Me Out to the Ballgame," "Wait Till the Sun Shines Nellie," and "I Want a Girl."

The year 1910 was meaningful for the freelance songwriter. Hits included "Let Me Call You Sweetheart" and "Down by the Old Mill Stream." People were purchasing more inexpensive upright pianos and phonographs, and sheet music sales soared.

The Rise of Ragtime

Donald Clarke, author of *The Rise and Fall of Popular Music* (St. Martin's Griffin, 1995), offers a shrewd evaluation when he comments, "The history of modern popular music may be seen as the repeated rescuing of a moribund scene by the music of African Americans." Certainly this statement was true when rock and roll exploded in the mid-1950s, and *ragtime* was an early example.

Ragtime started in Chicago, St. Louis, and Louisville and spread like wildfire. Nearly 3,000 ragtime songs found their way into print, including over 100 ragtime waltzes. Many of these songs were created by the legendary Scott Joplin, whose music was adapted for *The Sting* by Marvin Hamlisch, who won an Oscar for it in 1973.

Joplin was born in Arkansas and began selling his early songs in 1895. "Maple Leaf Rag" was his biggest hit. Fifty piano rags and dozens of ragtime waltzes established Joplin's reputation. He died in 1917 in a mental hospital, 59 years before his opera *Treemonisha* was awarded a Pulitzer Prize.

Lyrical Lingo

Ragtime is a style of music that includes a series of 16-bar themes. When this music is played on the piano, the left hand provides accompaniment, and the right hand's playing is generally syncopated. Scott Joplin, Eubie Blake, and Jelly Roll Morton are the ragtime figures best known today.

Beyond Blackface

Some of the most popular vaudeville performers and ragtime singers were Al Jolson, Sophie Tucker, and Bert Williams. Al Jolson, who was famous for singing songs in blackface, was an early commercial equivalent of Elvis Presley and The Beatles: If he sang a song, it became a widespread smash. Unfortunately, Jolson was also one of the early major performers to steal credit from songwriters.

One significant performer who eventually refused to appear in the demeaning blackface was Sophie Tucker. Tucker built her identity as "the last of the red-hot mamas." Her signature song was "Some of These Days."

"Give My Regards to Broadway"

The golden age of songwriting kicked off in 1914 and lasted until 1955, the start of the rock era. Early, still-admired figures include Rudolph Friml, who had a big hit in 1914 with the show *Rose Marie,* and Sigmund Romberg, composer of the crowd-pleasing *Maytime* in 1917.

Songs reflected the first global conflict of the twentieth century with such right-on titles as "We're Going to Hang the Kaiser on the Linden Tree" and "We'll Give the Stars and Stripes to the Kaiser." Other World War I tunes, such as Richard Whiting's "Till We Meet Again," depicted the sadness of separation.

George M. Cohan

George M. Cohan can be seen as an early prototype for today's performers. Before the 1960s, most singers didn't write their material or produce it. Cohan, by contrast, was a composer, actor, dancer, singer, lyricist, producer, and director. His song "Over There" received the Congressional Medal of Honor. Songs dramatizing World War I included "The Man Who Put the Germ in Germany" and "Someday They'll Be Coming Home." Cohan also scored with such standards as "Yankee Doodle Dandy," later the name of a film based on his life. James Cagney won a 1942 Best Actor Oscar for his portrayal of Cohan.

Jerome Kern

Jerome Kern was another pioneer. Prior to 1927, when *Showboat* revolutionized Broadway, shows had flimsy *librettos* and songs that entertained but had no dramatic, character-driven value. World War I made people increasingly impatient with theatrical silliness, and they were ready for realism, even in their musicals.

Showboat's "Ol' Man River" was a startling departure. Without spelling it out, the song portrayed rootlessness, the plight of African Americans at that time, and an often hopeless search for stability and happiness. Other tunes in the score, such as "Bill" and "Can't Help Loving That Man," had the same gritty underpinning of reality.

Trouble Clef

Be cautious if singers, publishers, or producers want to put their names on your songs, even though they had nothing to do with writing them. Jolson claimed authorship and royalties from many standards he had no part in creating, including "Me and My Shadow," "The Anniversary Song," and "Avalon."

Lyrical Lingo

A **libretto** is the script, also called the book, of an opera or musical.

George Gershwin

Gershwin is remembered for such masterpieces as "Someone to Watch Over Me," "How Long Has This Been Going On?" and "But Not for Me." But popular songs were only one arrow on his musical bow.

In Gershwin's heyday, the 1920s and 1930s, people typically made the snobbish assumption that popular music writers were not capable of creating "serious" music. Gershwin changed that perception forever with *Rhapsody in Blue, An American in Paris,* and *Porgy and Bess.* The latter was a magnificent opera, arguably Gershwin's greatest achievement.

Trouble Clef

Never be afraid to take a chance and stretch your talents. Like Gershwin, Billy Joel and Paul McCartney have both written classical works.

Irving Berlin, a Man of the People

Irving Berlin understood the man in the street. He knew instinctively which of the public's musical buttons to push, and he wanted to reach everyone. "God Bless America" demonstrated how songs could tap into a listener's patriotic feelings. "White Christmas" and "Easter Parade" reached millions and permanently shaped the way that Americans have looked at those holidays ever since. With "Alexander's Ragtime Band," Berlin revived America's love of ragtime music (though there are those who question whether the song qualifies as an authentic representation of the form); ragtime pianists and orchestras became the rage.

Backstage Banter

In 1937, Cole Porter suffered a crippling riding accident that later led to the amputation of a leg and sentenced him to being an invalid for the rest of his life. Despite this situation, he created his Broadway masterpiece, *Kiss Me Kate,* which opened in 1948.

The Elite Cole Porter

Cole Porter's reign began in 1929 with his hit song, "I'm in Love Again." Unlike Berlin's style, Porter's musical and lyric voice was sophisticated, chic, and risqué. It was what critics called "naughty," and it slyly furthered open sexuality. "Night and Day," "I Get a Kick Out of You," and "Just One of Those Things" sustained that witty tradition, although Porter successfully tried his hand at down-to-earth, accessible material with "Don't Fence Me In."

Songs of the Great Depression and World War II

E. Y. Harburg and Jay Gorney wrote a classic Depression song, "Brother Can You Spare a Dime?" But upbeat, cheery songs that could distract Americans from their financial woes were more prevalent during that period. A definitive example was "On the Sunny Side of the Street," which told everyone that if they never had a dime, they'd be rich as Rockefeller.

As in World War I, romantic songs ("I'll Never Smile Again," "I'll Be Seeing You," and "Sentimental Journey") flooded the market during World War II, expressing the hope of enduring reunions between GIs and the women who waited for them at home.

Rodgers, Hart, and Hammerstein

The wit and polish of Cole Porter were also characteristic of Lorenz Hart's lyrics, and he paired up with Richard Rodgers to write "With a Song in My Heart," "Mountain Greenery," "My Heart Stood Still," "My Romance," and many other standards. Rodgers and Hart turned out some of the best songs ever written, but the shows that contained them (*Jumbo, The Boys from Syracuse, Babes in Arms*) had weak, disjointed librettos.

Rodgers solved the problem of having his superb songs undermined by substandard books when he teamed with lyricist/librettist Oscar Hammerstein, who was responsible for the dramatically powerful lyrics from *Showboat*. The Rodgers and Hammerstein team made theater history with *Oklahoma* by integrating every song into the plotline. No one broke into song without reason; everything had to fit naturally.

Rodgers and Hammerstein dealt with pressing social issues. After two World Wars, theater audiences wanted songs that reflected the people and problems they knew. Songs such as "You've Got to Be Carefully Taught (To Hate and Fear)" from *South Pacific* centered on racial prejudice. *The King and I* stressed the importance of democratic change. Even the wholesome family story of *The Sound of Music* spotlighted the encroaching threat of Nazism.

Crosby, Sinatra, and the Pop Singers

Opportunities for songwriters exploded when pop singers started to dominate the airwaves. Bing Crosby became record and box office gold in the 1930s, and by the 1940s Frank Sinatra was in the limelight, along with Perry Como, Rosemary Clooney, Peggy Lee, and Jo Stafford.

Equally popular was the velvet-voiced Nat "King" Cole, who sang "Mona Lisa" and "For Sentimental Reasons." His hit recording of the mellow and idealistic "Too Young" demonstrated—to the delight of a teenage audience on the verge of taking over the pop song market—that adults were clueless, and would discover The Truth: Very young lovers could have a genuine and permanent relationship.

The Role of Rock

World War II had greatly influenced such bittersweet tunes as "I'll Be Seeing You," "For All We Know (We May Never Meet Again)," and "P.S. I Love You." After peace broke out, these tender, genuinely moving hits gave way to such impersonal, bland nonsense as "Shrimp Boats Are A-Comin'," and "How Much Is That Doggie in the Window?" Such safe, sexless tunes had no personality or cultural significance, and they had no relevance to young people and their preoccupations. The stage was set for a hard-driving, hostile takeover. Cleveland disc jockey Alan Freed was the first to sense this dissatisfaction and act on it.

At the time, black music was played only on small Harlem stations, and these raunchy, flesh-and-blood blues songs were referred to by *Billboard* as "race" records. Freed knew they would create a sensation with white teenagers, and he was the first disc jockey to play them for a white audience. Freed also championed integrated concert bills, a move that made civic officials and concerned parents apoplectic.

Rocking the Clock Forward

After the Korean War, the 1950s were a relatively calm period, a period during which television spotlighted the perfect family and a Gee-Whiz-Dad-Can-I-Borrow-the-Car attitude prevailed. It was also a time when rhythm and blues, so long suppressed, could no longer be held back. Chuck Berry, Fats Domino, Buddy Holly, and Jerry Lee Lewis (who announced, "This is the killer, baby") blasted all traces of sentimentality from pop music.

Trouble Clef

Songwriters of the 1940s, such as Sammy Cahn, kept insisting that rock was a passing fad and refused to write for it, figuring that it would go away. This resistance to new trends stopped their careers cold. A songwriter should always keep an open mind and move with the times.

Bill Haley's "Rock Around the Clock" in 1955 turned rock music into a lasting sensation when it thundered over the credits of the film, *The Blackboard Jungle.* Once it became evident that rock was here to stay, squeaky-clean artists such as Pat Boone and the Crew Cuts immediately released sanitized versions of the funky originals. For example, "Work with Me Annie" by Hank Ballard turned into the respectable "Dance with Me Henry."

Fans began to clamor for the original, sexually charged versions of the songs Freed was broadcasting. Shaking his way into the center of this national hunger was Elvis Presley, protégé of Sun Records President Sam Phillips, who wanted to promote "a white boy who could sing black." Presley unleashed a tornado of controversy, which only made him more popular.

Bob Dylan

Bob Dylan was rock's first major social spokesman. "Blowin' in the Wind" became an anthem for the growing civil rights movement. His subjects ranged from the evils of war to the value of Christianity. Musically, he blended blues, folk, and rock, and his lyrics were the first rock words to venture heavily into poetry. Most of all, he told other songwriters that they could speak about vital subjects, spew out their discontent, and use music as a means of changing the world. Dylan's messages were particularly inspiring to the songwriters who wrote of their anger and despair during the Vietnam War.

Sex in a Red Jumpsuit

A jumpsuit that James Brown wore had the word *SEX* stitched across the front. If you didn't catch the message from his clothes, you could hear it in his music: Sex was a natural thing. Brown screamed, "I'm black and I'm proud," and along with his blues and gospel shouting, he demonstrated rock as theater with a live show that included pirouettes, whirls, and splits. He let everyone know, "I Got You (I Feel Good)" and "It's a Man's Man's Man's World."

The Beach Boys

The world continually seesaws between dark and light, yin and yang. There's always a need for sunshine to balance bitterness, and The Beach Boys supplied that sunshine. Through the period of the assassination of the Kennedy brothers and the marches against Vietnam, The Beach Boys offered an antidote with "Surfin' USA," "Be True to Your School," and "Fun, Fun, Fun." The message seemed to be: No matter what horrors surround you, there's a magic place, an Oz with palm trees called California.

The Beatles' Artistic Fearlessness

Although Elvis was designated and remained "the King," crushing competition arrived in 1964 with The Beatles. The Beatles offered more than a performing alternative: They wrote brilliant material. Lennon and McCartney (and occasionally George Harrison) were tuneful, and beyond that, they were wildly inventive and experimental—a point conclusively proved with their *Sergeant Pepper's Lonely Hearts Club Band* album.

The Beatles' run of hits began with "I Want to Hold Your Hand" and moved on to "A Hard Day's Night," "Ticket to Ride," and "Yesterday." They were—and are—to aspiring songwriters, an example of the power of versatility, and how much is possible if you allow varying influences to affect your writing style. Lennon and McCartney digested Chuck Berry, the Everly Brothers, and the Brill Building pop of Carole King and Gerry Goffin, Leiber and Stoller, and Barry Mann and Cynthia Weil.

Lennon and McCartney jumped from sweet ballads ("Yesterday") to gospel ("Let It Be"); "Lady Madonna" and "Get Back" were tough and edgy. "Something" by George Harrison was unabashedly romantic. There was no genre, no beat, The Beatles wouldn't try, and this artistic bravery made them unique.

The Beatles caused cultural change in small and big ways. A highly visible but minor change was hair length; half the world imitated their haircuts and their clothes. They also fostered the attitude that marijuana and LSD ("Lucy in the Sky with Diamonds") were the answer to social and personal problems.

19

From a writing point of view, The Beatles endangered the status of freelance songwriters by encouraging record labels to focus on singer-songwriters. As artists wrote more and more of their own material, the freelance writer's role was diminished until its rebirth in the 1990s (largely through Diane Warren), although such freelancers as Carole Bayer Sager had continued success.

The classical establishment certified Beatles music as art, elevating them (and rock and roll in general) to intellectual respectability. Journalists from *Time, Newsweek,* and *The New York Times* treated The Beatles' music with respect, and a major music critic said that they were as talented as classical composer Franz Schubert.

The Rolling Stones

If The Beatles initially reassured parents with their clean-cut faces and Edwardian suits, the Rolling Stones terrified them. Mick Jagger screamed, "I Can't Get No Satisfaction," sang about "Honky-Tonk Women," and ordered, "Get Off My Cloud." The Stones have represented rebellion throughout their career.

Motown Magic

Berry Gordy's contribution to social change is reflected in the definition he gave his company: "The Sound of Young America." Berry, a former boxer and songwriter ("Reet Petite," "Lonely Teardrops") was determined to reach the largest possible audience. His combination of gospel and blues was exciting, unforgettably singable, and nonthreatening. More than any other label, Gordy's Motown made pop R&B acceptable to everyone, teenagers as well as adults.

The Supremes, Smokey Robinson and the Miracles, Marvin Gaye, Martha and the Vandellas, Michael Jackson, and Stevie Wonder turned out hit after hit for Motown. Ross, in particular, was elegant, feline, a society belle who could appeal to people mingling at the Copa and to those who didn't know where the Copa was.

Independent Women

While the girlishly enticing Diana Ross and the Supremes sang of "Baby Love," Atlantic Records' explosively emotional Aretha Franklin stared down any man who dared to oppose her, demanded respect, and told her lover, "You make me feel like a natural woman."

When the women's movement arrived, its voice was both reflected in the pop songs and amplified by them. Helen Reddy's "I Am Woman" was the most heavily played. Loretta Lynn's "The Pill" was also a groundbreaker.

Backstage Banter

When President Reagan used Springsteen's "Born in the USA" as his basis for citing Springsteen as a positive example of American values, and conservative columnist George Will offered further endorsement, Springsteen used his concert forum to let audiences know that he was politically poles apart from Reagan and George Will.

Bruce Springsteen

Bruce Springsteen appeared simultaneously on the covers of *Time* and *Newsweek,* and the world heard Jann Wenner's proclamation, "I've seen the future of rock and roll, and his name is Bruce Springsteen."

The Rap Revolution

Originally dismissed as temporary, the way rock and roll was in 1955, rap is now never out of the Top 10, and its influence continues to grow. Unlike other rock genres, rap isn't something a songwriter can study. It has to be in your blood and your culture. Songwriters can wear multiple musical hats, as Lennon and McCartney demonstrated; as Diane Warren does today. But rap, whether you plan to write it or not, should be listened to, because of the power and awareness of the spoken words, the pounding percussion and rhythm.

Listening to the controversial Eminem, Cuban Link, Too Short, X-Con, and Dr. Dre provides a reminder that modern music is all about emotion. Rap emphasizes the necessity of throwing your entire body and soul into writing today's music. It also paints a sharp, sometimes shocking, portrait of inner-city life and problems.

Backstage Banter

With the arrival of MTV and VH1, stars had to do more than just sing; they had to have a "look." Suddenly, what singers wore meant as much as what they sang.

Michael Jackson and the MTV Explosion

Writing songs that offered visual experiences was always a good idea; when the 1980s were in full swing and 24-hour music cable channels MTV and VH1 were launched, it became mandatory.

Quick Cuts

Movies such as *Flashdance* featured the MTV style: The plot was minimal, the camera never stayed still long enough to develop a character, and dance numbers were chopped into fragments. Viewers hardly had time to decide whether they liked something before it disappeared from the screen.

The MTV approach, dramatic as it was, had a negative effect on the public's attention span. If a story wasn't told with roller-coaster speed, viewers rejected it and switched channels. Despite this drawback, superstar directors saw a new future, and luminaries such as Brian DePalma and Sam Peckinpah did videos, respectively, with Bruce Springsteen and Julian Lennon.

Videos Come of Age

The musical possibilities of MTV emerged forcefully when Michael Jackson became its artistic spokesman. Jackson's videos were short movies; for example, he employed movie director John Landis to give dimension to his video for "Thriller," which resulted in a mini horror picture with elaborate makeup and dance sequences and vocal participation by horror king Vincent Price.

Videos continue to grow more imaginative, so if you as a songwriter hope to keep up with changing trends in commercial music, you should watch MTV or VH1 at least twice a week. Even overproduced videos or theatrical flights that bear no relationship to the lyrics sharpen the visual sense.

Hirschhorn's Hints

When MTV's *Total Request Live* or VH1's *Top 20 Countdown* is on, tape it. Listening to radio or CDs is not enough anymore. Music is as much about the eye as the ear.

A Rock Genre Mini Guide

No music has ever splintered into so many groups and spawned so many hybrids as rock and roll. Here are some of the genres:

➤ **Brill Building pop.** Hit songs composed in two New York buildings housing music publishers (1619 Broadway and 1650 Broadway). The Brill Building pop era featured hits by Carole King, Gerry Goffin, Barry Mann, Cynthia Weil, Neil Sedaka, Howie Greenfield, Neil Diamond, Burt Bacharach and Hal David, and Al Kasha and Joel Hirschhorn.

Backstage Banter

Carole King sang the majority of her songs on demo tapes from the early 1960s to the 1970s. These tapes were so effective that hundreds of artists recorded her material. The word around the Brill Building was that King sang her songs better than the performers who cut them. She had one minor hit, "It Might As Well Rain Until September," in 1962, but she had to wait nine more years before full acceptance as an artist on her album *Tapestry.*

➤ **Bubblegum.** Nursery-rhyme melodies with a rock beat. Some of the biggest bubblegum records are "Yummy Yummy Yummy" and "Sugar Sugar."

➤ **Disco.** Dance music that started in the early 1970s and centered around clubs that provided recorded (rather than live) music, lighted dance floors, and high-tech sound systems. Donna Summer was disco's undisputed queen.

➤ **Doo wop.** *A capella* harmonizing of rock groups.

Lyrical Lingo

A cappella is singing without any instrumental accompaniment.

➤ **Folk rock.** The marriage of folk music with a rock and roll beat. The Byrds were closely identified with this style.

➤ **Girl groups.** All-girl singing groups were hugely popular in the 1960s. Some of the best were The Crystals ("Uptown," "He's a Rebel"), The Dixie Cups ("Chapel of Love"), Chiffons ("One Fine Day"), The Shangri-Las ("Leader of the Pack"), and Angels ("My Boyfriend's Back").

➤ **Gospel.** A blend of black spirituals and Southern folk music. Gospel, folk, and blues originally combined to create rock and roll.

➤ **Hard rock.** Music packed with bluesy riffs and distorted guitars.

➤ **R&B (rhythm and blues).** Pop and dance music derived from the blues of the 1940s, with a pounding backbeat.

➤ **Rap/hip-hop.** Spoken street lyrics over pounding rhythm, with frequent use of sampling (using bits of music or rhythm from other records).

➤ **Rockabilly.** A blend of blues and country that evolved into rock and roll. Elvis Presley got it rolling with his early Sun sessions in Memphis, and Jerry Lee Lewis, Carl Perkins, and Johnny Cash continued the tradition until the form lost momentum in the 1950s.

➤ **Soft rock.** Gentle, middle-of-the-road melodies by bands such as Bread, The Carpenters, and Air Supply.

➤ **Soul.** Combination of rhythm and blues and gospel. Notable representatives of soul are "Lady Soul" herself, Aretha Franklin ("I Never Loved a Man the Way I Love You"), Don Covay ("Mercy Mercy"), and Wilson Pickett ("In the Midnight Hour").

Of all the musical genres in history, none has produced so many popular variations as rock and roll. Today more than ever, a songwriter has to be familiar with every kind of music, because rock forms overlap. From classical to tin pan alley, country to soul and rap, they meld into a creative stew. That's how pop/rock, folk/rock and every other hybrid came about. Don't just lock yourself into current hits or the current era. Influences that spring from a century ago, as well as last month, can be blended into unique new forms of music.

The Least You Need to Know

➤ Vaudeville provided a forum for popular songs.

➤ During the first half of the twentieth century, many of the best songwriters wrote for Broadway shows.

➤ The rise of radio and stars such as Bing Crosby and Frank Sinatra increased opportunities for songwriters.

➤ Evolving from rhythm and blues in the 1950s, rock and roll appealed to the rebelliousness of the young.

➤ MTV made the music business a visual world.

Chapter 3

The Idea Is King

In This Chapter

➤ Ways to banish writer's block

➤ Studying people around you for inspiration

➤ Media sources for hit material

➤ Titles of every kind and color

➤ A song written as a four-minute screenplay

➤ The self-hypnosis highway to hit-writing

As Chapter 2, "A Century of Songwriting," pointed out, hit songs are not created in a vacuum. To some extent, they reflect the historical conditions and social consciousness of their time. It's essential to be aware of the trends and currents that influence what's in the Top 10, but when the time comes to sit down and do the writing, ideas are the support system of a song. Without them, lyrics, tunes, and arrangements mean nothing. Before you begin thinking about embellishments, make sure you have a basic concept that excites you and justifies all the hard work.

There's a saying in the motion-picture business, "A great score won't save a poor film." But a wonderful idea, even imperfectly executed, usually shines through. Ideas are everything in songwriting. The tips in this chapter will help you generate them.

Banish Writer's Block

Composers and lyricists all have the same emotional reaction when they start writing a song: uneasiness, insecurity, and even terror. If you experience these feelings when you're trying to write, don't panic. If you feel the need to walk around the house, water the flowers, wash dishes, or hang a picture, do it! With each passing minute, your subconscious is gathering the courage to start creating. Eventually, you'll find yourself in front of a piano, a guitar, or a computer.

Backstage Banter

Billy Joel on the writer's block experience: "The thing you don't have control of is writing. You have to pull it out of yourself. You pace the room with something like the dry heaves, having no control over the muse, horrified that it won't come. All that's out there with you is the piano, this big black beast with 88 teeth."

—Fred Bronson, *The Billboard Book of Number One Hits*, Billboard Books, 1992

Once there, tell yourself that it doesn't matter what you write. Suspend all conscious judgment. Never be a third party evaluating whether your work is good or bad. Just jump in and get started. If the chords are ordinary and the lyrics are hackneyed, ignore it. Keep moving, and your sluggish creative engine will rumble into gear.

Dig Deeper

Once you've started writing, the next step is to find ideas that strike you as special. These ideas generally surface with increased focus and concentration, but not always. Sometimes you're just not satisfied, no matter how much effort you put into the song. Before indulging in self-flagellation (a typical response from writers), remember that there are numerous methods to stimulate the brain and dig out worthwhile ideas.

Keep Your Eye on the Idea

When you have your story and you sit down to begin the lyric, it's easy to lose sight of the main idea and wander off in a dozen directions. Stephen Sondheim has a neat trick to keep himself on course. He writes a synopsis of his idea at the top of the page and keeps referring back to it. Sondheim is also known for writing down every detail of his characters: how they dress, the cars they drive, their career aspirations. Keep yourself rooted in the main premise by putting reminders of what it is on every page.

Backstage Banter

The prolific songwriter Diane Warren had a friend who confided that her ex-husband still hoped for reconciliation, even though she had met someone else she wanted to marry. Diane's friend had to tell her ex that the relationship was beyond salvaging. Diane recognized that this situation would make a great song and told her friend, "I hope you're not too mad at me, but I used your life." That spark became the number-one hit "Look Away" by Chicago.

—Fred Bronson, *The Billboard Book of Number One Hits*, Billboard Books, 1992

Satisfy Yourself

Country great Tom T. Hall warns against writing to please others rather than creating what you personally want to write. "My blocks come when producers, publishers, agents, managers, people are on my back," he says. Don't become too concerned with the expectations of others, or your inner idea mechanism will get jammed.

Inspiring Characters

Hit songs always feature characters and conflicts that are familiar and universal. The Eagles understood the "New Kid in Town." Who hasn't been a newcomer, a fish out of water, breaking into unfamiliar circles? Billy Joel showed us the chic "Uptown Girl," Madonna pointed out the "Material Girl," and Garth Brooks defined his "Friends in Low Places."

These songwriters developed an acute awareness of individuals around them, a grasp of their hopes, dreams, and tragedies; then they utilized that knowledge to create interesting characters. These characters are all around you. All you need to do is develop your powers of observation: Study people you've never noticed before or those you've taken for granted. Once you've begun to look closely at the people around you, make it a daily habit.

Hirschhorn's Hints

Everybody has an image of themselves that they want to project. Often, however, that image is their cover; it's not the real person. The trick is to notice eccentricities that shine a light on the true individual.

The trick is to allow your imagination complete freedom. You're a hundred different people inside. Think of yourself as an actor, prepared at any moment to assume roles much different than your daily personality. The basic emotions exist in everyone, no matter how different they appear.

The People on the Street

All people are colorful and unique. Go to a club, and you'll encounter Abba's "Dancing Queen." Look around on a bus, and you're bound to spot the Allman Brothers' "Rambling Man." Any beach in California will produce Brian Wilson's "Surfer Girl." Lennon and McCartney created a wonderful portrait of a "Paperback Writer." And every high school student has met or observed Dion's "Runaround Sue."

Suppose you have a neighbor who always wears custom-made suits. Yet one day you see him in a short-sleeve shirt and notice that he has tattoos. Or you've noticed an elderly woman who wears her hair loose and flowing, like a young girl. These clues define character. The conservatively dressed neighbor whom you know to be an accountant may once have been a Hell's Angel. The elderly woman may live in the past and wish she was still in college.

Some people want to be kind even if they act tough. Some seem shy, but are boiling with aggression inside. Some are wildly sexual even though they present a bland, passionless front. Your job is to find out the real personality and write about it with depth and compassion. Ask yourself: Is the tough person disguising the pain of a childhood trauma? Is the shy person terrified of expressing his or her true emotions because they may be violent?

You can be a lyricist who reaches millions if you break through that first, superficial layer and uncover hidden truths. Just remember: Don't take any person or situation at face value.

Trouble Clef

Some songwriters, particularly new ones, are afraid to write what they feel because it might touch upon other peoples' lives. Don't censor yourself. My first hit was called "Why Can't You Bring Me Home?" by Jay and the Americans, and it dealt with a girlfriend who wouldn't bring me to her house because she was ashamed of her family. She didn't resent the truthful lyrics, and the song put me on the charts for the first time.

Loved Ones

That "hit" character may be someone close to you. Emilio Estefan Jr., Gloria Estefan's producer and husband, was inspired to write the touching number-one single "Coming Out of the Dark" after his wife nearly died in a bus accident. He wanted to capture the pain and heartbreak of her long rehabilitation and poured all his feelings into a song that portrayed her struggle.

Your Own Life

Sometimes the one you want to study is yourself. Maybe a relationship has gone sour, or the one you love doesn't return your feeling. R. Kelly, who had a hit with "I Believe I Can Fly," expressed his unrequited love for a girl through "Bump and Grind."

Universal Themes

Successful songs tap into the emotions that everyone feels. If you're feeling depressed, suffering a loss, being betrayed, ending a relationship, falling in love, feeling grateful to your parents, longing for the carefree days of youth, or wanting to ask forgiveness, there's a song for you. Thinking about these themes in terms of the characters you've observed is a good way to generate ideas for songs that everyone can relate to.

The Blues

When you're feeling depressed, you can do three things: give in to the despair, try to ignore it, or write about it. Using your heartache creatively will get you over the rough spots. John Lennon admitted that the song "Help" wasn't just a lyric to fulfill a movie assignment. He was expressing desperation because, "It was my fat Elvis period. I was depressed and crying out for help."

The Tragedy Trigger

Personal tragedy, such as the loss of a friend, a spouse, a parent, or a child, can trigger a great song. B. A. Robertson, in collaboration with Mike Rutherford of Mike and the Mechanics, wrote "The Living Years," a haunting story of a son who loses his father before ever being able to express his love. Robertson's father died immediately after the first verse was written. Rutherford's dad also passed away that same year.

GREATEST HINTS ALBUM

Hirschhorn's Hints

Janet Jackson claims, "My mother always said that ever since she could remember, I've been concerned with other people before myself." You'll be a much better writer and observer if you get off the subject of yourself and focus on the needs and feelings of others.

—Fred Bronson, *The Billboard Book of Number One Hits*, Billboard Books, 1992

Eric Clapton's "Tears in Heaven" centered on the heartbreak of losing a child. Clapton himself experienced this tragedy when his son, Conor, fell from a window the maid had left open. Millions of parents experiencing similar tragedies could identify with Clapton's grief.

Cheating Hearts

One painful but timeless theme is faithlessness. "Lyin' Eyes," popularized by the Eagles, presents a portrait of a girl who can't be true, a conscienceless climber who uses friends and lovers in her quest for position and money. "Me and Mrs. Jones" dramatizes sexual betrayal and the guilt involved. So does Elvis Costello's "Baby Plays Around."

Breaking Up

Divorce is another increasingly relevant topic in today's society. Cher took on the subject when she informed her family, "You'd Better Sit Down, Kids," and "D-I-V-O-R-C-E," sung by Tammy Wynette, dealt with a young mother spelling out the D word so her children wouldn't understand what painful issue was confronting her.

Endless Love

Who hasn't been so overwhelmed by consuming attraction that they could hardly think straight? Write down these feelings, the way Billy Joel did in "Shameless." The song scored with Joel and then became a hit for Garth Brooks. Undying devotion has always been a staple of songs in every genre. Examples are Faith Hill's "Breathe," Marc Anthony's "You Sang to Me," Michael Bolton's "How Am I Supposed to Live Without You?" and Celine Dion's "The Power of Love."

Backstage Banter

Writing about intense, eternal love has been one of the secrets behind Diane Warren's success. She has had 63 Top 10 records, and 300 artists have recorded her tunes.

Pride in Your Parents

For those who believe that pop music revolves primarily around the seamier aspects of life, consider the song "My Greatest Fan?" performed by the Backstreet Boys. This memorable ballad is a tribute to mom, who is always pushing her son to excel and believing in him. Tributes to family are invariably songs that move the public.

People will always warn you to avoid being sentimental and corny. Don't listen. There's nothing wrong with sentiment if you do it with honesty. Axl Rose of the band Guns n' Roses feels that many rock bands are too wimpy to have any sentiment or emotion.

Traveling Back in Time

Nostalgia always touches the heart, from "The Way We Were" to "Yesterday." Al Kasha and I wrote a nostalgic song with Charles Aznavour, "The Old-Fashioned Way," that was a hit all over the world because it externalized the longing people have to re-experience a past when times were sweeter and simpler and return to lost lovers and dreams that have faded.

Close your eyes and let your mind float back, or as a Diane Warren title wistfully expresses it, "If I Could Turn Back Time." All sorts of memories will bubble up from your subconscious, and you'll be deluged with first-rate song ideas.

Hirschhorn's Hints

Save everything you write. File it away for future use. Felice Bryant saves every scrap of paper, never throws *anything* out. Rejects re-examined at a later date have resulted in hits for numerous composers who followed Bryant's pattern.

All Apologies

In love, people explode, say tactless things, and risk destroying their relationships. A common theme in pop music is a request for forgiveness. Brenda Lee, John Denver, and the Platters sang different songs titled "I'm Sorry," and Connie Francis said, "I'm Sorry I Made You Cry." This approach is commercially successful because so many people who are hurt long for an apology, and so many others have difficulty offering one. You as a songwriter can speak for them.

Mining the Media

Hirschhorn's Hints

Using an overheard comment creatively worked for Steven Stills, but if you try it, always make sure—particularly if the line came from a fellow songwriter—that you have full permission to use it so you won't be surprised with a lawsuit later on.

Television, books, movies, newspapers, and magazines are rich avenues for ideas. Songwriting is synonymous with emotion, and the ongoing conflicts portrayed in the media provide countless sagas of love, hate, fear, rivalry, and rebellion.

Don't forget the wealth of input available online. The Internet combines information from every possible source: news, movies, stage, music, and biography. Let this electronic library fill your mind with ideas, titles, and tunes.

Chance Encounters Lead to Hits

Johnny Cash went to see a film called *Inside the Walls of Folsom Prison* to kill time before catching a plane and found himself captivated by the picture's main character, a convict. During the flight, he wrote lyrics and then composed the melody for the composition that subsequently became a number-one country smash, "Folsom Prison Blues."

Even something as simple as a chance remark might stimulate creativity. Steven Stills was attending a party when he overheard another guest, Billy Preston, say, "Love the one you're with." His ear latched onto that provocative phrase, and he asked Preston if he could pinch the line. Preston consented, and "Love the One You're With" became the title for a big hit.

I Am Woman

When you're selecting ideas, try to tap into current attitudes. For example, women used to be seen as sweet, demure, and helpless, embodied by Debby Boone and other apple-pie heartthrobs one could take home to mother. Then in the 1970s, Helen Reddy screamed, "I am woman, hear me roar." Donna Summer and Barbra Streisand gave men a double-barreled lecture with "Enough Is Enough." Today, Cher clenches her fists and shouts, "I'm strong enough to live without you," adding "There's no more to say, so save your breath." Celine Dion informs her lover that he was history with the slamming of the door, and she's never wasted any time on him since then.

Simple Starting Points

If no character intrigues you, offers any inspiration; the grand song themes leave you cold; and the media is not inspiring you, start with something small, such as an interesting image, phrase, or title. The following sections provide examples of how these small pieces can turn into big hits.

Devil or Angel

Religion is a fertile arena for ideas. George Harrison sang to "My Sweet Lord," and Brian Wilson told us that "God Only Knows." Elvis Presley spent his time "Crying in the Chapel," and Madonna warned her dad, "Papa Don't Preach."

On the flip side of the spirituality coin are songs spotlighting the devil, from "Little Devil" and "Devil Woman" to "The Devil Went Down to Georgia." A sure-fire commercial contrast to these devil songs are angel songs, from "Angel Baby" to "How Do You Talk to an Angel?"

"Barbara Ann" to "A Boy Named Sue"

Using names, male and female, has often been a direct route to the Top 10. Think of how many name-based hits you've heard: "Barbara Ann," "Delilah," "Maybellene," "Gloria," "Sara Smile," "Jean," "Mrs. Robinson," "Little Jeannie," "Michelle," and "Joanna."

There aren't as many songs on the male front, but we still have "Tommy," "Daniel," "(Billy) Don't be a Hero," "Big Bad John," "Hey Jude," "Jesse," "Sir Duke," and even "A Boy Named Sue."

Location, Location, Location

Chances are you've done some traveling. Even if you haven't, you know the neighborhood where you grew up, nearby cities, a mountain resort where you spent the summer. Use those backgrounds for a story. You've seen them, so you can depict the details realistically. Places provide a wonderful framework for hits: "Creeque Alley" and "California Dreaming" (The Mamas and Papas), "Detroit City" (Tom Jones), "Down in the Boondocks" (Billy Joe Royal), "On Broadway" (The Drifters), "(Girl from) Ipanema" (Astrud Gilberto), and "South of the Border" (Frank Sinatra).

Writers often conclude that song settings have to be exotic and far removed from everyday reality in order to make an impact. They can be, as "Xanadu," "Montego Bay," and "Jamaica Farewell" testify. But Dolly Parton made life in an office entertaining and colorful with her buoyant "9 to 5." "Five O'Clock World" did the same thing, as did "Take a Letter, Maria."

The Songwriter's Paintbrush

Colors are the key to many hit songs, such as: "Nights in White Satin," "Blue Suede Shoes," "Purple Rain," "Red, Red Wine," "Crystal Blue Persuasion," "Yellow Submarine," and "Brown-Eyed Girl." A great way to sharpen your sense of color is to become interested in art. Look at paintings, either in a museum or in a catalogue of color reproductions. Study the cinematography in a movie rather than just immersing yourself in the plot.

Animal Magic

Did you enjoy visiting the zoo as a child? Do you have pets? Do you have an affinity for nature? Draw upon those feelings and utilize animal imagery. These hit songs did: "Hound Dog," "Let Me Be Your Teddy Bear," "When Doves Cry," "The Lion Sleeps Tonight," "Muskrat Love," and "Bird Dog."

Backstage Banter

Birds figure in 24 of the Top 100 rock songs of all time. Dogs are second, with 11, and cats are next with 9.

Good Days and Bad Days

How often do we say we hate Mondays, because we have to go back to work? Do you love Fridays, because the weekend is coming up? Do you dread Saturday nights because you don't have a date? Do you resent Sundays, because the weekend is almost over? There's a wealth of material in free-associating about the seven days of the week. Hit songs do it all the time: "Monday, Monday," "Ruby Tuesday," "Friday on My Mind," "Saturday in the Park," and our own Top 10 hit by the Peppermint Rainbow, "Will You Be Staying After Sunday?"

Questions and Answers

Madonna and Patrick Leonard asked, "Who's That Girl?" and Frank Wildhorn and Chuck Jackson were desperate to learn "Where Do Broken Hearts Go?" Questions are excellent ways to intrigue and pull in the listener. A skillful writer can then answer the question well enough to give listeners complete satisfaction.

Holiday Songs

Because Christmas happens only in December, getting a Christmas song recorded is not easy. If you write one, be sure it's completed early in the year, because Christmas music is usually chosen and slated for albums by late summer or early fall. The advantage of a Christmas cut is its longevity. If a yuletide number catches on, it often turns into a perennial, such as "Silver Bells," "The Christmas Song," or "White Christmas," which is one of the biggest-selling singles in history. Christmas standards are re-recorded over and over again. The payoff is high if you hit, so it's worth the gamble.

Hirschhorn's Hints

Titles are more than subjects. They also allow you to bend the language cleverly. "Hurts So Bad" became "Hurt So Good." "We've Got to Stop Meeting Like This" was turned into "We've Got to Start Meeting Like This."

The Four-Minute Screenplay

When searching for subjects, you can express a straightforward emotion, as in Mariah Carey's "Vision of Love," or you can create a story song so fully fleshed out that the song is a miniature movie. Examples of this are "American Pie," "Harper Valley PTA," "Ode to Billie Joe," "Escape (The Piña Colada Song)," and "By the Time I Get to Phoenix." A life-altering event can also be utilized for a dramatic story, whether it's a wedding ("Wedding Bell Blues") or a funeral ("Green Green Grass of Home" and "He Stopped Loving Her Today").

Do you have the storytelling gift? If you do, you're way ahead of your competitors. Absorbing stories are always in demand, and most writers lack the talent to create them. If you suspect that your talent lies in story songs, give them your full concentration. I guarantee that the effort will pay off.

When you have the story clearly etched in your mind, with a beginning, middle, and end, the song will flow. To facilitate this process, you may want to emulate Stephen Sondheim and work backward by devising the end first and then moving in reverse to the beginning.

Priming the Idea Pump

The process of developing ideas can be urged on even more quickly with a method I employ: Close your eyes and say to yourself, "I have dozens of great ideas." Do this over and over again, particularly before you drop off to sleep. To heighten the effect, say it into a tape recorder, put on earphones, and listen to your own voice repeating the thought, "I have dozens of great ideas." Within two or three days, your mind will be bursting with fresh ideas and concepts.

Just coming up with ideas isn't enough, though. You have to trust them and act on them and not let insecurity prevent you from completing them. You can conquer the fears that limit your creativity in these ways:

Hirschhorn's Hints

If you blend inner motivation and outward observation, I promise you'll never again say, "I can't find any ideas." The problem will become, "I have too many ideas. Which ones will I use, and which will I discard?"

> ➤ Don't put songs aside in the middle because you're afraid of criticism.

> ➤ Don't rewrite too much; you may lose the special quality the idea started with.

> ➤ Don't automatically put ideas aside because someone you tell about them isn't enthusiastic about the premise.

> ➤ Don't shelve a song because a recording of it didn't turn out as well as you moving. If the material is strong enough, record it again.

> ➤ Don't drop an idea because you get the feeling that ideas by other writers are superior.

Travel the Highway to Hits

Good songwriters are observant. Be a student of all you see around you. All too often, we retreat into our private worlds, rarely gazing outward at the parade of events moving around us. Developing an intense fascination for this parade will guarantee the arrival of platinum ideas.

The Least You Need to Know

➤ Ideas are the support system of your song.

➤ Don't let pre-work jitters intimidate you.

➤ Think of tragedies and triumphs in your own life and utilize them.

➤ Write about problems such as divorce, sexual betrayal, the loss of a child, or tragic love.

➤ Explore universal themes such as love and religion; and use names, places, animals, colors, and anything that engages you for ideas.

➤ Keep your ideas flowing. Trust them and act on them.

➤ Study everybody around you as character material.

Chapter 4

What Comes First, Words or Music?

> ### In This Chapter
>
> ➤ The importance of flexibility
>
> ➤ Writing for an artist
>
> ➤ Words vs. music for Rodgers, Rice, David, and Newman

Should music or lyrics come first? As a composer/lyricist who has collaborated and also written alone, I can answer this question from both sides of the fence. There are no fixed rules, despite the insistence of songwriters on all sides that one method is superior to the other. The only rules necessary are the ones you personally apply to each individual partnership.

If you begin collaborating with a partner who demands that you adhere strictly to his or her style of working, you should cut off the relationship immediately and search for someone else to work with. You both have to function in a way that's natural to your basic style and personality.

Working Styles

Sometimes the songwriting process is extremely simple and friction-free: The lyricist comes up with a complete set of words, and the tune writer hands his or her partner a finished melody. Whether the words or music come first or second is irrelevant. The division of labor in such cases can be clear to the point where each partner accepts the other's contribution without any suggestions.

Backstage Banter

An example of a clash between lyric and melody occurred when Carole Bayer Sager and the late Peter Allen were writing a song called "Ah My Sister." Carole had her own definite ideas about it, as did Peter. Peter was talking about his actual sister, and she was talking about a kind of sisterhood for women. The result disappointed her, and she referred to it as a mixture of thoughts that sounded schizophrenic.

More often, though, writing roles vary. Even if the lyricist doesn't contribute a specific note of music, he or she may have some strong ideas about how to strengthen the tune. The melody writer might notice a cliché and feel that some word substitutions would make the line fresher and more original. Both people must remain open to the other's viewpoint.

My first encounter with the big what-comes-first question came when I was a teenager and RCA signed me as a writer/recording artist. After being told to buy collegiate sweaters, wear dark glasses, and get a crewcut, I sat down to write songs for my first record session.

Hirschhorn's Hints

Newscaster Ted Koppel became a stutterer because he was forced to write with his right hand when he was a leftie, and the problem was solved when he did what his brain demanded. Forcing your thoughts along one channel when they ache to go in a different direction is equally destructive. Be open-minded and receptive, especially if the person giving advice has years of experience. But if the advice feels wrong, and you've weighed it as objectively as possible, then don't go along with it just because of your adviser's seniority. Trust your instincts and remember that no one, no matter how confident he or she may sound, has all the answers.

I had written some material (recorded by long-forgotten names such as Wayne Rooks, Tony Cosmo, Bob and Joe, and Ellen Tracy), but I'd never given the process much thought. Now I was told by an executive, "You'll only have a hit if you write the music first." He seemed knowledgeable, so I tried it his way on a song called, "Will You Stay in Love?" I found myself bursting to finish the lyric, but I repressed the desire and nearly drove myself crazy laboring on a tune instead of following my instincts. I missed my first deadline, and arranger Norman Paris, who was set to do my recording session, asked what the trouble was. I told him, and he said, "Write the lyric. That's the way your mind works. It's like forcing yourself to be a right-handed pitcher when you're left-handed."

Preparing to Create Songs for Artists

If you're creating material for artists who cut *outside* songs, you'll want to do an analysis of their previous work before you make a what-comes-first decision.

As a Composer

Study former hits of those artists for the following elements:

> ➤ **Chords they particularly favor.** It helps to buy sheet music and listen to records until you become familiar with their signature chords.

> ➤ **Chord progressions.** Does this particular artist like songs that frequently use C Am F G7 or G Bm C C/D? If you study the catalogue of any particular artist with care, you'll begin to notice progressions that keep resurfacing.

> ➤ **Rhythm.** Does the artist like waltzes? Bossa novas? A Bo Diddley rhythm?

Lyrical Lingo

When an artist is willing to record songs composed by other writers, those songs are known as **outside** songs.

As a Lyricist

Look for these lyrical elements:

> ➤ **Recurring themes.** Determining that the artist cuts love stories is not enough. What kind of love stories? Does he or she lean toward the optimistic or the tragic? Is the artist's approach cheerful or cynical?

> ➤ **Attitude.** For example, does the artist lean toward middle-of-the-road conservatism or is he or she rebellious?

> ➤ **Style.** Does the artist prefer pop poetry, or is he or she bluntly straightforward?

After doing this pre-work, you can move to the writing. You'll have a sense of that individual artist, both personally and artistically.

Major Songwriters Weigh In

Examining the way skillful composers and lyricists handle the what-comes-first problem is the best way to clarify your own ideas on the subject. The following examples describe how different songwriters work.

Was Richard Rodgers Wrong?

Those who claim that music must come first should think about Richard Rodgers. One of our greatest melodists, Rodgers composed his immortal tunes after Oscar Hammerstein had written the lyrics. This order was followed for such masterpieces as *Carousel, Oklahoma,* and *The Sound of Music.*

Tim Rice

Tim Rice, lyricist for *The Lion King, Aida,* and *Jesus Christ Superstar,* recalls that while working with Andrew Lloyd Webber …

> "We had the tune first every time. He'd play it for me and I'd pick it up. If I couldn't pick it up quickly, obviously it wasn't a very good tune. I'd tape it on a recorder … or if not, I'd just have it in my skull."
>
> —Bruce Pollock, *In Their Own Words,* Collier Books, 1975

Hal David

Hal David always felt comfort and freedom in his daily writing routine with Burt Bacharach, a routine that resulted in such classics as "Don't Make Me Over," "Close to You," and "Raindrops Keep Falling on My Head." In the Bacharach/David relationship, neither words nor music came first; it was a constantly evolving, changeable mode of working. David describes it this way:

> "On occasion, I just think in lines, but most of the time the idea comes to me with a title. And often it occurs in two lines. I see things in hunks, rather than specific sentences. I'll think of an eight-bar phrase. Burt and I would meet in one room, and I was very hardworking, as he was. I was always writing lyrics; he was always writing melodies. The question most repeatedly asked was, 'What do you think of this? What do you think of that?' Either my lyric would set him off to write a melody or vice versa."

Randy Newman

Randy Newman, composer of the scores for *A Bug's Life, The Natural,* and *Toy Story,* says that an inspiration might come to him in the middle of the night, but more often it takes place while he sits at a piano.

> "I hardly ever have the words first. A piece of a melody or a figure of some kind will be enough to get me going, and sometimes I'll be right there where you can see the end of it. Sometimes I won't, and I'll change it and go someplace different from where I thought."
>
> —Bruce Pollock, *In Their Own Words*, Collier Books, 1975

Bob Dylan writes alone, and he starts out with melody before words. The same is true of Paul Anka, Stevie Wonder, and Paul Simon. Yip Harburg agrees, although he overstressed the case when he said, "The tune inspires. It *must* come first!" Charlie Fox has done just fine writing music to Norman Gimbel's lyrics ("Killing Me Softly with His Song," "Ready to Take a Chance Again," and "I Got a Name").

Backstage Banter

Marvin Hamlisch feels that having lyrics first hems him in, and when we wrote together, he gave me the tune first. Legendary composers from the prerock era such as Jerome Kern, Harry Warren, Harold Arlen, and Arthur Schwartz agree that lyrics as a starting point are stifling.

The Rhythm in Your Mind

If you're a lyricist, hearing a tune before you begin can make things easier. The leaps in the melody direct you in your emotional approach. The rhythm is also spelled out. In any case, lyricists, even those who don't write tunes, are generally musical. They hear tempos in their heads. If they have dramatic thoughts, they can imagine a melody swooping up or dropping down as they write.

Practice Wearing Both Hats

Although most composers and lyricists have a preference about whether music or words come first, others easily slide back and forth, equally relaxed with any order the process takes. Some writers, particularly those who handle all the music and lyrics, do things only one way, but would prefer to be more flexible. My advice is to take a musical track, either from an instrumental or a hit song, and write words to it. Then try it the other way around, taking a famous lyric and providing your own tune. Regardless of whether you wind up favoring one method over the other, you'll expand your musical perceptions, and the results will reflect that creative testing and freedom.

Backstage Banter

Stephen Schwartz, winner of two Oscars for Best Song, says, "I always get down as much of the lyric idea as possible. I think music is much easier than lyrics, because lyrics are craft, and music is an emotional response to a situation or a particular feeling. So I handle the lyric first. It's important that I get as much of the lyric done as possible, because once the music is done, that's it for me. I'm trapped in that form."

No Borders

Without a melody to give a lyricist defined borders, he or she may occasionally wander. The lyricist doesn't need the entire tune; a verse is enough to provide structure. The structure could be AABA (verse, verse, bridge, verse) or ABABCA (verse, chorus, verse, chorus, bridge, chorus). It doesn't matter what the structure is, as long as the lyricist is given the basic foundation. (See Chapter 8, "Cooking Up Your Hit Ingredients," for more about common song structures.)

A melody writer might have the same problem as a lyricist and require words to organize his or her thoughts. In that case, lyrics, whether in fragments or fully conceived, are needed to bring out the melody writer's best work.

Trouble Clef

Alan Jay Lerner once told me, "If you tell your partner you don't like something, be prepared to say why. Don't just say, 'It doesn't appeal to me.' If you're putting thumbs down on something, have good reasons and be able to express them."

Take This Song and Shove It

Certain titles proposed by the lyricist demand a direction from the tune writer. David Allan Coe's "Take This Job and Shove It" could never (let's hope) be turned into a Tony Bennett ballad. The thought compels a tune writer to provide pulsating, angry music. "Colors of the Wind" (Alan Menken/Stephen Schwartz) is reflective and spiritual and would be jarringly inappropriate as a title for a pulsating rap song. "I Will Remember You" (Sarah McLachlan) suggests a mood of nostalgia and sadness.

If a tune writer plays lush, jazz-oriented chords, those chords will lead a lyricist in a different direction than if the chords are harsh and dissonant. Throbbing hip-hop rhythms are emotional explosions; a slow ballad pace cries for sensitivity.

Don't Stick to Your Own Area

When partners are compatible, they're totally open to input from each other. The process begins with a single line, and then addresses issues of range, altered lyrics, and rhythm. No one is saying, "That's *my* area; stick to your own," whether subtly or directly.

A lyricist may write four verses that make perfect sense, yet the words lack emotional build. At that point, an astute partner might realize that the first and second verses, if switched around, would make the song far more powerful. Or the lyricist will see that the ending should rise for more impact.

Trouble Clef

When writers start out, they often oppose the idea of partnership and insist on writing alone. If you find that your work is being rejected, don't close your mind to the idea of working with other people. Sometimes an individual who does words and music lacks objectivity. That second pair of ears will hear flaws and correct them so that a competent song evolves into a fine one.

Positive Disaster

Each project follows a different path. When Al Kasha and I wrote our Oscar-winning song, "The Morning After," for the 1972 movie *The Poseidon Adventure,* we knew that a unifying concept was mandatory before a single note or word was written. The producer Irwin Allen told us, "A ship is turning over. People are drowning. The boiler room is exploding. So make it positive!" In other words, we had to convey a message of hope in the midst of devastating catastrophe.

Once we landed on "The Morning After" as a title and followed that line with "if we can make it through the night," our overall concept was nailed. Then we worked together, line by line, testing out alternatives on each other. The melody was also achieved with this line-by-line approach.

Backstage Banter

Diane Warren wrote the "Solitaire" lyric for Laura Branigan; the song became Branigan's first Top 10 record. Warren began at nine o'clock on a Wednesday night and had to have it done by nine o'clock the next morning. She got the B side, "I'm Not the Only One," too.

We functioned as one person, one mind, and this intensely collaborative mental state ensured that the song would be completed by the next morning in order to meet the insane deadline Twentieth Century Fox had imposed on us.

For "The Old-Fashioned Way," which became a worldwide standard with Charles Aznavour, Al and I received a melody from Charles. He made it abundantly clear that not a note, rhythm, or phrase was to be touched. Our job was to do lyrics only. Fortunately, the tune was so beautiful that we had no desire to change anything.

Writing "Wake Up" with Marvin Hamlisch for the Chambers Brothers was another case of here's-the-music-write-the-lyric. On the other hand, Nelson Riddle gave us a fragment of melody for a television movie starring Nick Nolte (*The Runaway Barge*), and we were told, "Play around with the tune. Feel completely free."

Lyrical Lingo

A **dummy line** is one that uses words to get the writer started, to give him or her a sense of rhythmic or musical pattern. These words are throwaways and rarely, if ever, make it to the final draft.

Hooked on a Feeling

In today's rhythm-oriented world, a hit song can start without melody or words: a "feel" (rhythmic pulse) is enough. Once the tune writer supplies the beat, the song is set in motion. When Al and I wrote with the great Maurice White of Earth, Wind, and Fire, White listened to me play a few chords and melodic ideas, and then waved them aside saying, "Never mind that. Give me the feel."

The all-important feel or groove is the key to pop songwriting today. The tune writer can play it on an instrument or tap it out; a lyricist can come up with a *dummy line* that conveys the needed syncopations and tempo.

Backstage Banter

Hold on to your melodies if you can't get the right lyric. Joan Baez, discussing her song, "Speaking of Dreams," says, "I had the luxury of having written the melody about a year and a half before, and I bumbled around with it whenever I was in a piano-playing mood. So I knew it was there, and I knew some day the words would come to claim it."

—Paul Zollo, *Songwriters on Songwriting*, DaCapo Press

Steve Tyler of Aerosmith also emphasizes the value of an instrumental riff in launching hits. According to Steve, "Walk This Way" started out as a Joe Perry guitar riff. After that, Tyler put his rhythm licks, that stem from his early days as a drummer, on top. The Rolling Stones's "Start Me Up" also began as a Keith Richards riff. With that as a basis, Mick Jagger wrote the rest.

Feel Your Way to Creativity

Rules are meant to guide, not to strangle. Thousands of composers and lyricists torture themselves in their efforts to do the "right" thing. Any composing system that produces quality material is the right one. The right system is the one that can be mutually agreed upon by two or three collaborators or even, as in the case of "Say My Name" by Destiny's Child—seven collaborators (R. Jerkins, F. Jerkins III, L. Daniels, B. Knowles, L. Luckett, K. Rowland, and L. Robertson)! For composers such as Jerry Herman, Randy Newman, and Billy Joel, who work alone, the right system is the one that feels comfortable.

Lindsey Buckingham of Fleetwood Mac makes another point worth remembering. A writer should exert a certain amount of craftsmanship and conscious control, but not so much that a sense of spontaneity and inspiration are eliminated. Buckingham says:

> "You may start off with a certain intent, and you start putting strokes on the canvas, but because it's so intuitive and one on one, the colors will lead you in a direction you didn't expect to go, or you may have a preconception of what the song is going to be, melodically and otherwise, and you may end up in a totally different place. And that is probably more the norm than the exception.

> —Paul Zollo, *Songwriters on Songwriting*, DaCapo Press

The Least You Need to Know

➤ There are no rules written in stone about whether music or words come first. What works best is the best way to work.

➤ If you're a lyricist, have a rhythm in mind when you write.

➤ If you're a tune writer, imagine words that correspond to the mood of your melody.

➤ Be tactful, but truthful, about your collaborator's contributions.

➤ Learn the craft, but don't get so locked into it that you sacrifice spontaneity.

Chapter 5

Finding and Keeping Collaborators

In This Chapter

➤ The trials and rewards of partnership

➤ Work habits that need work

➤ Ways to find a partner

➤ International songwriting collaborations

One of the most remarkable partnerships in music history is the team of Jerry Leiber and Mike Stoller. Their collaboration began in the early 1950s, and now, nearly half a century later, they're still together. Leiber and Stoller wrote Elvis Presley's biggest hits, as well as "Charlie Brown" for the Coasters and "Is That All There Is" for Peggy Lee.

From the theater world, we can see equally impressive evidence of durability with John Kander and Fred Ebb, who composed *Zorba*, *Chicago*, and *Cabaret*. These collaborators are heartening proof that a songwriting partnership can endure permanently, surviving all the inevitable stresses that arise in the course of day-to-day creativity.

A Roller Coaster Worth Riding

Partnerships don't just coast along blissfully without traumas and trials. Even the best of them take dedication, work, and compromise. But if you're willing to put forth that effort, the rewards are often emotionally and financially satisfying.

Alan Jay Lerner and Frederic Loewe enjoyed a harmonious partnership that began with *Paint Your Wagon* and reached an artistic peak with *My Fair Lady*. They followed

Hirschhorn's Hints

Some people look upon writing as a grim, backbreaking chore. Compatible partners don't see it that way. As John Kander says, "Writing is never hard, even if it takes a long time. Freddy and I never don't have a good time when we're writing." His positive approach is part of an overall attitude that sustains collaborations.

this with MGM's Oscar-winning musical *Gigi* in 1958. It was such a triumph that few remember its first, disastrous review from *Time* magazine. As Lerner put it, "Fritz was in an oxygen tent at the time. When I read that notice, I wished I was there with him." Despite that, the team's bond didn't fray under pressure. They never shifted responsibility or blamed each other. Lerner and Loewe went on to write *Camelot* and the film version of *The Little Prince.*

Sometimes a partnership with lifetime potential collapses over an artistic disagreement. If you're part of a team that has tremendous personal and creative chemistry, try to distance yourself from the emotional crisis. If it builds, you may sacrifice something you'll later regret losing.

Songwriting partnerships are like marriages. They involve much more than the ability to turn out hit songs. New writers are usually bewildered when they see such a team as John Lennon and Paul McCartney go their separate ways. But temperament, philosophy, and long-range goals are as crucial to a partnership as creative ability. If the divisions are too wide on these issues, the relationship comes apart.

Backstage Banter

Sheldon Harnick and Jerry Bock, creators of *Fiddler on the Roof*, *The Rothschilds*, *She Loves Me*, and *Fiorello* had 14 years of uninterrupted success. Unfortunately, while in production with *The Rothschilds*, they disagreed violently over the choice of the show's director, Derek Jacobi. Harnick felt that Jacobi, who specialized in dramas, couldn't handle a musical. Bock took the opposing view, and the clashing viewpoints provoked a rupture in their relationship that never healed.

If at all possible, heed producer Lynda Obst's words when you sense that a partnership of value is threatened: "Resist all impulse to turn incident into drama." Search for areas of compromise. You'll be glad you did.

Work Habits

Suppose you're a night person and your collaborator is only able to think clearly during the day. You have to ask yourself if you can adjust to a different time schedule. How about if you work together evenings for three days a week and early mornings for the other four?

How Important Is the Job?

One of the most remarkable things about the creative brain is its ability to rise to the occasion on demand. If you and your partner think you need a minimum deadline of a month and someone says, "have this for me in a week," you'll meet that deadline—I guarantee it. Everything depends on how much the job means to you.

Backstage Banter

When Al Kasha and I were asked to do the song for *The Poseidon Adventure,* producer Irwin Allen and director Ronald Neame wanted the material completed in one night. We never thought for a second that completing a song in one night was impossible. As Marvin Hamlisch says, "the answer is always yes." Then you find a way.

Punctuality Problems

One of the major difficulties in maintaining a partnership is punctuality. According to legend, Larry Hart was always late (or didn't show up at all), and it drove Richard Rodgers to distraction. In the interests of the team, Rodgers swallowed his anger to save the collaboration until it became an unbearable pressure and he turned to Oscar Hammerstein.

The best you can do is try to convince your partner how much his or her tardiness disturbs you. Keep emphasizing it, without letting your feelings flare into open hostility. After a while, if nothing changes, you have two choices: Break up the relationship or live with it. Remember this fact: In any relationship, individuals rarely change when someone else pushes them. They have to make the decision to change on their own.

Keep in mind that no partnership flows evenly without some bumps and bruises. You probably have traits that annoy your collaborator, who also has to repress his or her emotions for the greater good of your creativity.

Last-Minute Blues

Another common conflict between partners is the attitude toward deadlines. When a team is given three weeks to complete a song, one person may want to work slowly and methodically every day, analyzing and discarding dozens of different alternatives. The other person might let two and a half weeks slide by, and then rush frantically to complete the song.

Frequently you'll hear the cry, "That's the only way I can work!" Again, compromise is called for. The person who functions only at the last minute is perfectly capable of working on the music and lyrics throughout the allotted time given. Or the more methodical person could provide the last-minute person with a list of ideas to review closer to the deadline.

Trouble Clef

Cy Coleman, the composer of Broadway's *Sweet Charity, Seesaw,* and *I Love My Wife* worked with a lyricist named Joe McCarthy. Together they wrote a Frank Sinatra standard, "Why Try to Change Me Now?" But the work process, as Coleman admitted, caused him constant frustration. "It took Joe days and days, and I hated it because you had to sit with Joe. I didn't want to sit with him while he contemplated." Remember that excessive dependency and emotional neediness can undermine a partnership. Be independent.

Deferring to the Larger Ego

In most songwriting partnerships, one person is more extroverted, and the other is more retiring. If your partner wants to grab and seize the limelight, are you content to let him or her dominate, or do you need equal appreciation? Two people who want dominant, highly public positions rarely maintain their creative connection for long.

If you're the introvert, you have to decide whether you're capable of or willing to subordinate your personality to your partner's. If you're outgoing and your partner is shy and subdued, you may want him or her to pitch in more and get more involved rather than linger in the background. Ideally, your two personality types can blend, but most teams shatter because one feels neglected or deprived of proper credit; and resentments quietly escalate.

It's the Song, Stupid

The key element of a writing partnership is the song! Don't get too caught up in competition with your partner, or you'll lose focus on the main issue. Competition, left unchecked, poisons everything. Remember, success has many fathers, and failure is an orphan. There's plenty of glory to go around if the song hits the charts.

"Let's Try It Another Way"

Sammy Cahn once told me that he never directly criticized a melody brought to him or bluntly said he disliked it. Sammy was wise. If you criticize a collaborator, you should suggest alternatives and say something diplomatic, but you should never be cruel and harsh. Your lack of tact will be resented and will undermine the partnership.

At the same time, you shouldn't write lyrics to a melody you don't care for or a tune to words that fall short of your standard. Eventually a language evolves between co-writers, and their true feelings are clearly communicated by a word, a gesture, or a joke. These tactful ways of expressing reservations don't ever come across as attacks.

Stick to Your Guns

Be open to the opinions of your partner, but also be willing to fight for a tune or lyric you passion-ately believe in. Listen without being defensive if your collaborator doesn't seem as enthusiastic as you expected him or her to be. In the end, if you reach an impasse and your collaborator is dead set against a particular product, you have to capitu-late. But try to defend your point of view if it's a strong one. Otherwise, you'll hate yourself for giv-ing in too easily.

Trouble Clef

Voice your anxieties; don't let them fester. If you become a walking mass of hidden agendas, you'll one day explode with accu-mulated resentment and destroy the partnership.

I Do (but Sometimes I Don't)

People often say, "Don't get too professionally involved with your partner, and above all, don't marry her (or him)." Like all dogmatic, black-and-white statements, this one fails to ac-count for differences in individuals. Barry Mann and Cynthia Weil are together after more than 30 years. Jeff Barry and Ellie Greenwich divorced, but Alan and Marilyn Bergman are still married and are more professionally active than ever.

Songwriting spouses can find life wonderfully satisfying and productive if they both have the same goal. In a situation like this, work usually continues after the sun goes down. Writing is the cornerstone of a composing partnership between husbands and wives.

If you're a person who lives and breathes work 24 hours a day, marriage to a partner will be ideal. If you want to escape and tune out your musical career for large chunks of time, major adjustments will have to be made. There is, however, great, unmatch-able satisfaction in creating a bond that means so much to you both.

Part-Time Collaboration

The collaborations I've mentioned, as well as the partnership Al Kasha and I had over 25 years, were or are all exclusive. Even when we wrote with other people, Al and I were both on the song. At different times, we partnered up with Maurice White of Earth, Wind, and Fire; James Ingram; Marvin Hamlisch; Billy Goldenberg; and David Shire.

Hirschhorn's Hints

Whatever the structure of the partnership, the vital thing is to agree on the terms up front. Your co-writer can feel threatened if you decide to write "just one song" with another collaborator. His or her security may rest in keeping your pact exclusive.

Certain composers and lyricists like to work primarily with one person while having the freedom to occasionally partner with someone else. This arrangement is often an ideal way to avoid the sense of being confined.

Carole Bayer Sager composed frequently with her ex-husband Burt Bacharach ("That's What Friends Are For," "On My Own") while providing lyrics for the late Peter Allen, Albert Hammond, and Melissa Manchester. Johnny Mercer teamed up several times with Henry Mancini, yet he also wrote with Harry Warren and Marvin Hamlisch, among dozens of others.

You might prefer to write rock with one person, country with another, rap with a third, and a motion picture theme song with a fourth.

How to Find Your Partner

You might be the kind of person who expects a partner to be a psychotherapist, a mother/father confessor, or a pal. Or you may prefer a collaborator who's all business. Hooking up with a songwriting partner is very similar to finding a lover or a friend. The right partner is out there if you keep searching.

Don't wander around, praying that an elusive, ideal co-writer will magically appear. If you choose to write with someone else, rather than alone, you have to conduct your search in a thoroughly organized fashion.

Start Locally

Partners are everywhere. The logical place to start is to turn to those in your immediate vicinity. Consider members of local bands. Chances are that some of them have songwriting ambitions. Go to clubs in your area and form friendships with performers. If they write, fine. If they don't, they might put you in touch with people who do. The musician's union is another rich source of potential partners.

Look up the addresses and phone numbers of locally based publishers and producers and try to meet them personally. You can mail in the material, but unsolicited songs are generally disregarded and returned. A face-to-face encounter is always preferable.

If possible, look beyond local opportunities. Go where the action is in the main music circles of Los Angeles, Nashville, New York, San Francisco, Chicago, and London. Write to every publisher you can and set up appointments well in advance of your arrival. Find out who reviews material in each firm and establish a running dialogue with him or her, so you won't be a complete stranger when you show up. Be prepared with lead sheets and recordings of your songs when you walk in.

Advertise

If you're a student, run an ad in your school newspaper. State your desire to team up with someone and spell out your specific needs. On a broader level, *Songwriter* magazine prints similar ads, and many rewarding collaborations have materialized through this fine publication. Put up notices in music stores, churches, synagogues, and music clubs.

Your ads can be as simple as the following:

> Young composer looking for lyricist in the Chicago area. Ron Garvey, 124 Rosemont Drive, Chicago, Illinois 00000

> Lyricist seeks composer of Latin/rock music for collaboration in Enrique Iglesias/Marc Anthony style. 619 N. Kingsbridge Road, Bronx, New York 00000

Hirschhorn's Hints

Making contacts is rough at first. A shortcut, if it's creatively feasible, is to work with someone who has more connections. It's also an asset if your collaborator has a studio setup which will save you a fortune in recording fees.

NAS (the National Academy of Songwriters) has a collaboration service for its members, or you could turn to SGA (Songwriter's Guild of America) for help in locating a partner. Mention the type of music you specialize in (pop, R&B, rap, country), specify whether you're interested in a tune writer or lyricist, and include information about how interested parties can reach you.

Establish Industry Contacts

Getting to top people in the recording industry isn't easy. You can't just stride into the office of a record company president or *Billboard*'s number one producer of the year. To establish a link, you need middlemen.

Never forget: One introduction leads to another. Chat with a gatekeeper, a secretary, or an assistant. They may be forbidding and cold, but not always. Some are sympathetic, friendly, and helpful. They might mention your name directly to the boss, but they can also tell the vice president and the office manager, who are people in higher, though still secondary, positions. Eventually, your name will filter upward to the person in charge.

Talk to background singers, arrangers, and copyists. Start a favorable buzz going. Everybody in the industry is a possible contact, a possible lead, a possible partner.

Be in the Right Place at the Right Time

Sometimes just being on the proper turf is enough.

When I was 17, a famous songwriter named Charlie Singleton saw me wandering in the hall of Manhattan's Brill Building and took me to a well-known publisher, Robert

Mellin Music. Charlie's compassion for a lost-looking newcomer brought me my first record, "All About Love," sung by Clyde McPhatter. After I was armed with an important cut, other, better-known songwriters wanted to write with me, and I started collaborating with a host of talented composers and lyricists.

Contact ASCAP, BMI, and SESAC

ASCAP (the American Society of Composers, Authors, and Publishers), BMI (Broadcast Music, Inc.), and SESAC (Society of European Stage Authors and Composers), the three societies that log music around the world and pay writers for accrued airplay, are supportive and helpful in making introductions. Put together a tape of your material and take it to these societies to evaluate.

BMI has many workshops for new, as well as experienced, writers. The Lehman Engel Theatre Workshop has taught and encouraged such composers as Maury Yeston (*Titanic, Nine*) and given them the background to achieve great success. Whether as a member of a workshop or a member of a performance society, you'll be provided with opportunities to meet other writers searching for a partner.

Go for a Lucky Long Shot

Billboard lists the national hits weekly in all categories, along with names of their songwriters and producers. Make careful note of these names and study the styles they compose in. Armed with this information, you can try to get in touch with those you particularly admire. When you do eventually connect, you'll be sufficiently well informed about them to see if a partnership is possible.

If entertainment attorneys feel you have talent, they can offer direct access to their illustrious clients. Agents might also be coaxed into arranging valuable introductions.

Backstage Banter

Al Stillman wrote dozens of hits for Johnny Mathis, including "Chances Are." My mother remembered that she had dated Stillman in high school, so I called him and reminded him of their friendship. This call led to our working together, and it gave me a start in the industry.

Work an Artist's Muscle

On a practical level, writing with producers and artists increases the chance of getting records. These people have total control, and unlike publishers, they automatically supply the recordings. Working with an artist (such as Bernie Taupin's collaboration with Elton John) can guarantee entire albums of your music or lyrics.

Cold, Hard Business

As I mentioned, getting a partnership's emotional ground rules worked out from the beginning is vital. Just as important are the business decisions. Here are some questions that must be answered before you start working with a partner:

➤ Will you each get 50 percent of the royalties, or will one get the larger share? Will the partner who accepts the smaller share feel resentful later on if the song is a hit?

➤ Will you both co-own the song's publishing? Again, there's fuel for rage if one person owns the entire copyright and has the power to sell it later on and collect the profits.

➤ If a song doesn't succeed, will one writer or the other have the power to take his or her lyric or melody back and find another writer to put fresh words or music to it?

I've had writers say to me, "We began with a 50-50 split, but I wrote more. Don't you think it's fair that the percentages be amended to 60-40 or 75-25?" My answer is a thunderous NO! In an ideal partnership, there should be no list-making or toting up of scores of who did less or more. In the long run, the contributions even out, and a you-did-this, I-did-that attitude is the death knell for the partnership.

Trouble Clef

One arrangement that should never be made with a collaborator is agreeing to pay him or her to put words or music to your material. True collaborators share royalties and operate on an equal basis. A similar situation may occur with a record company that the writer or writer/artist pays for his or her session and pressing costs. Reliable, trustworthy labels don't function that way. If they like your work, they'll shoulder the investment.

Inspiration from Across the Sea

Collaborators can be as close to home as the next room. But sometimes they can be on another continent.

Hirschhorn's Hints

Be prepared for strange ways of collaborating. Al and I discovered that when an opportunity came to write with Charles Aznavour, who gave us a melody and asked us to write English lyrics. When we completed it, we had to sing it for him via a long-distance phone call. From his den in Paris, he made the decision to cut the song, which ultimately became "The Old-Fashioned Way."

Long-Distance Gold

"The Old-Fashioned Way" has had over 300 recordings to date, including those of Charles Aznavour himself, as well as Petula Clark, Jack Jones, Liza Minnelli, and Frank Sinatra. We had no idea when we collaborated with Charles on this romantic, lilting (but completely nonrock) tune that it would take the world by storm.

Paul Anka probably didn't suspect what an impact "My Way" would have on the world when he co-wrote the lyrics (with C. François, J. Revaux, and G. Thibault). Other Euro-American classics include: "Volare" (Migliacci, Modugno, Parish), "You're My World" (Sigman, Bindi, Paoli), "Yesterday When I Was Young" (Aznavour, Kretzmer), "Never on Sunday" (Towne, Hajidakis), and "More" (Newell, Cioclolini, Oliviero, Ortolani).

Traveling in Your Mind

Writing to foreign melodies allows the imagination to stretch beyond conventional bounds. The flavor of different countries is a powerful influence. Music from Mexico may inspire your thinking in a certain way; music from Germany may inspire you in another direction. We all have images and impressions of exotic places, and these impressions shape how we react to tunes from far off shores. The same holds true if we write music to words of a different culture.

Certain lyricists have practically based their entire careers on long-distance collaborations. The name Carl Sigman ("Losing You," a hit for Brenda Lee in 1964; "You're My World"; and "What Now My Love") is synonymous with long-distance composing. Al Stillman, Buddy Kaye, Norman Gimbel, and Rod McKuen all recognized the value of foreign collaboration early.

Starting Out with a Hit

From a practical standpoint, songs written with collaborators from different countries frequently are *cover records*. Generally, they're already hits in their country of origin, and this past success increases their chances of acceptance in the United States by both the artist and radio.

Sometimes European material comes to an American lyricist with words already written in a different language. Two things may happen:

➤ The American writer may be asked to adhere, verse by verse, to the ideas in that lyric.

➤ The American writer may be granted the freedom to conceive entirely new ideas of his or her own.

European collaborators generally indicate a preference. Creating something new is less restricting, but the alternative has advantages. Following a foreign lyric line by line, word for word, is impossible because English words fall on different syllables. You, as an author, must find fresh, interesting ways of making the meanings come alive in your native tongue. This challenge will sharpen your tools as a lyricist.

Lyrical Lingo

A **cover record** is a new recording of an already existing cut. Cover records are valuable, because the more a song is covered, the better chance it has of lasting permanently.

Jerry Herman sums up the value of finding and keeping a collaborator when he says that working by yourself is very lonely. He admits envying his composer-friends John Kander and Fred Ebb because John can say, "Hey, Fred, what do you think of this?" and vice versa. Partnerships provide the joy of sharing, and also the comfort of having a permanent support system when you're forced to deal with disappointment.

The Least You Need to Know

➤ Try not to let the stress of conflicts pull apart a productive partnership.

➤ Organize a mutually acceptable work schedule and stick to it; don't leave assignments until the last minute.

➤ Increase your opportunities by writing with producers and artists.

➤ Decide on your royalty split with your partner in advance.

➤ Collaborate with international writers to increase your visibility.

Chapter 6

Title Power!

In This Chapter

➤ What makes a hit title

➤ Title characters, plots, and themes

➤ Words with universal appeal

Titles are so important that many composers can't even begin to write without one. Titles suggest a story, convey a mood, and establish a flavor. They imply or state outright what kind of characters the song is about. They spell out the conflict.

Most of all, intriguing titles attract people. It's no different with songs than with books or movies. When you have a choice between "I'm in Love" and "Let's Get It On," which one would draw your interest right away? This chapter looks at title types that have been successfully used for hits.

Titles That Tell the Story

The ideal title for a song is one that announces the entire plot. Hundreds of titles are general, and they can be made to work, but your job is half done if the title reveals your overall concept right away. Most hit titles tell you if the *protagonist* is happy, angry, or frustrated.

Simple and Straightforward

In the beginning, try to write titles that deal with subject matter the public cares about. As Frank Zappa says, "Basically what people want to hear is: I love you, you

love me, the leaves turn brown, they fell off the trees, the wind is blowing, it got cold, you went away, my heart broke, you came back, and my heart was okay" (Pollock).

Lennon and McCartney's "I Want to Hold Your Hand" sets an easy, obvious direction. The music and rhythm may vary, the words may be simple or sophisticated, but the emotion is clear and direct. The song is not going to be dark and convoluted; it's an open, happy expression of affection. "You Light Up My Life," Debby Boone's Oscar-winning song by Joe Brooks, forces the songwriter to be spiritual and romantic at the same time.

"I Don't Wanna Miss a Thing," Aerosmith's recording of a Diane Warren song, is another title that writes itself, as is Van Morrison's "Have I Told You Lately?" Others in this straightforward category include the following:

"Can You Feel the Love Tonight" by Elton John (E. John and T. Rice)

"Let Me Let Go" by Faith Hill (D. Morgan and S. Diamond)

"Please Remember Me" by Tim McGraw (W. Jennings and R. Crowell)

"You Don't Send Me Flowers" by Barbra Streisand (Neil Diamond, A. Bergman, and M. Bergman)

Title Characters

Producers and artists love titles that draw a character. Jim Croce introduced us to "Big Bad Leroy Brown," who's "meaner than a junkyard dog," and the characterization was so vivid that it became Croce's first number-one single. Mick Jagger and Keith Richard sang a loving tribute to "Angie," and Simon and Garfunkel portrayed the adulterous "Mrs. Robinson."

The Everly Brothers told the story of "Cathy's Clown," and Michael Jackson sang an award-winning love song to a rat, "Ben," and then switched to the story of Billie Jean, whom he tells, "the kid is not my son." "Lucy in the Sky with Diamonds" was about the hallucinatory sweetheart (LSD) devised by John Lennon and Paul McCartney. The Four Tops filled us in on "Bernadette," and we heard about a variety of different women from the Four Seasons, when Frankie Valli's falsetto sobbed loudly about "Sherry," "Candy Girl," "Dawn," "Rag Doll," and pleaded "C'mon Marianne."

Character studies can be light and adolescent, such as Rick Springfield's "Jessie's Girl," or have more depth, as in Don Henley's "The Boys of Summer." The character could be someone we all know, such as Carole King's "Jazzman" or Madonna's sanctimonious father in "Papa Don't Preach."

Titles That Set the Tone

The common denominator that unites all titles is exaggeration. Quiet, calm, mellow attitudes have little place in a song that aspires to world acceptance. Motion pictures are not accurate reflections of life, but distorted, heightened exaggerations of it. Songs have three or four minutes to do what a movie does in two hours. Unless your title is strong, unless it explodes with violent, raw emotion and raises that emotion to fever pitch, few listeners will become engrossed in what you have to say.

Built-In Drama

Titles don't always lay out the plot in detail, but the best of them set an intriguing mood, provoke curiosity, and contain built-in drama.

Paul Revere and the Raiders had two emotionally-charged hit titles, "Kicks" and "Hungry," which were both written by Barry Mann and Cynthia Weil. We don't know immediately whether the kicks indicate sexual frenzy or drug addiction; we're not sure if they represent destructive rebellion or a solid relationship. But the word "kicks" promises excitement. The word "hungry" sounds urgent, desperate. Both supply drama, and drama is something you should always consider when you make a title list.

Another provocative title is "Coward of the County," sung by Kenny Rogers. What kind of coward is he? Will he fight and redeem himself? Is he battling for the love of a woman? Once these questions occur to you, you're hooked.

Backstage Banter

You never know what kind of competitors you'll be faced with as a writer. My first Oscar-winning song, "The Morning After," was pitted against "Ben," the story of a rat. My second, "We May Never Love Like This Again," faced opposition from a love song to a dog, "Benji."

Backstage Banter

Songs that portray an era and voice protest have to begin with passion. Billy Joel's "We Didn't Start the Fire" hit us with Harry Truman, Doris Day, Red China, and Johnnie Ray, all in the first line. Rarely have four images been so unrelated, yet they paint an unforgettable picture and draw you into the spell of Joel's vision.

The following are examples of titles that signal a fascinating dramatic tale:

"Maneater" by Hall and Oates (D. Hall, J. Oates, and S. Allen)

"Gangsta's Paradise" by Coolio featuring L.V. (A. Ivey Jr., L. Sanders, and D. Rasheed)

"Wind Beneath My Wings" by Bette Midler (L. Henley and J. Silbar)

The Message in the Music

Titles aimed at changing society reached a peak in the 1960s with Bob Dylan, but some composers are always eager to influence the masses and improve world conditions. If you're politically conscious, the following examples should inspire you:

"The Times They Are A-Changin'" by Bob Dylan (B. Dylan)

"Give Peace a Chance" by John Lennon (J. Lennon)

"Give Ireland Back to the Irish" by Paul McCartney (P. McCartney)

Pleading, Hoping, Begging

In pop songs, lovers beg, get down on their knees, and cry out in despair. Michael Bolton said, "How Am I Supposed to Live Without You?" Rick Astley vowed, "Never Gonna Give You Up." Little Anthony sobbed, "Take Me Back." These titles also beg you to listen:

"Don't Be Cruel" by Elvis Presley (Otis Blackwell, Elvis Presley, Jerry Leiber, and Mike Stoller)

"Please Don't Go" by KC and the Sunshine Band (Harry Wayne Casey and Richard Finch)

"Please Mr. Postman" by The Carpenters (B. Holland, R. Bateman, W. Garrett, and G. Dobbins)

"Don't Go Breaking My Heart" by Elton John and Kiki Dee (E. John and B. Taupin)

Hot-Blooded

Titles that are purely sexual automatically command attention from publishers, producers, and artists. Robert Palmer's "Addicted to Love" falls into that group, as do the following:

"Hot Stuff" by Donna Summer (P. Bellotte, H. Faltermeyer, and K. Forsey)

"Kiss You All Over" by Exile (M. Chapman and N. Chinn)

"D'ya Think I'm Sexy?" by Rod Stewart (R. Stewart and C. Appice)

"Do That to Me One More Time" by The Captain and Tennille (T. Tennille)

"I'm In You" by Peter Frampton (P. Frampton)

Hot blood also courses through angry titles, many of which have risen to the top. "I Will Survive" is a cry of rage and a declaration of independence that has just as much relevance to this generation as it did when it made the Top 5 in March of 1979. Aretha Franklin demanded "Respect." Jennifer Holliday blended hysteria and vulnerability when she cried out, "And I Am Telling You I'm Not Going," the standout song in the Broadway musical *Dreamgirls*. Jon Bon Jovi told his girl, "You Give Love a Bad Name."

Frank Sinatra let the world know that he did it "My Way," and Sammy Davis proclaimed "I've Gotta Be Me." Paul McCartney told us "I've Had Enough," and James Brown made his position clear with "Say It Loud, I'm Black and I'm Proud."

Hirschhorn's Hints

Hit titles should never be passive. When a singer stands up against adversity, the public is put on the singer's side.

For All the Victims of the World

Powerful emotion in song isn't only direct, confrontational, and angry. It can also take the form of masochistic, long-suffering, pathetic cries from victims of love. Linda Ronstadt portrayed herself as "Poor, Poor Pitiful Me," and Little Anthony was on his knees "Goin' Out of My Head."

Anyone who has tossed and turned or walked the floor till morning will identify with Kris Kristofferson's agonized plea of "Help Me Make It Through the Night" and Peter Frampton's "I Can't Stand It No More."

Titles that offer a cathartic release for people bruised by bad relationships will reach millions. The important thing to remember as a writer is: Don't be embarrassed by what you feel. Be as frank with the world as you would be with your best friend or your psychiatrist. The more self-protective you are, the less power your lyrics will have. Say to yourself, "I'm not afraid to show myself, to be known."

When Richard Marx wrote the heartfelt title, "Right Here Waiting," he resisted putting the song on his album. He felt it was far too personal and it would expose his inner-most thoughts to the world, like writing a love letter to his wife and having it printed in the tabloids. Later on, Marx realized that part of his job as a songwriter was to communicate with as many people as possible.

Title Triggers

Titles can come from anywhere. For example, your favorite book or a word may inspire your song. Some titles come from the subject of a song, anything from a move on the dance floor to a visit to a small town. Wherever you get your titles from, make sure you save the good ones; you never know when you might need them.

Go from Text to Title

Gone with the Wind was a book title that became the basis for a standard that Frank Sinatra sang. Another book title was *I Never Promised You a Rose Garden*, a hit country tune for Lynn Anderson.

Find the Right Word

Sometimes one word says it all. The following songs with one-word titles all made number one:

"Emotions" by Mariah Carey (M. Carey, D. Cole, R. Clivilles)

"Romantic" by Karyn White (K. White, J. Jam, and T. Lewis)

"Shout" by Tears For Fears (R. Orzabal and I. Stanley)

"Runaway" by Del Shannon (C. Westover and M. Crook)

"Escapade" by Janet Jackson (J. Jackson, J. Harris III, and T. Lewis)

"Batdance" by Prince (Prince)

Dance to the Music

Songwriters frequently hit the jackpot when they write dance songs. Some well-known dance titles are the following:

"The Twist" by Chubby Checker (H. Ballard)

"The Loco-Motion" by Little Eva (G. Goffin and C. King)

"Mashed Potato Time" by Dee Dee Sharp (G. Dobbins, R. Bateman,
W. E. Garrett, K. Mann, B. Holland, and F. C. Gorman)

"Vogue" by Madonna (Madonna and S. Pettibone)

"The Hustle" by Van McCoy and the Soul Symphony (V. McCoy)

Cover the Country

You may be one of the writers who enjoys viewing stories from a geographic angle. Those who feel as you do have created major standards:

"Penny Lane" by The Beatles (P. McCartney and J. Lennon)

"I Left My Heart in San Francisco" by Tony Bennett (Douglass Cross and George Cory)

"Hotel California" by The Eagles (Don Felder, Don Henley, and Glenn Frey)

In addition, modes of transportation are always popular themes with writers and with the public. The Monkees took "The Last Train to Clarksville," and Peter, Paul, and Mary soared to the skies with "Leaving on a Jet Plane." Natalie Cole rode in a "Pink Cadillac," and Harry Chapin drove a "Taxi."

Keep Your Titles in the Trunk

After you've written songs for a while, you'll find yourself compiling lists of titles. Place a star next to the ones you like best, but don't throw out the others. Your composing priority one week may be a gentle country ballad, but six months later you might want to produce an up-tempo R&B song. Some of your earlier titles (even un-starred ones) will be perfect at that time. George and Ira Gershwin, Cy Coleman, and Cole Porter saved songs they didn't use for future projects. Work that doesn't strike you one day could very likely excite you the next.

Backstage Banter

Sometimes a great title can have different meanings for different writers. Lyricists Phil Galdston and Wendy Waldman both liked "Save the Best for Last," but Galdston thought it indicated a sad and cynical song, which it wasn't. Waldman argued that the title was a positive one. Over Galdston's protests, Waldman prevailed, and the romantic "Save the Best for Last" became a number-one hit for Vanessa Williams on March 21, 1992.

Words That Work

Some words have such strong universal appeal that songwriters use them over and over again in titles. Hit titles are even sometimes used again for completely different songs.

"Come On, Baby, Light My Fire"

Candles have a particular attraction for writers. Al and I wrote a song called "Candle on the Water," which received a Best Song Academy Award nomination. Elton John's "Candle in the Wind" was a tribute to Marilyn Monroe and then to Princess Diana. "Sixteen Candles" was a number-two smash for the Crests, and "(Lay Down) Candles in the Rain" made it to number six for Melanie.

Letters

Everyone likes to receive mail, particularly love letters, so letters are frequently referred to in hit titles. Pat Boone sang about "Love Letters in the Sand," and the Box Tops told us "my baby wrote me a letter." "Love Letters" also achieved popularity with this theme.

Trouble Clef

You can't copyright a title, so many songwriters use titles that have been hits in the past. Try to avoid this if possible. It creates confusion in the public's mind. Also, when identical titles are being logged by ASCAP, BMI, and SESAC, payments may go to the wrong person.

Cry Your Way to the Charts

Certain words are commercial magic, and they unfailingly touch a universal chord. "Tears" is one such word:

"96 Tears" by Question Mark and the Mysterians (R. Martinez)

"Tears of a Clown" by Smokey Robinson and the Miracles and by Stevie Wonder (H. Cosby, W. Smokey Robinson, and S. Wonder)

"Cry" works wonders as well:

"Cry Me a River" by Julie London (A. Hamilton)

"Crying" by Roy Orbison (R. Orbison)

"I Won't Let You See Me Cry" by Trini Lopez (A. Kasha and J. Hirschhorn)

A Taste of Sugar

Some words have an automatic appeal. "Sour" doesn't work too well, but you can find "sweet" all over the charts. In fact, it's one of the most utilized words in popular music:

"Sweet Blindness" by The Fifth Dimension (L. Nyro)

"Sweet Caroline" by Neil Diamond (N. Diamond)

"Sweet Child o' Mine" by Guns 'n Roses (Guns 'n Roses)

"Sweet Dreams Are Made of This" by Eurhythmics (A. Lennox and D. Stewart)

"Sweet Little Sixteen" by Chuck Berry (C. Berry)

One Is the Magic Number

Numbers are always popular in titles: "Two Hearts" (Phil Collins); "Three Times a Lady" (Lionel Richie); "Four Walls" (Jim Reeves); but none has the commercial impact of the number "one." The following are just a few of the chartbusters with "one" in the title:

"One Bad Apple" by The Osmonds (G. Jackson)

"One More Night" by Phil Collins (P. Collins)

"One More Try" by George Michael (G. Michael)

"One of These Nights" by The Eagles (D. Henley and G. Frey)

"The One That You Love" by Air Supply (G. Russell)

Only

Maybe because we all want to be someone's "one and only," the word "only" has potent title appeal. Neil Young summed it up best when he said, "Only Love Can Break Your Heart," and Roy Orbison sang about "Only the Lonely." The Platters, the Hilltoppers, and Ringo Starr all sang "Only You," demonstrating the power of the emotion that "only" expresses. Carole King concluded, "Only Love Is Real."

Kiss

Artists, publishers, and producers all respond when they see the word "kiss" on a lead sheet or hear it on a recording. Prince went to number one with "Kiss," and Charley Pride had a country smash with "Kiss an Angel Good Mornin'." Elvis Presley told his lady friend, "Kiss Me Quick," and the Manhattans sang, "Kiss and Say Goodbye."

GREATEST HINTS ALBUM

Hirschhorn's Hints

If you have a chance to write a song for a film, fight for the title you believe in. We were asked to write a song called "The Poseidon Adventure" for the film of the same name. No song with "The Poseidon Adventure" as a title could have become a hit. Fortunately, we convinced the producer to let us use "The Morning After" instead.

First-Line Fever

Titles and first lines are the lure, the come-on to draw the audience in. If they're bland or colorless, you've lost your listeners. In an age of diminished attention spans and relentless bombardment by new stimuli, no one will give you more than a few seconds to score an impact. Movies succeed or fail after one weekend. If ratings for a television series are mediocre, it's instantly yanked from the schedule.

I've heard novice songwriters say, "I'm not going to be so blatant and commercial." This attitude is musical suicide in the rock world or even in theater, where Andrew Lloyd Webber felt he had to dangle a monster-sized chandelier in front of his *Phantom of the Opera* audience to guarantee its attention. Your title has to project power in order to obliterate the competition.

A memorable tune, a rousing rhythm, or a superb vocal performance can break through and hand the writer a hit, but spending some extra time and energy in creating an outstanding title and a mesmerizing first line will yield surprising and exciting results.

The Least You Need to Know

➤ A title has to suggest a story or create a mood.

➤ Sexually oriented titles are always in demand.

➤ The best titles are powerfully emotional exaggerations of life that offer a rich experience packed into a three-minute song.

➤ The audience's diminished attention span and increased exposure to new stimuli make captivating titles more important than ever.

➤ A dynamic title grips the audience, and a powerful first line mesmerizes them.

Part 2

Dressing Up the Song

People respond to sight, smell, taste, hearing, and touch, but in the twenty-first century, the visual sense dominates. This part shows you how to become a visual songwriter and how to think with all five of your senses.

Smooth rhyming, alliteration, and the proper use of vowels and structure are the building blocks of any superior song. Repetition and the right rhythmic groove are the lifeblood of popular songwriting; beyond that is the big H—the hook! "Give me a hit hook," is the cliché uttered by all publishers, producers, and writers. In this part, you'll learn what a hit hook is and how to write one. You'll also study sample repetitions and rhythmic grooves until these elements become second nature to you.

Finally, rewriting is a necessary evil. In this part, you'll learn how to face it and do it.

Chapter 7

The Visual Songwriter

In This Chapter

➤ Concentrate on what you see

➤ Live the visual lifestyle

➤ Create drama with details

➤ Write with all your senses

➤ Connect colors and music

Lyrics have to be emotional. From the time pop music was new, they expressed such feelings as "I Want You," "I'll Never Stop Loving You," and "Be My Love." Today those emotions are just as valid, but in this MTV and video age, generalities aren't enough to draw the attention of producers and recording artists. To stand out from the pack, you have to bring your words alive with visual images.

Boyz II Men don't just say, "I adore you." They sing "On Bended Knee." We see their emotional need through action. Titles such as "Black Cat," sung by Janet Jackson, and "Wind Beneath My Wings," sung by Bette Midler, bring the story brilliantly alive. You can improve your visual sense through awareness and practice.

A Unique Visual Personality

When I started, one of the first songs I brought to a publisher read like this:

> Nothing matters but your love
> Nothing matters but your kiss

> Without your touch my life is lonely
> How can I go on like this?

The publisher studied the song and said, "It's nice, but I see a hundred lyrics like this every day." When I pressed him for an explanation, he shrugged. "They have no special personality. How would I know if it's you or someone else?"

It all comes down to seeing with concentration. The majority of us walk through life with blinders on, more preoccupied with our private thoughts than with the external stimuli blazing around us. You can develop a visual sense effectively and rapidly by embarking on a whole new lifestyle.

The Visual Lifestyle

A visual lifestyle is a daily pattern, one that should kick off in the morning and be part of your schedule all day long. Tell yourself:

➤ This visual lifestyle is a new and permanent existence.

➤ Developing a visual lifestyle means success and recognition.

➤ A visual lifestyle is going to make me a much better writer and change my whole life.

Start with Cereal

As you're eating breakfast, try to think visually. Nothing interesting there, you think, just a plate of oatmeal with raisins and strawberries. But wait! The raisins and strawberries are much more like a painting than you ever imagined. The bowl is green and gold. You never noticed it before.

Read the newspaper for visual images, not simply for information. If the statement is, "President Bush stumbled off Air Force One, stooped forward with exhaustion, eyes lined as he told the press about his Mideast Conference," forget the Mideast Conference. Hone in on "stumbled … stooped forward … eyes lined."

As you peruse every page, circle the visual phrases. Within a few weeks, your lyrics will gain color. Bland phrases will drop out of your writing, and everyone who hears your language will relate more deeply to it.

Live in the Visual Landscape

Take a walk every morning. While appreciating the walk's cardiovascular benefits, tell yourself, "I see everything around me." Notice the cars, trees, flowers, and the runners waving as they pass by. If you're in a suburban area, observe the homes. Are they one-, two-, or three-level? Are they painted in conservative black and white? Is the trim blood-red or blue? Are kids in the front yard? What are they wearing? What game are they playing?

Now you've reached the park. Other walkers and runners have joined you. Old people sit on the benches. What expressions are they wearing? Optimistic? Sad? Resigned? You might notice a water fountain you've never been aware of before or a fence that needs painting.

Backstage Banter

"Madonna described how the words of the number-one hit, 'Like a Prayer,' developed. 'Originally, when I recorded the song, I would play it over and over again, trying to get a visual sense of what sort of story or fantasy it evoked in me. I kept imagining this story about a girl who was madly in love with a black man, set in the South, with this forbidden interracial love affair.'"

—Fred Bronson, *The Billboard Book of Number One Hits*, Billboard Books, 1997

If you live in a big city like New York, with an apartment in Manhattan, you'll find yourself awash in imagery if you bother to look around. Look beyond the obvious high-rise buildings, speeding yellow cabs, and expensive restaurants and study the gray-haired, overweight vendor on the corner selling salt bagels or the sax player blowing his heart out while indifferent crowds push past him.

Twain and Conroy

Read incessantly, and *not* only the bestsellers. Today's writing is fast, concise, and stripped for action. Few books can, for example, match Mark Twain's *Tom Sawyer* or *Huckleberry Finn* for language. But if you want to see modern visual writing at its finest, read Pat Conroy. *The Prince of Tides, The Water Is Wide, Beach Music,* and *The Lords of Discipline* are definitive demonstrations of how words can achieve the height of cinematic excitement.

The Drama in the Details

Film critic Pauline Kael once remarked in *The New Yorker,* "Do producers think we go to movies for the sets?" Most of us don't, but you, as a songwriter, should. Watch movies for more than the car chases or the explosions. From this day forward, watch how the characters dress, walk, talk, and gesture. Zero in on the set design, the architecture, and the furnishings of rooms ranging from the middle ages to today.

Everything from the gardens of Venice to the ghettos of New York is in the movies, and you should be studying it with an eye to recreating details.

In the end, lyric writing is all about the details that individualize people and situations. It's often more vital to notice a food stain on a coat than the coat itself. A food stain hints at the type of person you're watching. This kind of observation protects you from settling for clichés.

Hirschhorn's Hints

Tom T. Hall says that some songs require a mental picture of a train wreck. Some others require, melody-wise, a flower waving in the breeze. Allowing random mental pictures to float through your mind not only produces beautiful lyrics, but beautiful melodies as well.

Songwriter Sol Marcus, who wrote a hit song for the Animals, "Don't Let Me Be Misunderstood," once took a new writer to task for saying, in one line: "I love the morning sun and I wanna grab you, babe." These lines are certainly visual, but the same person would never speak both of them, particularly in one sentence.

Brides and Brothers

Visual lyrics are just as vital for theater writing as they are for rock songs. When Al and I were hired to compose the Broadway musical *Seven Brides for Seven Brothers*, Alan Jay Lerner (*My Fair Lady, Camelot*) told us, "If you want to write for Broadway, make sure the audience sees everything you say through visual action."

We took Lerner's advice seriously, and it worked. Our music received a Tony nomination for Best Score and has been playing to packed houses around the world for the past 20 years.

Analyze Nonvisual Lyrics

A highly effective approach to jump-starting your visual sense is to analyze both good and bad lyrics and rewrite them by deleting generalities and finding ways to make them more specific. Many songs reach the top of the charts based on their well-produced tracks, powerful vocal performances, or basic idea, but the lyric lines are banal and clichéd. You'll discover yourself improving quickly if you rework those throwaway lines and make them visual.

Look for Consistently Visual Writers

Some lyricists have a much more visual flair than others. Study the market to find out who these artists are and then give special attention to their work. Certain names spring immediately to mind:

Marilyn and Alan Bergman	Jimmy Webb
Garth Brooks	Sheldon Harnick

The late Howard Ashman	Bob Dylan
Tim Rice	Bernie Taupin
Stephen Sondheim	Paul Simon
Paul McCartney	Chuck Berry
Dan Fogelberg	Jerry Leiber
Bruce Springsteen	Smokey Robinson
Billy Joel	Joni Mitchell
Bob Seger	Pete Townshend
Bob McDill	

Describe Everyday Experiences Visually

Another process that expands your visual sense is concentrating on ordinary, mundane activities. Paint them visually in ways that heighten the actions and bring them alive. Think of small details that give them individuality and freshness. It's been said that you can take an orange and find dozens of characteristics about it worth describing.

These seemingly static situations can lead to interesting lyrics. For example, the following lines describe the act of waking up:

> My legs were crooked, my top undone
> My hair was in my eyes
> My knees were stiff from too much sleep
> The sun took me by surprise

Taking a picture off the wall becomes an emotional experience in these lyrics:

> Tore your picture from the wall
> The tears ran down my face
> I stared into your evil eyes
> and cursed your last embrace

Describing the ordinary act of picking up a child at school creates an image all parents can relate to:

> My six-year-old was bundled up
> Shivering at the gate
> He ran to me, leaped in the car
> Angry I was late

Keep in mind what famed author and scriptwriter Adela Rogers St. John once said: "Creative people have story reactions to the most average situations." Make those visual stories, and you'll be on your way to becoming a visual songwriter.

Visual, but Not Verbose

Books sometimes have descriptions of sunsets, rivers, and mountains that are beautiful in themselves, but they slow the story down to a crawl. Expert writers use imagery to dramatize emotions and events, but never at the expense of pacing. All visual details must serve a purpose in the song. If they don't move the story and the emotions forward, discard them.

The Other Four Senses

Most people are oblivious to their visual surroundings, and they're even less aware of the sounds, smells, tastes, and tactile experiences that fill every day. Only by responding to everything around you with all your senses will you reach your highest potential as a lyricist. Seeing is the firs but not the only step toward giving lyrics a pulse and making them breathe.

Sound

Sounds roar from every direction. Cars don't simply go by; they zoom, screech, groan, and rumble. A bus comes to a sharp, squealing stop. Two people are having a bitter argument. Someone yells across the street to a friend.

Life has a soundtrack, but most of us have the volume turned way down. Adjust the dial and listen to everything. What you hear will make your lyrics more compelling.

Smell

Take a deep breath. Stop and smell the roses, a woman's perfume, the chicken or steak from a local diner, and the stench of garbage. Not every smell is pleasant, but all of them help to set a scene and make your words more vibrant.

Trouble Clef

Do not trust your memory! It will let you down every time. You'll remember the broad outlines but not the specifics, and specifics are what make your lyrics magical.

Taste

I used to have a bad habit, one I overcame with superhuman effort. I would gulp down my lunch or dinner, and an hour later I wouldn't even recall what I'd eaten! All of us have been given the great gift of taste, so chew slowly and savor your food.

Touch

The softness of our hand on another's skin is one kind of pleasure; the feel of the person's hair and the warmth of his or her lips are also pleasurable. Yet touching is a sensual experience that extends far beyond contact between two human beings. We're rarely aware of all the things we touch. Consider the softness of old blue jeans, the bristly stab of a beard, or the leathery texture of shoes. A tablecloth has a gentle coolness; the mahogany finish of a piano is smooth and pleasing.

Writing with the Five Senses

Writing is always more memorable when it encompasses the five senses. Consider this verse from "Hearing the Wind":

> Eating cherry pie
> Watching the sun in the sky
> Waiting for love to let me in
> Smellin' the fries
> Smoke in my eyes
> Touching your hand—and hearing the wind

Every sense—taste, sight, touch, sound, and smell—is engaged in this lyric.

Brushing your teeth is admittedly routine and boring. You've probably never bothered to ask yourself, what sensation am I experiencing when the toothbrush moves across my teeth? The same goes for combing your hair, buttoning your shirt, and tying your shoelaces. These are moments when your psyche switches to automatic, and you have to catch yourself and pay attention.

GREATEST HINTS ALBUM

Hirschhorn's Hints

Make sure all your senses are functioning; don't close any of them off. Nuno Bettencourt, co-author, with Gary Cherone, of "More Than Words" by Extreme, was sitting on his porch when he wrote the song. He heard the cars go by, and that street sound inspired him.

Look at Who's Talking

Pay attention to the way people talk. Both a forest ranger and a Philadelphia debutante speak English, but they might as well be speaking two different languages.

I worked twice with Shelley Winters, on *The Poseidon Adventure* and *Pete's Dragon,* and had this experience: She was telling me a story about an argument she'd once had when, in the middle of the story, she lost track of her point and became acutely aware of her gestures, the tone of her voice, and her body language. Actors respond this way to what they hear; songwriters should, too.

Write It All Down

As the impressions mount, as your senses begin to feast on the barrage of input you receive, one thing is absolutely crucial: Keep a record! You can do it the old-fashioned way by writing in a notebook, or you can carry a tape recorder and speak about all you see, touch, hear, taste, and smell.

When you listen to music, jot down every interesting, unusual, original word or phrase you encounter. It sets the mental machinery buzzing. You won't necessarily use any of these lyrics, but they'll stimulate you to think of your own. The same applies to magazines. The authors who contribute articles to *Vanity Fair* and *GQ* are masters of writing that employs all the senses.

Lyrical Lingo

Synethesia is the process by which a certain color or colors provokes the hearing of a certain sounds.

Hirschhorn's Hints

Thunder, deep voices, and drums often invoke dark images. The imagery is light when people hear squeaks from string instruments, flutes, or piccolos. High pitch makes the colors more powerful and vivid. If you see red with middle C, C-sharp will be a brighter red. You'll see a more brilliant color if D is played rather than C-sharp.

Music and Colors

Thinking in colors can stimulate musical composition. Let waves of purple, red, blue, green, and black flood your mind. Be receptive without straining for tunes. Gradually, if you're patient, the imagery will be accompanied by sound (this is called *synethesia*), such as the tinkling of a distant piano, bells, a lone fiddle, drums, or bagpipes. Every mind is individual, but before long your brain will explode with sound, and that sound will channel itself into exciting melodies and rhythms you can utilize.

To encourage musical creativity, listen to music before you start to write and let your mind bring up imagery in a free-floating way. Psychologist Chuck Loch says:

> "Imagine hearing music that deeply affects you emotionally. You close your eyes. A cloud or filmy veil of color begins to billow. Spreading sheets of color overlay each other. Bands or ribbons of color develop and flow with the music."

> —*Songwriter* magazine, June 1979

Loch's research revealed that high-pitched music tends to produce small, sharp-edged images; low-pitched music brought on dark, round images. Graceful lines of color accompanied smooth music; syncopated music yielded jagged lines.

Don't be concerned whether your mental imagery conforms to the majority. For half an hour, give yourself over to the sounds and let your mind choose its own visual equivalents. After the power of your imagery dissipates, start to write. Your music will gain richness, color, and freedom.

The Least You Need to Know

➤ Experience your surroundings visually.

➤ Even mundane events can translate into exciting and visually appealing lyrics.

➤ When you write, think with all five senses.

➤ Thinking in colors can stimulate musical composition.

Chapter 8

Cooking Up Your Hit Ingredients

In This Chapter

➤ Rhymes that work and rhymes that don't

➤ Ways to build your rhyming skills

➤ Rhyme schemes and song structures

➤ Amazing alliteration and powerful vowels

Rhyme doesn't seem like a controversial word. It's love and above, moon and June, and sing and spring. Or is it down and around, shine and mind, and laugh and pass? It's both. The issue that continues to rage is: Do rhymes have to be true or can they be false soundalikes? If you ask the master craftsman of Broadway, Stephen Sondheim, if false rhymes are acceptable, you'll be hit with a resounding no.

I used to stand with the Sondheims and I still prefer the true rhyme, but I'm not as dogmatic about it because attitudes toward rhyme have changed. But other lyric ingredients stay the same. As this chapter points out, learning structure will prevent you from wandering formlessly and ensure that every thought comes across with emotional clarity. Alliteration (in which two or more words in a line start with the same letter) makes the line flow easily and effortlessly. And using vowels such as "e" and "o" helps singers to achieve greater vocal passion and power.

Rhyming Time

There's more latitude in rhyming today than there used to be, but one thing is still certain: On Broadway, where standards of craft are mercilessly strict, you have to rhyme perfectly. If you don't, critics will pounce on you and probably close your show before anyone gets a chance to see it. The pop world is different. Pop music is not just for educated sophisticates, but for the masses, and the byword is honesty. Singers and writers have to relate to the man (or woman) on the street. If the words are too slick, they'll be rejected as pretentious.

Types of Rhymes

Most rhymes fall into one of the following categories:

➤ **Perfect rhyme.** The sounds are exactly alike, as in day/play, joy/boy, blaze/craze, and ease/knees.

➤ **False rhyme.** Still a matter of controversy among writers, this rhyme pairs words that contain similar sounds, such as time/mine, down/around, and hard/car.

➤ **Masculine rhyme.** This rhyme involves a single syllable. That syllable may be the entire word as in store/floor or the last syllable in longer word, as in venerate/segregate. In a masculine rhyme, the final syllable is accented, as in these words: resound, avoid, reply, and consume.

➤ **Feminine rhyme.** In this two-syllable rhyme, the stress falls on the first part of the word: walker/stalker. The final syllable of the word is unaccented, as in softness, careful, and fairest.

➤ **Open rhyme.** This rhyme ends softly as in flow/toe or sky/pie.

➤ **Inner rhyme.** "The wall is tall and close to the mall" illustrates multiple rhyming within a single sentence.

A Hit Mixture

In most cases, professional songwriters know how to rhyme. But more often today they go by what feels emotionally right, even if it means sacrificing the perfect, obvious rhyme word.

This combination of false and true rhyme is used in Celine Dion's "The Power of Love" as well as in "I've Waited All My Life."

> The morning sun is shining
> We made love through the night
> I pray the feelings still go on
> When I look in your eyes
> I've waited all my life for you
> And if you leave, I'll break
> You've everything I've waited for
> So stay here for my sake

"Night" and "eyes" don't even sound alike, except for the vowel sound of "i." Yet "break" and "sake" would satisfy any purist. Your intuition has to tell you when such false rhymes as love/touch or again/rain best serve your thought and when a true rhyme would make the point more effectively.

Endings That Set You Free

The following endings will give you maximum rhyming freedom:

-ay	-ee	-in	-ore
-ade	-eer	-ine	ot
-ain	-el	-ist	-ote
-ake	ence	-it	-ow
-ar	-ent	-ize	-ow (o)
-are	-ess	-ock	-ude
-ate	-ew	-oke	-y
-ean	-ide	-oom	
-eat	-ill	-oon	

These are by no means the only alternatives, but they make a writer's life much simpler. I'm not a person who shuns rhyming dictionaries. But sometimes you're in the midst of a song, and no rhyming dictionary is available. Train yourself to automatically know as many rhymes as possible by using these sounds and writing as many rhymes as you can think of.

Inner Rhymes

The best inner rhymes give lines rhythmic grace, smoothness, and professionalism:

I see your face—it's everyplace
I hear you talk—I see you walk—when I close my eyes
The smile I wear is just a disguise
I'm gonna crack—'cause I want you back
The smile I wear is just a disguise

Listen to the classic record of "Ain't Nothin' Like the Real Thing" by Marvin Gaye and Tammi Terrell, and you'll see how perfectly the rhymes coast along, beautifully integrated into the overall structure.

Wayward Rhymes

When you're creating a rhyme, keep the word "flow" in mind. Whether a rhyme is false or true, it must maintain a comfortable, natural flow. That's the only thing that matters. Use words that offer dozens of rhyming alternatives and avoid lines that lack any rhyme, unless you feel that your thought is so brilliant it can survive without safety nets of craftsmanship.

Rhymes Without Reason

My advice is to learn to rhyme perfectly before you settle for false rhymes. If possible, avoid words that aren't rhymes in any sense of the word, such as new/knew or bare/bear. Combinations like these call attention to themselves and sound amateurish.

Another amateurish approach is twisting a line unnaturally:

> You're all that I've been thinking of
> Because I find, in you, my love

No one talks that way. Don't wrench words like pretzels for a rhyme.

Trouble Clef

Cole Porter used *puberty* and *Shuberty* as well as *flatterer* and *Cleopatterer.* Show writers often employ this device, distorting words out of shape and then pronouncing the result witty, sophisticated, and playful. But we're not in the age of Lorenz Hart and Noel Coward. Unless you're a brilliant wordsmith, an attempt to bend words this way might sound more like a mistake than an inspiration.

Rhymes That Box You In

Although love is the main theme behind all songs, the word itself offers few interesting rhyming possibilities. Love/above was a dated combination in the 1930s, and love/of always sounds clichéd. What's left? *Glove* is not a pop word; *shove* sounds hostile rather than romantic; and *dove* sounds pristine in the rock era.

In Search of Colorful Rhyme Words

If you're hitting a brick wall searching for interesting rhyme words, these sources can sharpen your lyric writing:

➤ *Roget's International Thesaurus.* This invaluable resource was first printed in 1852 and has been a treasure chest of synonyms ever since.

➤ *Slang!* by Paul Dickson. This book is packed with expressions relating to fields such as business, computers, the automotive industry, counterculture, the drug trade, fantasy, the future and science fiction, food and drink, medicine, sailing, performing, politics, real estate, sex, sports, and many other areas.

➤ *The Dictionary of Clichés* by James Rogers. Over 2,000 popular expressions, their meanings, and origins are listed in this book.

➤ *Instant Quotation Dictionary* will spark your rhyming and lyric writing.

➤ *Dictionary of Modern Quotations* by J. M. Cohen and M. J. Cohen.

➤ *The International Thesaurus of Quotations* compiled by Rhoda Thomas Tripp.

➤ *A Dictionary of American Idioms* contains such expressions as "get down to brass tacks," "far-out," "bolt from the blue," and "zero in on."

➤ *Dictionary of American Slang* compiled by Harold Wentworth and Stuart Berg Flexner.

➤ *20,000 Quips and Quotes* complied by Evan Esar.

E. Y. (Yip) Harburg, who wrote the songs for *The Wizard of Oz*, once said, "Rhyme, schlime—it's the thought that counts. The thought is more important than the rhyme." Another of his favorite lines was, "It's all for naught without the thought."

Fresh, original, interesting thoughts matter more than any surface craft. But craft can provide the key that expresses those thoughts clearly, and rhyme is one crucial way of achieving this clarity.

Rhyming Dictionaries

Many rhyming dictionaries are so detailed that they confuse rather than enlighten. I like the pocket-sized *Random House Rhyming Dictionary,* edited by Jess Stein. In a pinch, this tiny volume has never failed me.

These rhyming dictionaries are also useful:

➤ *The Songwriter's Rhyming Dictionary* by Sammy Cahn

➤ *The Complete Rhyming Dictionary* by Clement Wood

➤ *Dell's Complete Rhyming Dictionary, Revised Edition*

➤ *The New Rhyming Dictionary and Poet's Handbook* by Burge and Johnson

➤ *Songwriter's Rhyming Dictionary* by Jane Shaw Whitfield

➤ *The Writer's Rhyming Dictionary* by Langford Reed

➤ *The Modern Rhyming Dictionary* by Gene Lees

➤ *Penguin Rhyming Dictionary* by Rosalind Fergusson

➤ *Webster's Compact Rhyming Dictionary*

➤ *The New Comprehensive American Rhyming Dictionary*
➤ *Words to Rhyme With* by Willard Espy

Rhyme Schemes

Successful writers utilize a variety of popular rhyme schemes. This section points out several important ones.

My Oscar-winning song, "The Morning After," written with Al Kasha, demonstrates the rhyming of lines 2 and 4:

> There's got to be a morning after
> If we can hold on through the night
> We have a chance to find the sunshine
> Let's keep on looking for the light

Trouble Clef

Don't be too proud to use a rhyming dictionary or feel that this aid is a copout. Stephen Sondheim never works without one, and he's considered by many people to be our greatest living lyricist.

To add even more rhyme, you can rhyme lines 1 and 3 and lines 2 and 4:

> You've broken my heart
> Our bridges have been crossed
> 'cause he broke us apart
> It hurts to know I've lost

Another hit rhyme scheme is to rhyme lines 1 and 2 and lines 3 and 4:

> I want you more than I can say
> So promise you won't go away
> If I can't have your love I'll die
> So baby, please don't say goodbye

Some writers rhyme all the lines:

> Baby I'll be there
> You know how I care
> There's so much to share
> Love beyond compare

Or a writer may rhyme the first two or three lines and leave the last one without a rhyme:

> I hate to sleep alone
> It's painful on my own
> I want you back
> I just want you to know

I'll never let you go
I only want to show
That I need you

Yet another popular rhyme scheme is to rhyme
lines 2 and 3:

I hate the rain
It just reminds me of my tears
How much I've cried through all these years
I hate the rain

Sometimes writers only rhyme the first line of
verse 1 and verse 2:

I'll never be free
You've got me in chains
I'm praying that I can escape
You're part of me
When I try to run
I never get far

Backstage Banter

Writers sometimes decide not to
rhyme at all. John Denver's
"Annie's Song" had no rhymes.
The sincerity and emotional honesty of the lyrics carried Denver's
melody along and turned it into
a major hit. "I Got Rhythm" by
George and Ira Gershwin also
became a standard without
rhymes.

Or the last line of each verse rhymes, as in this example:

The minute we met
I wanted your love
And girl, I still do
With each passing day
This ache only grows
My whole life is you

These often-used, thoroughly dependable rhyme schemes can work for all writers.
If you're a new songwriter, stick with them until they feel comfortable and natural.
When they seem automatic, stretch out and try others.

Other Hit Ingredients

Using rhyme effectively is basic, buy other hit ingredients such as structure, alliteration, and the right vowel sounds will add form, flow, and vibrancy to your songs.

Structure

Without structure, your song would be shapeless and sprawling. Within it, however,
there is a surprising number of variations.

Bruce Springsteen's "Born in the USA" uses this form:

A (Verse) A (Verse) A (Verse)

The most accessible and familiar form is this one:

A (Verse) A (Verse) B (Bridge) A (Verse)

"Raindrops Keep Fallin' on My Head" (H. David, B. Bacharach), "Saving All My Love for You" (M. Masser, G. Goffin), and "Just the Way You Are" (Billy Joel) use the AABA structure. Al and I also used the AABA format on our two Oscar winners, "The Morning After" and "We May Never Love Like This Again."

Another familiar form is the following:

A (Verse) B (Chorus) A (Verse) B (Chorus) A (Verse) B (Chorus)

"Killing Me Softly with His Song" utilizes the ABABAB structure, as does the driving "Big Bad Leroy Brown." This structure has no *bridge* in it, just two sections alternating with each other.

B. J. Thomas used the following format in "Don't Worry Baby":

A (Verse) B (Chorus) A (Verse) B (Chorus) C (Bridge) B (Chorus)

A variation on ABABCB would be this structure:

A (Chorus) B (Verse) A (Chorus) B (Verse) A (Chorus)

Sometimes the verse is repeated four times or more, without any chorus or bridge. Johnny Cash's "I Walk the Line" uses this structure.

The Eagles demonstrated that basic forms can be stretched, extended, or molded into any shape that makes sense. For "Lyin' Eyes," they did the following:

A (Verse) A (Verse) A (Verse) B (Chorus) A (Verse) B (Chorus)

This structure is daring because it delays the appearance of the chorus until nearly halfway through. If you're a new writer, it's safer to stick with more familiar forms. The Eagles were powerful enough when they recorded "Lyin' Eyes" to experiment and buck commercially conservative trends.

Alliteration

Nothing makes a line flow more smoothly than *alliteration,* as in this example:

Tell me you'll be true
Trust my love for you

Note the three *T* words: tell, true, and trust.

Alliteration is something to concentrate on. You can overdo it, as in "How wonderful to walk with you this Wednesday," but if kept in check, it's the best friend any lyricist can have.

Vibrant Vowels

A, E, I, O, and *U* are the magic letters. Think how often you hear big, powerful notes on words such as *go* and *say* and *me*. Think how wrong it would be to sock out a roaring note on *the* or *but*. When you're writing, stress vowels on your crucial notes, and you'll keep the singer happy. You'll also increase your chances of having a hit.

Act Out Your Lyrics

When used properly, rhyme, alliteration, and vowels pay off the ultimate dividend: Your words will talk. Whether sung or spoken, lyrics should never sound stilted. After you've completed your lyric, give it the talk test. Be an actor. Read every word out loud, dismissing all music from your mind. Pretend you're speaking to a loved one or a friend.

Is there any phrase that sounds awkward when spoken? It will be equally awkward in combination with music. Speak the lyrics two, three, or four times. Your ear will latch onto the lines that sound real and reject the ones that seem artificial. You'll notice right away which words are fillers, throwaways, or pieces of a first draft that should have been discarded.

Once the talk test identifies your weak lines, be ruthless and get rid of the verbal dead weight. Don't rationalize, as so many beginning writers do, that the line "works," that the overall feeling is fine, or that it's the best you can do. You may be tempted to do that if you're tired or discouraged or bored by the process. If this is the case, stop working, and then return to the problem and deal with it in a renewed frame of mind. An absolute truth about all writing is: As good as something is, there are always ways to make it better.

Lyrical Lingo

A **bridge** (or release, as it's also called) is the mid-section of a song. It's completely different from the rest of the tune.

Lyrical Lingo

Alliteration is the use of the same first letter to begin several words in the same line.

Hirschhorn's Hints

Get sheet music of the Top 10 and speak the lines. You'll begin to see how the best ones sound like natural human speech.

Before you play your material for anyone, make sure that you've done as much as you possibly can with your rhymes, alliteration, and vowels. When the lyrics talk to you, they'll talk to the listener as well.

The Least You Need to Know

➤ Try for pure rhymes first.

➤ Be constantly aware of inner rhymes.

➤ Keep in mind that the thought behind the lines counts most.

➤ Learn the basic rhyme schemes used by the pros.

➤ Alliteration gives your material a flow and polish.

➤ Lyrics have to sound like honest, colloquial human speech.

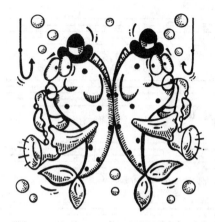

Chapter 9

Repetition and Hooks

In This Chapter

➤ Simplify your style with repetition

➤ Factor in the tempo

➤ Improve your hook consciousness

➤ Add magic with riffs and figures

The core of all popular music is repetition. A song may repeat only one note or one lyric line or, more commonly, an entire section. The importance of repetition can never be emphasized too strongly, because composers, particularly new ones, tend to resist it. In their quest for originality, they drop basic form, as though adopting a structure will compromise their art. They often come up with tuneful themes and then replace them, never to return to the melody they started with!

When people complain that they can't sing a song, it's because the tune is difficult or even impossible to remember. Repetition can make your songs more memorable and more likely to become hits.

Styles of Musical Repetition

You can work miracles within a tight, organized framework. Some familiar ways repetition can be applied include the ones illustrated in the following figure.

Samples of repetition.

(© Joel Hirschhorn)

Hirschhorn's Hints

Don't look at the few exceptions to the repetition rule. Yes, Bob Dylan's "Rainy Day Women #12 plus 35" never even gives us the title in the song, but most of Dylan's hit singles are repetitive and instantly memorable: "Blowing in the Wind," "I Want You," and "Mr. Tambourine Man."

As a new writer, I once told Irwin Schuster, an A&R (artists and repertory) man at Screen Gems Music, that I was afraid I would bore the audience *if* I repeated the chorus too much. His answer: "You can *never* repeat too much, not in pop music."

The Strength of Simplicity

The late Irving Berlin is still one of the most performed composers in ASCAP history. Reviewers often criticized Berlin for being too commercial and simple. But as *Hello, Dolly!* composer Jerry Herman comments …

> "That's like saying the bride is too pretty. To me the ultimate compliment is to be called commercial. I'm writing for the people out there, and if I can't reach them by having them hum something of mine, I've failed."

Simplicity allows people to hum, whistle, and sing songs after one or two listens. Simplicity equals *repetition.* This formula pertains equally to a Broadway standard and a rock song, whether the song is Webber and Rice's "Jesus Christ Superstar" or an early 1950s hit such as "Maybe Baby," with this catchy opener:

> Maybe baby, I'll have you
> Maybe baby, you'll be true
> Maybe baby, I'll have you for me

Paul McCartney made sure listeners would remember his title when he sang the phrase, "band on the run," four times in a row!

Lyrical Lingo

Repetition can refer to one note, full lines, or a complete verse. When an entire section is repeated, this section is known as the song's **hook.**

Repeat Hits

When repetition is skillfully utilized, it can produce songs that become hits two or three times. Goffin and King's "The Loco-Motion" was a gold record for newcomer Little Eva (their daughter's baby-sitter) and reappeared at the top of the charts with Grand Funk Railroad. This rousing dance record kept repeating, "Come on, baby, do the Loco-Motion." Diana Ross and Phil Collins benefited from the repetition of the title "You Can't Hurry Love," which was a number-one smash for both of them.

Repetition and Tempo

When a tune races ahead quickly, keep the lyrics simple. That's why there are so many repetitive sha-na-nas, tra-la-las, and doo-wop-doo-wops when tempos pick up steam. On a tune such as "Staying Alive" by the Bee Gees, the rhythm plunges ahead rapidly, so the words are simple, and the title repeats unceasingly. The words can be more varied and sophisticated when the tempo is slow, because listeners have time to digest them.

Hooking the Audience

It doesn't matter if the material is pop, country, R&B, hip-hop, hard rock, soft rock, punk rock, Latin, or adult contemporary: The lifeblood of a song is its *hook*. Hook is a perfect word for pop writing. A pop song doesn't seduce, coax, or invite; it hooks people with an assertive, repeating demand.

You don't have to open a song with a hook (hundreds of hits don't), but for chart insurance, Berry Gordy, founder of Motown, used to urge his writers to jump in hook first. Number One was Gordy's goal, and he once referred to number 9 on the charts as a major disappointment and number 28 as "dismal." He took no chances.

A hook is often based on a sound, such as "Hi-De-Ho" by Blood, Sweat and Tears, "Be-Bop-a-Lula" by Gene Vincent, and Al Green's "Sha-La-La." The ideal hook contains three elements:

➤ A danceable, pulsating rhythm

➤ A melody that sticks in people's minds after one listen

➤ A lyric that propels the story forward

Hooking the Emotions

A hook line has to connect viscerally with all the senses. If you were to take a sentence such as "I should brush my teeth" or "It's time to do the dishes" and base your song around that phrase, no great performance or explosive orchestration could rescue it. An outstanding hook always puts across the song's basic, overall point of view.

Hooks should represent the most powerful part of your lyric and melody. For example, "Dancing in the Streets" by Martha and the Vandellas sought to combine exuberance, a sense of celebration, and a feeling of future hope; the pounding hook captured all three.

It doesn't matter what kind of emotion you're projecting, as long as that emotion deeply affects people. In Sting's "Every Breath You Take," the hook line, "I'll be watching you," conveys suspicion and paranoia. The melody here is more low-key and insinuating. It portrays the feeling of a lover's desperation and creates a strong setup for the rest of the song.

"Killing Me Softly with His Song," written by Charles Fox and Norman Gimbel, is gentler and more subdued than the previous two songs, but the effect is just as forceful. The spare, guitar-driven arrangement and Roberta Flack's sensitive vocal brought out all the emotions felt by someone who finds herself falling in love at first sight.

Trouble Clef

Don't let your focus on a hook mislead you into thinking that the rest of the song doesn't matter. Writers often give short shrift to the second verse in particular, figuring the hook will compensate. Keep this in mind: Every part of the song has to be worked over and made as strong as possible.

Lyricist Gimbel knew that the words in a hook had to be vivid. When Johnny Mercer commented, after first hearing the song, that the word "killing" was too shocking and tonally harsh, Gimbel obeyed his instincts and used the word he believed in. He had enough confidence not to emasculate the hook and make it tame.

Hirschhorn's Hints

Listen to songs in your car (or when you're walking or riding the bus). Gerry Goffin felt he could tell if a song had a hit hook and lyric if he listened to it on the car radio. He never listened at home. It was just something about the resonance of the car that caught the sound of a hit single.

Marvin Gaye's "What's Goin' On?" is a definitive example of the hook as chant. "What's Goin' On?" he cries over and over again, with increasing despair, to a world brimming with prejudice and hostility. Jackie De Shannon's classic rendition of "What the World Needs Now Is Love" is also a chant, but in a waltz tempo. The note on the word "world" leaps up, underlining the intensity of her plea for tolerance, love, and understanding.

The test of a Top 10 hook is its ability to exist without verses, bridge, or orchestral icing. A good hook should have tremendous impact and stand completely alone.

If you write a hook first, you know right away if you have something special. You've established the story, the rhythmic feel, and the song's crucial repetitive element.

Hirschhorn's Hints

To emphasize and hammer home the hook, writers like to attach a strong, rising section right before it begins. This section is called a pre-chorus. It's not mandatory, but pre-choruses are riveting announcements that the big musical wave is coming. Whenever you feel a pre-chorus works comfortably within your song's context, you should consider using it.

Developing Your Hook Consciousness

Try thinking in hooks. As a practice exercise, listen to the radio and ignore everything except the hook. Treat the radio dial as you would your television remote; stay on a pop station for a couple of songs, and then switch to country for a few more. After that, move to R&B. Scan an oldies program. Cover all genres. Do this for an hour a day, listening to nothing but the hooks.

This exercise will develop and sharpen your hook consciousness. It will simplify any tendency you have to wander and ramble. Then listen to CDs you have, one or two in each style. Play the hooks over and over again. Listen to them a couple of times, without analyzing anything. Once the general hook is in your head, concentrate on individual notes and words. What is repeated? How many times? If you can write music, write the hooks down. If you can't notate music, write down the lyrics from each hook you hear.

Ask yourself what the hooks contain that catch your ear most powerfully. What, in your opinion, makes them special?

Creating and Testing Your Hooks

Sing the hooks you've heard without backing yourself up on an instrument. Get a sense of how simple they are and how little they depend on chords and arrangements to be appreciated. In writing your own hooks, do the same thing. Never think this thought: It may not sound perfect just now, but when it's produced or an arrangement is added, it will be just right. If the hook doesn't work without embellishment, you need to re-examine it, rewrite it, or discard it.

Verse vs. Hook

The verse and the hook (chorus) are from the same family, but you must never make them so similar that no distinction exists. It's always better to hear the complaint, "I can remember the hook, but not the verse," than to hear someone express the opposite thought. Make sure the chords don't fall in exactly the same places, and that the rhythms differ. The lack of contrast between verse and hook will cost you a hit, even if you're lucky enough to land an important artist and get top promotion.

When you've completed a song, make sure there's enough variety in story, lyric, and melody to avoid tedium. Eager young songwriters often take the message about repetition so much to heart that they practically eliminate all the other song elements needed. If you feel the slightest bit uneasy or bored, examine your tune again. The trick is to be memorable without being monotonous.

Instrumental Breaks

Instrumental breaks allow musicians to let loose. Sometimes these breaks are spontaneous creations in the studio. Other times the composer works out every note with care. But either way, the instrumental break allows room for another hook. It can be utilized in the intro or repeated at the end. It can become part of a background chorus. When writing your song, keep its value in mind.

Sleep on It

In the rapturous rush of a completed first draft, you'll tend to love what you've written. Your hook will seem like the next Number One. My advice is to get away from it for a while and re-evaluate your masterpiece the next morning. You may still be impressed with your own brilliance; you may even feel that the work is better than you originally thought. But you may also notice notes, words, or chords that could benefit from rewriting. When that happens, don't be depressed. With the clarity of distance, you'll be able to make the song far better.

What Hooks Your Friends?

When your friends listen to music, what hooks them? What do they respond to? Your job, as a commercial songwriter, is to develop a keen awareness of what appeals to other people. Even though you must stay true to yourself, you're also writing for the public.

Keep in mind that before your song reaches the ears of the public, it has to win the approval of radio program directors who decide what music will be aired and emphasized. The song must be immediately singable or it will never be added to a Top 40 playlist. Occasional exceptions are made for icons like Whitney Houston or Madonna, but even superstars have a tough time if they don't offer a memorable hook. Today, more than ever, program directors are conscious of ratings. They were never risk-takers, but in this era, the word risk is poison.

Tell Yourself the Truth

Remember: Your friends and family are your public. So are your children and your nieces and nephews. You don't want intellectual reaction or analysis of your work; you want to judge the emotional response. If you're honest with yourself, you can always tell the difference between "It's nice" and genuine excitement. Don't be so self-protective that you program your pals to react the way you want them to. Don't start out by saying, "I wrote a new song you're going to love." People, particularly family members, take their cues from the need you project.

Criticism is tough to take. We all want our work to receive unqualified praise. I used to think, after I won my Oscars, that I would have less difficulty accepting negative reaction, that success had insulated me against hurt feelings. My shell is a little tougher now, but if friends give me a less-than-ecstatic reaction, I still feel as though one of my children has been criticized. When that happens, I try to keep my main goal in mind: I need the truth so I can improve my work and win world acceptance for my songs.

Instrumental Icing: Figures and Riffs

A song is a blend of melody and lyrics, and many songs have succeeded by coasting on these two components alone. But the real magic comes when you add *figures* and *riffs*. Publisher Irving Mills of Mills Music once referred to them as "the golden glue."

Don't make the mistake of saying, "Figures and riffs aren't my job. They're the job of the arranger or producer." Anyone who studies hooks and develops an acute case of hook consciousness will be cured of that attitude.

Lyrical Lingo

A **riff** is a short, rhythmic pattern repeated with no melodic variation (*ostinato*, in musical language). A **figure** is a melodic fragment repeated through the song, often serving as an extra hook.

Figure on Catchy Figures

Stevie Wonder's "Superstition" supplies a rocking guitar intro that repeats after every line in the song. This record wouldn't have had half the impact without Wonder's superb guitar riff.

Lennon and McCartney based many of their early tunes on riffs. Think of "Daytripper," and you'll hear the repetitive 11-note riff in your mind before you hear the melody. "You Keep Me Hangin' On" achieves immortality through its SOS figure.

These records all have unforgettable, built-in background figures:

"All Night Long (All Night)" by Lionel Richie (L. Richie)

"Fame" by Irene Cara (M. Gore and D. Pitchford)

"Live and Let Die" by Paul McCartney (McCartney/Eastman)

"Take My Breath Away" by Berlin (G. Moroder and T. Whitlock)

Write Cool Riffs

Rock fans treasure the wailing sax in Leiber and Stoller's comedic Coasters recording "Yakety Yak." Whether it's a movie tune such as "What's New, Pussycat? (wa-wa-wa-wa)"; or George Harrison's "My Sweet Lord," with its repetitive and romantic guitar riff; added words, notes, and sounds become fresh, delightful hooks of their own.

In other words, you can't have too many hooks! After a while, it becomes an enjoyable game to see how many you can include. Try writing a tune that contains the following hook elements:

➤ The hook verse itself

➤ A vocal part that keeps repeating in every verse

➤ A bass part that repeats every other bar

➤ A guitar part that opens the record and then repeats in every hook section

➤ A recurring piano figure

➤ The lead vocalist doing a high, recurring falsetto part

The following figure illustrates how it can be done.

Backstage Banter

A famous music publisher used to give his staff writers an assignment: to write a song and think of as many hooks as possible, both lyrically and melodically. He wouldn't accept less than 10, and someone on the staff would occasionally come up with 15 or more.

"Nobody Knows How Much" (Joel Hirschhorn). A 32-bar computer-generated song demonstrating four hooks, a recurring piano figure, and a recurring falsetto part for the lead vocalist.

Always remember what people say when they like something: "I can't forget it." "I can't stop singing it." "I heard it in my dreams." "I found myself whistling it." If you can write unforgettable, repetitive hooks, your songs will always attract the attention of artists and producers.

The Least You Need to Know

➤ Repetition of lyrics, notes, or whole sections of the song simplify the song and make it more memorable.

➤ Keep the hook simple.

➤ When the tempo of the tune is rapid, keep the lyrics simple.

➤ Put as many figures and riffs in your songs as possible.

Chapter 10

The Secrets of Hit Melody Writing

In This Chapter

➤ The elements of an appealing melody

➤ Chord progressions of Top 100 songs

➤ Rhythms that drive the chords

➤ Prosody, the marriage of words and music

What is a good melody? Opinions and tastes vary, but a melody with popular appeal is usually …

➤ Singable.

➤ Easy to remember.

➤ Based on a pleasing chord pattern.

➤ A combination of creatively arranged notes on top of a captivating rhythm.

➤ A blend of intervals that mix innovation with a sense of the familiar.

Successful popular melodies can be different, but not *too* different. Neil Sedaka, composer of "Breaking Up Is Hard to Do," "Bad Blood," and "Love Will Keep Us Together," used to say that he included at least one "oy gevolt" chord in his music, a chord that was adventuresome and daring and took the listener by surprise. That chord was a dash of color that made the melody special, but the rest of the chords in his songs were comfortably familiar to the listener's ear. The same applies to rhythm. You can slip in a 5/4 or 7/4 bar rather than the more typical 2/4 or 4/4. But put in too many of them, and you have jazz, not pop music. Danceability is always a major factor in commercial songs.

What Makes a Tune Singable?

A melody consists of intervals, which are the distances between one pitch and another. The choice of appealing intervals determines whether your song makes an impression with the mass audience. A major second (C to D) leaping to an augmented octave (C to C-sharp) would be likely to alienate your public. But a major third (C to E) moving to a perfect fifth (C to G) is something listeners can greet with enthusiasm.

Record buyers automatically embrace certain chord progressions. These buyers don't intellectually know why particular chord patterns draw them in; the response is emotional.

The following chord progressions are utilized in Top 100 songs. Without attempting to analyze which songs they provide foundations for, write your own tunes over them. Do this with other progressions you hear on the air or have on sheet music. It will sharpen your commercial ear immeasurably.

➤ G Em Am Am C/D D7

➤ C C/Bb Am7 D7/F# C/G (F/G G7) C

➤ F F F/E Dm7 G7 C F F/E Dm7 G7 C

➤ Ema7 Ema7 F#m7 F#m7 C

➤ Ema7 Ema7 F#m7 F#m7 A B A B A B E

➤ Am Dm G Cma7 Fma7 Bm7-5 E7 E7

➤ C Cma7 F C Cma7 F

➤ C G (Am F) (C G) (F C/E Dm7 C)

➤ D D G A A7 A7 D

➤ Cma7 Cma7 Am7 Am7 A7 A7 D

➤ Cma7 Cma7 Am7 Am7 Dm7 Dm7 Fm7 F/G

➤ C Em7 Fma7 Fma7 Em7 Fma7 Fma7

➤ C C G G G G C C

➤ C7 F Bb C7 F

➤ Gm C7 F F Gm7 C7 F

➤ Eb F7/Eb Fm7 Bb7 Eb

➤ D D/F# G Bm Em D/F# C G

➤ G A7 D7 G

➤ Eb Fm7 Bb7 Fm7 Bb7 Eb

➤ D A7 Bm D/A Gma7

➤ C G7 C G7 C E7 Am E7

➤ C#m C#m B C#m

➤ F F Fma7 Fma7 Bb Bb C C

➤ Eb Ab Ab Gm Eb Ab Gm Ab

➤ D A/C# G A D

➤ F#m D A F#m D A

➤ Db F7 Bbm Gb Db Ab7 Db

Reliable Rhythms

Chords and intervals are two thirds of the puzzle; rhythm is the support system that gives those chords a groove and makes them pulse with excitement.

The following figures show examples of frequently used, always reliable rhythms. These rhythms should be studied, played, and internalized. When you're running through them, learn the range of moods they can convey by picking varying numbers on a metronome and getting to know how the rhythms sound in all tempos.

Hirschhorn's Hints

A rhythmic groove can be utilized in a dozen ways. If you play certain beats slowly, they convey an entirely different mood than if you play them in an upbeat manner.

Frequently used grooves.

(All © Joel Hirschhorn)

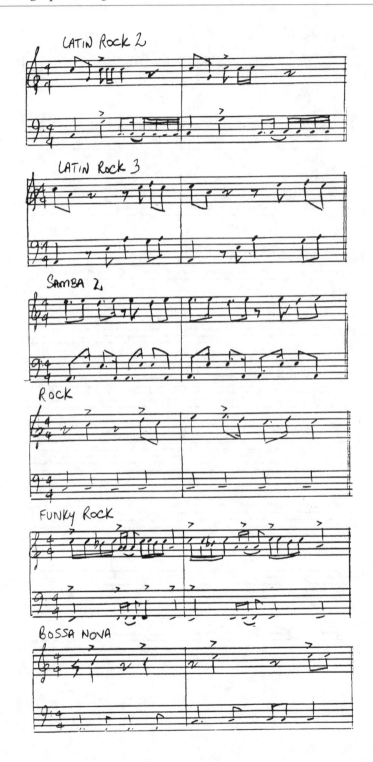

Prosody

Now you have a tune that incorporates all the vital elements. But how does it match up with the lyrics? *Prosody,* the union of words and music, is like a marriage. When a powerful emotion is being expressed, it makes no sense to drop the notes or to keep them on one repetitive level.

Lyrical Lingo

Prosody is the proper, seamless blending of words and music.

Music's basic function in a song is to dramatize the words that are being sung. When lyrics are put to a melody, the same applies in reverse: The words dramatize the melody.

Consider the song "When You Wish Upon a Star," and how effectively it uses octave leaps. The octave leap on *you* has a plaintive, yearning quality. Then again, on the word *no* in the phrase "Makes no difference," the octave leap appears again. The emotional level of the song and the lyric is powerfully heightened by these two perfectly chosen dramatic intervals. The following figure illustrates some examples of logical, effective prosody.

You Gotta Shop Around

What's the most intense thought in a line? Make sure you emphasize that emotion. Don't place your most powerful interval leaps on undramatic words. For example, "I went shopping today," doesn't scream out for melodic melodrama, unless, of course, someone robbed the store while you were at the checkout stand. Use common sense.

Hirschhorn's Hints

Think of yourself as a singer at all times. Imagine yourself on stage, facing a huge audience. Unless your words and music project excitement, you'll quickly lose the audience's attention. Sing each line individually when you've completed a draft. Do it several times. Each line is crucial to the overall impact.

There are no hard-and-fast rules in prosody, just your own artistic judgment. Sometimes the sadness in a heartbreaking line is dramatized best by going up, rather than down. Other times, a sense of joy can come across more vividly if the interval dips. The true test is if the prosody moves you. If you're not personally moved by what you're writing, no one else will be either.

Do a Prosody Search

Analyze all the current hits. How are the emotional effects achieved? After listening a few times, make note of the most emotional lyrics in the song. How does the melody highlight them? Do the notes go up or down? Ask yourself why the composer and lyricist made the choices they did. This exercise will help you to improve your prosody with amazing speed.

Examples of prosody.

(All © Joel Hirschhorn)

The Least You Need to Know

➤ The more interesting your chord progression, the better your chances are for a hit.

➤ Rhythm is just as vital as melody.

➤ Prosody is a key element to the overall emotion of the song. Develop a habit of analyzing prosody whenever you hear a new song.

Chapter 11

Rewriting

In This Chapter

➤ Overcoming your resistance to rewriting

➤ Becoming a better songwriter through rewriting

➤ Choosing the right rewriting environment and time

➤ Dealing with writing disappointments

Rewriting is just as much an emotional as a creative process. Songwriters recognize how important it is, but they resist it.

Sometimes the resistance is conscious. Other times, a subconscious conflict makes composers and lyricists put off rewriting as long as possible.

Every songwriter wants to feel that his or her music and words burst out perfectly formed. I'm not saying it never happens, but ordinarily a first draft is just that: assembling ideas and lines that only suggest a final, polished product. Refusal to rewrite is more than a mistake; it's a catastrophic blunder that could prevent your career from developing.

Bad Reasons to Avoid Rewriting

Songwriters use all kinds of weak reasons to resist rewriting songs that they know need it. If you find yourself thinking any of the thoughts in the following sections, recognize them as rationalizations for putting off the inevitable and think again.

The Best Things Will Be Thrown Away

The danger of throwing good stuff away during a rewrite is greatly overestimated. You're in the driver's seat. You have life-and-death control over what's kept and what gets discarded. Examine everything carefully, methodically, and slowly. If a line or a musical phrase feels comfortable, keep it. Trust your intuition. If something isn't working, you'll sense it.

Backstage Banter

Norman Gimbel, who wrote the lyrics to "Killing Me Softly with His Song," has said, "Very rarely do I get lucky and does it really explode. I usually have to work my ass off. Even after all the things I've written, I have a lot of problems to be looser ... to be freer. And yet I think it's valuable that I go through all that struggle. My songs aren't as much written as they're rewritten."

Above all, believe you can make it better. Writers, new ones in particular, throw up their hands and cry out, "I can't do any better." It's a perfectly normal fear reaction. You have to remind yourself that you can improve your song immeasurably.

The Rhyme Is Fine

Suppose the song is basically there, but a few rhymes feel like compromises. Don't tell yourself, "People won't notice them. They'll just react to the overall feeling." Even if nobody notices a specific compromise, listeners may know that you settled for a less-than-perfect rhyme. Lots of things work, but is adequate enough for you? It's worth it to find a rhyme word with more color, more cleverness. Don't say, "It's the feel that counts today. Rhythm is the main thing, and words don't matter." Everything matters.

Let rhymes flow. As the late Harry Chapin said …

> "Don't force it. Don't submit to what Robert Frost called 'the tyranny of rhyme.' I know when I write a bad line or a bad rhyme, I've got to throw the damn thing away. I've time and time again come up with a great line and I can't find another line that rhymes with it. So you try to change it around, you do something else. You've got to work with practical realities and be tough with yourself. I edit, I struggle, I throw away, and I resurrect."

Second Verses Aren't That Important

Just because people have a strongly positive initial reaction to melody or lyric doesn't mean they won't notice if the second verse is comparatively boring. Discounting the value of a second verse means that the lyricist doesn't know how to develop the story of the song. Melodically, the second verse usually repeats what the first verse does, so it's less of a concern for the tune writer.

The Bridge Is No Big Deal

When it comes to the bridge, resistance and rationalization take over powerfully. Those who want to avoid rewriting bridges often say, "Lots of songs don't even have bridges today, so it's not a big deal." That attitude is fine if you want to eliminate the bridge altogether. But if you plan to write one, it's just as important as any other part of the song.

I'm a big believer in bridges because they add a different color. You can launch into an entirely new rhythm and a fresh chord progression. Sometimes you can just talk the bridge rather than utilizing music at all. Even if you think you might not use a bridge, write one and then make up your mind about whether you want to keep it.

It's Just a Little Like Britney

It's one thing to use a common chord progression. You can hardly avoid it. But if three or four measures of your tune are exactly or almost exactly like the latest Britney Spears single (or another hit), change them! In this case, reluctance to rewrite can get you into big trouble. You don't want to find yourself in court like George Harrison, forking over a fortune because you duplicated someone else's work. (Harrison's "My Sweet Lord" ended up being the same tune as the 1963 hit "He's So Fine" by The Chiffons, written by Ronnie Mack.) Sometimes these things are unfortunate accidents, but if you're aware of the similarity, it would be madness to take a chance that "no one will find out."

Hirschhorn's Hints

If you write both words and music, and your first priority is words at the expense of movement, listen to records and concentrate only on the bass and drum parts. One of my earliest publishers said it best: "Lyrics will get a publisher interested, but only a great track and feel will make it a hit."

But the Rhythm Fits the Words!

Rhythm is the key to today's music, but it has to be the right rhythm. Is your melody written so that the backbeat (emphasizing beats 2 and 4 of the bar) is emphasized? Without that emphasis, the tune won't be danceable.

Is your lyric wordy? Too many words hold down the rhythm. When I started, I was too verbose and too concerned with an excess of poetic imagery, and publishers would tell me, "It's nice, but it doesn't swing!" You can sacrifice words to preserve the rhythm, but you can't sacrifice rhythm to preserve the words. Keep the lyrics simple and uncluttered; if they're not, you'd be wise to rewrite them.

When you're playing the song, do you find your body moving automatically? If you're playing it on piano or guitar, you won't be able to keep still if the beat is right.

I'll Fix It in the Studio

The problem with rewriting in the studio is that you don't have enough time, and the financial and emotional pressure is on. Yes, great ideas do sometimes spring up during the recording process. But is it worth taking a chance on this possibility when you can work out the kinks at your leisure?

Saying you'll fix it in the studio is just another way of avoiding what seems like an arduous and boring task. It's like an actor saying, "If the audience doesn't respond properly, I'll make up new lines," because he or she doesn't want to learn the scripted dialogue.

My First Draft Is Always the Best

Some songwriters say their best work is "spontaneous." Spontaneity is fine at the beginning, and a few first-draft melodies (though rarely lyrics) wind up being the final product. But this occurrence is so rare that it's not worth considering. There's always a chord that can be improved or a lyric line that can be phrased better.

Backstage Banter

Richard Sherman, co-composer with his brother Robert of *Mary Poppins* and two-time Oscar winner, says, "The key to our success is that we both have to feel 100 percent about every word, every note, every concept, before we show it to a third party."

I Just Want It Done

"I want it finished now," say many songwriters, as though speed were synonymous with artistic achievement. Unless you've been given a difficult deadline, there's no reason to rush. Everyone likes immediate satisfaction, but how about total satisfaction? No one is pointing a gun to your head. When you have the luxury of extra time, take advantage of it. Strive for perfection.

The Title Is Strong Enough

Suppose the song works and you're satisfied with the title. Yet that little voice is buzzing in your mind: "It's too ordinary ... It's good, but it's not a grabber ... I think people will like it ...." If those inner thoughts keep returning, I can assure you that you'll never be satisfied with that title. Weeks, months, or even years later, you'll say, "Why didn't I change it?"

Backstage Banter

While you're writing and rewriting, something mystical can happen. Barry Gibb of the Bee Gees says, "We can't think of something, and it just comes. We just leave it to the open spaces ... we play along and when it's time to do that line, it's not just a good line, it's an amazing line, and Robin and I look at each other and say, 'Where did that come from?' And we'll sit there looking at each other numbly, especially when we find out that that line connects all the lines before it, which wasn't planned."

Do you write down titles when they occur to you? Do you keep a title list? If you don't, you should. Even if you look over the list and nothing seems right, it will spark dozens of other title ideas. Rewriting titles may seem like a threatening process, especially when the song is completed. You can't help worrying, "What if a title change forces other changes? What if it changes the whole meaning of the song, and leads to massive rewrites from top to bottom?" These changes mean only that the song was not quite finished; those changes are needed.

The Ending Is Okay

When composers and lyricists don't want to rewrite, they frequently rationalize that the ending works perfectly. Even if it's not quite as exciting as it should be, even if it doesn't put a powerful button on the production, they resist tinkering with it. Here are just some of the rationalizations about endings:

➤ When the singer hits a big note at the end, it'll be exciting.

➤ A dynamite drum fill will give it the impact it needs.

➤ All that's needed are background singers in that section.

Nothing is more important than the right ending. The beauty of the song construction doesn't matter if the proper payoff is missing.

Backstage Banter

"I battle over songs and work," says Burt Bacharach. "It takes me a long time. I don't write easily now, and I didn't write easily at the beginning. I like to write and then look at it the next day, then a week later, and see if I can come up with something better than I've already got. Often I'll wind up back where I was."

It's Not Worth Bothering About

Suppose you show the song to a producer and he's not enthusiastic. Do you automatically toss the song into the wastebasket? No! If you believe in it, if you think it has something of value, re-examine and rewrite. Granted, rewriting something when you don't get a positive response is hard. The temptation is to start something new. This is like throwing out the baby with the bathwater. If you, as a writer, felt the song had something special, you might be more on the mark than the person you played it for.

A star may turn to you and say, "I don't feel this; it's not me." This comment doesn't mean that there's anything wrong with your work. Stars have an image they want to project. They sing certain notes more effectively than others. You may have written some notes that are out of their range, that would force them into uncomfortable registers that don't do their singing justice.

Remember, people judge subjectively. They have their own needs and their own prejudices. You may be showing the song for Mariah Carey when it would be perfect for Christina Aguilera.

I remember showing a song to a Disney executive, and he said, "I can't stand when a writer uses so many major sevenths." Fine, but someone else may love major sevenths. I had two options: Rewrite it and substitute some other chords for the major sevenths, or show it the way it was to someone else. I did rewrite it, but not by deleting the major seventh chords; I created an entirely new bridge and ending. The rewritten song was recorded by Maureen McGovern and put into a television show.

Trouble Clef

Don't be seduced by praise into feeling you've written a masterpiece. Don't rationalize by saying, "What do I know? I'm too close to it. If they think it's wonderful, it must be." The final voice, the only significant voice, is your own.

You're a Genius

Who doesn't love the sound of "Bravo!" when he or she completes an artistic work? But don't let compliments convince you that rewriting is unnecessary. As a songwriter, your objectivity has to be ruthless. It's not enough that your mom thinks the song deserves an Oscar or that your girlfriend feels Garth Brooks is an amateur by comparison to you. Do you love the song you've written? Do you feel that it's in such perfect shape that no rewriting is required?

You *Do It!*

You may not want to rewrite, but your partner does. Don't throw up your hands and say, "Go ahead, then." If your partner doesn't feel you've nailed it completely, he or she is probably right. Even if you think your partner is nitpicking, that no rewriting is required, go along. Respect the person's desire to improve the song, unless you feel that his or her perfectionism is too extreme. In some cases, you can rewrite until you've completely altered the product and removed the qualities that made it special in the first place. Unless the song is one of these rare cases, though, don't fight your partner. A resistance to rewriting could backfire when the song is rejected or when people pick up on the weaknesses in the record that you were too lazy to correct. At that point, your partner is likely to resent you for not rewriting. He or she may say so straight out or smolder inside; either way, unnecessary tension is created.

Starting the Process

If you have a partner, you may prefer to begin the rewriting process alone, and then show him or her what you've come up with. Or your partner might want to come up with changes and then show them to you. Find a rewriting approach that suits you both best. It doesn't matter how you accomplish it; it only matters that it gets done.

Hirschhorn's Hints

When is the rewriting process done? When the work is right. As Jerry Bock, composer of *Fiddler on the Roof*, put it, "[The song] 'Tradition' accumulated a bit here, a bit there. We must have written 20 versions of it, and we worked with Jerome Robbins. We didn't know how the hell to open the show, so we tried things. Some worked; some didn't. We'd have to draw it out."

When you complete a song, you always have special affection for particular notes or lyrics. So you say to yourself, "I'll work around these. I'll correct other places and try to match them up with the lines I like best." That's not total rewriting because it restricts creative freedom. If new ideas necessitate discarding old ones, don't be afraid to throw out the old stuff.

A big mistake is to come up with a sensational line and say, "I can't use it, because it will mean tossing something else out." If the old line or tune has to go, send it on its way without regret.

Take It from the Top

The best way to approach rewriting (especially if you're fighting it) is to think of your composition as a brand-new song. Look at it as though you've never seen it before.

It's His Song, Not Mine

Another method for maintaining emotional objectivity is to pretend someone else wrote the song. Tell yourself you're rewriting the material for a friend. That way, you won't have such a violent need to defend it or to personalize the process so much that you lose your grasp of the overall picture.

Tell Yourself It's Fun

Part of the reason songwriters dread rewriting is the fear that they won't be able to solve the problems, no matter how hard they try. Comedic as it sounds, just tell yourself over and over again that the rewriting process is fun. View it as an enjoyable challenge rather than a grim, deadly strain. Visualize the rewards that will come to you as the song gets into tighter shape. Visualize higher royalties with each chord and Grammies with each lyric change.

Create Your Own Time Patterns

If you're like many composers and lyricists who fight the rewriting process, it's best to work on rewrites when your mind is clear. If working at night is a trial for you, don't start your corrections at 10 or 11 P.M. Doing so will only add to your reluctance. You can often work through less-than-ideal hours when you're hatching your first draft, but when you rewrite, pick times you know you're absolutely at your best.

When you sit down to rewrite, you don't have to keep going until all the changes have been made. Stop if you want to. Have a soda. Walk around the block. Call a friend. Or maybe even put your music away and start fresh the next morning. You can direct your mind, but you can't exert tyrannical control over it. When you feel your rewrites aren't top-notch, that's the time to quit for a while. Sometimes, even with all the motivation and dedication in the world, the well runs dry. At other times, creative ideas pour out in a monumental flow, and you can't get them down fast enough.

Choose the Right Environment

An office can become claustrophobic. Your room at home might seem too routine and familiar to inspire creativity. Worse, some environments dampen initiative. If you're anywhere near a television set, you might use that as an excuse to slack off and watch *Survivor* or *Ally McBeal*.

When the environment interferes with your work, change it quickly. My first recorded song was written on a park bench. You can sit in the car with a notebook and finish a lyric. I know writers who operate best while having coffee in a restaurant. A writer friend of mine has done some of his most successful work on a rooftop.

Rewriting, in particular, demands a new way of seeing, a different point of view from what you've already composed. New backgrounds and new sights encourage that fresh perspective.

Trouble Clef

The only danger of rewriting is that you might use it as an excuse to avoid showing your work altogether. At a certain point, you just have to jump into the deep end of the pool and let the world evaluate what you've done. Don't be like a composer friend of mine who's been rewriting a song for three years and feels it's "almost done"!

Staying with It

Jerry Bock once said, "Songs aren't written. They're rewritten." The initial burst of inspiration is an emotional state; rewriting is the objective phase. Don't personalize rejection if you can help it, and don't get discouraged. You never want a publisher to say, "This sounds like a first draft."

The Record Lost Its Bullet

You've written a song, a major artist has recorded it, and it gets on the charts. It starts at number 100, and moves to 89—83—81—and then off! You can't believe it. In your despair and disappointment, you may want to throw the song into the trash. Don't. It was recorded and made the *Billboard* charts, so it has something special.

Let a little time go by and look at the song again. Maybe the reason it didn't reach the Top 20 is because of a weak line or lyric or a bridge that went on too long or not long enough. Rewrite the song again and try to get it recorded by someone else. Whatever attracted the first artist to it will inevitably attract another one.

If you've rewritten a lyric and left the melody alone, you can bring a singer back (or get a new one) and do another pass at the vocals. If the tune has been changed, however, you'll have to do another recording altogether. The thought of that may make you groan (for artistic or financial reasons), but it will be worth it if the song is vastly improved.

This Is Show Business

Writers are sensitive, and they frequently see critical response in a personal light. Such thoughts flood in as, "He has something against me," "She doesn't like young writers," "He doesn't like old writers," "She's old-fashioned and doesn't like the fact that I'm experimental," and on and on.

Hirschhorn's Hints

Rewriting isn't always a pen-and-paper process. Suppose you do a recording of the song, and it doesn't capture the feeling you had in mind. If the song is strong enough, it's worth recording it again. Maybe it's a question of overdubbing a few lines or adding a background part. Possibly the singer is wrong, even if the track is great. Studio stitching and pasting can bring the recording up to par in most cases.

The music business is a business. Or, as hit producer Peter Guber puts it, "This is not show friend." Most of the time, those evaluating your work are not judging you as a person. They just want to know if you're showing them something that will earn them money. If they suggest a rewrite, it's not because of the color of your shirt or where you went to school. They want a commercial product. The fact that they're asking you to rewrite at all is a positive sign. It means they think your work has possibilities. If they didn't like it, they would quickly dismiss you.

Backstage Banter

If you take Lamont Dozier's advice, you'll never look upon rewriting as a chore again: "Writing songs is a 24-hour-a-day job. You dream in it, you eat it, you sleep in it. It's my relaxation, my fun, my everything."

—Paul Zollo, *Songwriters On Songwriting*, DaCapo Press, 1998

Try a Different Instrument

If your rewriting isn't flowing as well as you'd like, you can trick your creative mind into submission. Suppose you play both piano and guitar. If you're trying to work the song out on the piano, try guitar instead. If neither feels comfortable, sing without any accompaniment.

Another way to stimulate creative rewriting is to turn on the radio or a favorite CD. Soak in the music without trying to relate it to what you're writing. Richard Rodgers was famous for listening to classical music for at least an hour before starting to compose.

Let the Song Breathe

When you're rewriting, you want the song to be as tight and professional as possible. But you don't want to rewrite endlessly until the song starts to sound slick and bloodless. If you see the chords becoming too complex and lush, the lyrics too self-consciously clever, catch yourself. Above all, no matter how much rewriting you do, you want to retain that sense of honesty and naturalness.

Going in Reverse

When you rewrite, there are times when you realize your early stuff was better than the corrections that came afterward. Be grateful when this occurs; it doesn't happen often. All it means is that you examined every alternative, analyzed it, tested new tunes and lyrics, and discovered that you'd hit the bull's-eye right at the start. You won't be any worse off for carrying the whole process through. Rewriting is a wonderful creative practice and a fine way to flex your musical muscles.

The Least You Need to Know

➤ Don't rationalize your way out of rewriting a song that needs it.

➤ Overcome your resistance to rewriting by remembering that it can make you a better songwriter.

➤ Take a positive approach and choose the most supportive environment and time periods for rewriting.

➤ Don't let disappointing results keep you from finding creative solutions.

➤ Look upon rewriting as a pleasure, not a chore.

Part 3

Genre Gold

All good songs follow certain rules, but each genre has its own individual characteristics. This part shows you what elements go into an outstanding country, R&B, and rap song, as well as tunes and lyrics for commercials, children's songs, movies, and theater musicals. You'll also learn how to write the kind of film song that works within the movie and functions as a hit outside the picture.

Chapter 12

Crossing Into Country

In This Chapter

➤ Country goes pop

➤ Realism reigns

➤ Country's chord patterns stay simple

➤ A country collection that holds everything from honky-tonk to rock

Country music, in its efforts to compete with rock for multiplatinum sales, has gone partially, and in some cases completely, pop. Garth Brooks initiated the process with his phenomenally successful songs, and records such as Faith Hill's "Breathe" are so completely pop that they're causing country purists to cry foul. Objections still linger about overuse of lush strings and synthesizers.

Pop hit-makers such as Diane Warren now concentrate on country songs as much as they do on rock music. Warren's acceptance by Nashville clearly announces that writers from Los Angeles, New York, or anywhere else can make their mark on the country charts. Her "How Do I Live?" became a simultaneous smash for Trisha Yearwood and LeAnn Rimes, and she has followed up with Mark Chesnutt's "I Don't Wanna Miss a Thing."

Nashville News

Nashville is no longer the somewhat insular city it used to be. At one time, the capital of Tennessee was a tight little society of its own, not given to embracing writers from out of town unless they made their Nashville moves permanent. Now the doors to non-Nashville composers are wide open.

Backstage Banter

Tony Brown, producer of Reba McEntire, Lyle Lovett, and Vince Gill, doesn't feel as though Nashville will change greatly as a result of the influx of New York and Los Angeles writers. Brown says, "We'll change them!"

Lyrical Lingo

The **Grand Ole Opry,** which started in 1926, is the longest-running radio broadcast in history. An invitation to play the Opry certifies country performers or performer/writers as superstars. Great names associated with it include Minnie Pearl, Roy Acuff, and Bill Monroe.

Barbara Mandrell once sang, "I was country when country wasn't cool." Today, country is cooler than ever, from both an artistic and a financial point of view. If country music calls to you, keep in mind that opportunities to write songs and have them recorded have never been greater.

A Little Background

Scottish, Irish, and English settlers brought their folk music to the South in the eighteenth and nineteenth centuries, and these folk songs became the basis for country music. The first country recordings were released in the 1920s. Radio stations recognized the genre's appeal and brought it to a wide audience, courtesy of such artists as Jimmie Rodgers and the Carter Family.

A pack of independent labels opened up in late 1940s Nashville: Nashboro, Republic, Excello, Dot, Bullet, and Tennessee. As recording activity proliferated and the *Grand Ole Opry* achieved fame, booking agencies and music publishers made the city their base of operations. The area on the southwest side of town that spawned this accelerating country world got the name Music Row.

Country sales were modest at first, and they sharply diminished with the advent of rock and roll. Three producers, Columbia's Don Law, Decca's Owen Bradley, and RCA's Chet Atkins, decountrified much of the music by subtracting steel guitars and fiddles. Vocal choruses, rhythm sections, and eventually strings took the twangy edge off the sound, broadening country's national appeal.

Traditional country stylings featuring honky-tonk and mountain music still exist, but the pop influence, spearheaded by Garth Brooks, is unlikely to disappear. Nashville records always stayed firmly rooted on the country charts in the past. Now dozens of them are represented on *Billboard*'s Top 100.

Hirschhorn's Hints

Garth Brooks was the first country artist to sell a million copies. He brought country to a mass audience. Brooks's album, *Ropin' the Wind,* made its debut at the top of the pop charts. But at the beginning of his career, every label in Nashville refused to sign him. He had to make a living singing recordings of songs by other writers until Capitol Records recognized his potential. The message in his story is: Don't give up. If you have something special, it will eventually be recognized.

The Currents of Country

To write country, you should be as familiar with Merle Haggard, Johnny Cash, and the Gatlin Brothers as you are with John Michael Montgomery, Jo Dee Messina, Tim McGraw, and Vince Gill. You should also have a basic understanding of the many ideas and emotions that make country what it is:

➤ **Honesty.** Whether pop-flavored or flat-out country, honesty is the key ingredient to Top 10 country music. This music is for the man on the street, without pretension and slickness. Country artists have no interest in lyrics and music that sound forced or fake.

➤ **Raw reality.** Country classics often reflect struggle. "Guitar Man," by Jerry Reed, follows the efforts of a guitarist to find success and the bitter rejections he receives. He sleeps in hobo jungles and bums a thousand miles of track. In another part of the lyric, Reed talks about nearly starving to death in Memphis, having run out of money and luck.

➤ **Down-to-earth drama.** Country is no place for fantasies. Tim McGraw contemplates the question of aging with his memorable "The Next 30 Years," and in "Middle-Age Crazy," the protagonist is 40 going on 20, with a "young thing beside him that just melts in his hands." The man in Bob McDill's "I May Be Used but I Ain't Used Up" strikes a positive note for older folks who still want to feel the pleasures of youth.

There's no self-delusion in country breakup songs, either. "Two Story House" tells of a couple who achieved fame and fortune, but despite the surface splendor, "there's no love about." Love is no simple matter in "When She Cries," because the protagonist has tried and failed to fulfill the dreams of his loved one, and sometimes in the night, he hears her crying. He wants to be the man that she deserves, and he dies a little each time she cries.

127

➤ **Honky-tonk heartache.** Stories of honky-tonk nightlife are *Grand Ole Opry* staples. In "Honky-Tonk Attitude," we hear about "tight pants, line dance, Stetson hats and cowboy boots" and the Friday nights when a man goes out with a honky-tonk attitude. Hank Williams's "Honky-Tonk Blues" tells of a man who went to a dance, wore out his shoes, and then woke up in the morning wishing he could lose the honky-tonk blues. As he concludes, "Lord, I'm sufferin' with the honky-tonk blues."

➤ **Turning to the Lord.** Spirituality is a current that runs strongly through country songs. Kris Kristofferson's "Why Me? (Why Me, Lord?)" takes an unusual slant on prayer; the protagonist is grateful for everything God has given him and now wants spiritual help and a chance to prove he deserves all his blessings. Another creative way to deal with spiritual strength is demonstrated by Merle Haggard in "From Graceland to the Promised Land," a touching story about Elvis Presley in which Haggard sings about Elvis going from Memphis to a mansion in the sky, keeping his faith in Jesus all along.

➤ **Feelings that touch everyone.** Many of us have loved someone only to have them call us by the wrong name. "I'm Not Lisa" touches that chord in all people who can't quite replace the person their lovers cared about before. Garth Brooks reminds us about our capacity for revenge when he sings, "Friends in Low Places," in which a rejected suitor shows up at his former girl's wedding and proceeds to wreak havoc.

➤ **Street poetry.** Visual imagery is a characteristic that makes country lyrics shine. A good example is "Rednecks, White Sox, Blue Ribbon Beer." "Country State of Mind" is a definitive example: The protagonist is chewin' on a hickory twig, asking someone to pass a bottle so he can have a swig. He ain't got a lot, but he's got it made in the shade, because he's in a "country state of mind."

The majority of country songs are miniature motion pictures. You, as a country writer, must draw every detail of the scene for the listeners so that they can see cracked paint on the walls, hear the railroad whistle, taste the food, and touch the people.

➤ **Dramatic overstatement.** Country lyrics don't hold back. When you're writing them, be as vividly emotional as the following:

> I was lying in the dark
> Screaming to the wall
> Praying I'd hear her footsteps in the hall
> Dying for her touch
> Aching for her smile
> Desperately I grabbed the phone and I began
> to dial

➤ **Exquisite simplicity.** The greatest education country can give you, as a writer, is to force you into writing specifically. It can also teach you how to edit out overblown phrases and shave your sentences down to exquisite simplicity. "Going Going Gone," "God Bless the USA," and "Got No Reason Now for Goin' Home" are perfect examples of this kind of simplicity.

➤ **Spoken dialogue.** When the words sound as though they just sprang into the protagonist's mind, you've reached the pinnacle of country composing. With urgency and immediacy, people in country songs confess, confide, share intimate feelings, and open up their souls to close friends or loved ones.

➤ **Get loose and playful.** The lyrics in country music have a looseness and freedom about them. Alan Jackson's hit "Right on the Money" uses free-flowing imagery with "She's a three-point jump shot" and "She's the best cook that ever melted cheese." Tracy Byrd's "I'm from the Country" is verbally playful when he talks about sleeping in the hay because he's from the country and he likes it that way.

Many country titles have the same far-out playfulness. Consider "I'm Gonna Hire a Wino to Decorate My Home," in which the protagonist tells her alcoholic husband that she's made this decision so he'll be comfortable and won't feel the need to roam. Another product of an inventive imagination is "God Must Be a Cowboy." These off-center, tongue-in-cheek approaches are typical of much country music. A country writer doesn't say, "She's leaving me for him," when he can just as easily say, "That ain't my truck in her drive."

Hirschhorn's Hints

You can't connect with country publishers or the public unless you dig deep down into yourself and the sources of your own pleasure and pain. Bob McDill, writer of 28 number-one country hits, says that country songs are more about loss and hurt than music, beat, or groove.

Trouble Clef

Just because country is frank, don't go overboard. A conservative, puritanical streak still runs through the country world. When Garth Brooks wrote "kiss my ass" as part of a last verse for "Friends in Low Places," the phrase was cut. "I'll Try," by Alan Jackson, originally said, "We both know damn well." The line eventually became "We both know too well."

➤ **Turning clichés inside out.** A characteristic of country lyric writing is taking common expressions and bending them in a clever way. Dean Dillon's "Nobody in His Right Mind Would've Left Her" is a perfect example with its "right" and "left" references. Another good example is "If I Said You Had a Beautiful Body Would You Hold It Against Me?"

➤ **Say it straight out.** Country songs have an appealing, down-home directness. When you're coming up with ideas and titles and you want to break beyond conventional thinking, remember these classics: "Please, Daddy, Don't Get Drunk This Christmas," "Ruby, Don't Take Your Love to Town," and "You Make Me Want to Be a Mother."

Musical Elements of Country

Country music is a combination of different genres. You should be familiar with the ones in this list:

➤ **Honky-tonk.** This music is what most people think of when country music is mentioned; it uses steel guitars, fiddles, acoustic guitars, and vocals. Stars that kicked off the movement were Ernest Tubb, Al Dexter, and Hank Williams. George Jones and Lefty Frizzell were also highly admired practitioners of honky-tonk.

Backstage Banter

Honky-tonk king Jerry Lee Lewis was enraged that Elvis Presley was treated as "The King" while he was treated as white trash. He regarded himself as a nice guy, and told the press that he couldn't understand why people hated him.

➤ **Country gospel.** This genre describes the sound of traditional country wed to spiritual lyrics.

➤ **Bluegrass.** The roots of modern country grew out of bluegrass, a style of music that blended fiddle, mandolin, and banjo with string bass and guitar accompaniment. Bill Monroe kept this traditional string music alive and flourishing. His band, The Blue Grass Boys, was responsible for the term "bluegrass." Earl Scruggs, Ricky Skaggs, and the Osborne Brothers are other bluegrass performers.

➤ **Hillbilly.** This term was the first definition used for country music derived from Tennessee, Kentucky, Virginia, West Virginia, and Southeastern Ohio. "Fiddlin'" John Carson, Henry Whitter, and Vernon Dahlert recorded hillbilly songs.

➤ **Western swing.** This music is a combination of string band music, blues, folk, jazz, and traditional pop melodies. Lyrics concentrated on the lives of cowboys and reached a zenith with Gene Autry and Roy Rogers. This genre attained a new popularity in the 1990s.

➤ **Rockabilly.** This music is rock-and-roll in its earliest form. A combination of rhythm and blues and hillbilly songs, Jerry Lee Lewis, Carl Perkins, Buddy Holly, and the Everly Brothers made it popular.

➤ **Country rock.** Country played by rock bands, with pop melodies, a strong back-beat, and powerful amplification typifies this genre. Neil Young, Gram Parsons, and the Byrds increased this genre's popularity.

➤ **Traditional country.** This country music has a distinctive twang and uncompli-cated instrumentation. Ernest Tubb, Eddy Arnold, Hank Williams, and Roy Acuff played it and helped launch the *Grand Ole Opry,* the weekly radio program that came to represent country music to the world.

➤ **Country pop.** Here's a genre that consists of country-flavored rock-and-roll songs such as "I Don't Wanna Miss a Thing" sung by Mark Chestnutt and "How Do I Live?" by Trisha Yearwood. The advent of rock and roll and its wildfire suc-cess encouraged country to absorb more pop influences. This pop Nashville sound smoothed out the rough edges of the earlier country records, and by the 1970s, country recordings were more accessible to a wide noncountry audience.

➤ **Outlaw country.** David Allan Coe, Merle Haggard, and Johnny Cash were representa-tives of this genre, which emphasized smaller bands and acoustic instruments.

➤ **R&B, gospel, and folk.** These music genres are mixed into the country brew for color.

➤ **Old-time country.** This style was heard in the nineteenth century and first recorded in the 1920s. Originally British folk songs played on the fiddle, the same folk songs were later played on banjos, Spanish guitars, bass, *dobro,* and washboard.

Lyrical Lingo

The **dobro** is a guitar with am-plification made of steel or wood. Musicians also know it as the Hawaiian guitar.

Chord Patterns of Country

Country is simple, although not as simple as it used to be. But behind the new, often lushly orchestrated country pop hits is a fundamental simplicity that can't be sacri-ficed. The songs build excitement, but they don't veer into strange, wild syncopa-tions.

A look at current country hits confirms their chordal simplicity: Tracy Byrd's "I'm from the Country" begins with D D G G D D A A D D. The melody is buoyant and infectious. "Wide Open Spaces," a hit for the Dixie Chicks, has a hook based on four chords that recur four times: E F#m7 A B.

Trouble Clef

Remember, too many chords weigh down a tune. Once you find a pattern, stick with it as the melody develops.

Trouble Clef

A prejudice against outsiders still exists in Nashville. One studio owner commented, "If you heard a country record cut in L.A., you knew it. It never seemed authentic." Your chances of doing recordings that inspire enthusiasm in the country music industry will improve if you go to Nashville and stay there, at least part of the time.

Musical progressions that move stepwise, up or down, allow for driving rhythm. They also offer room for the musicians to improvise. An uncomplicated but memorable progression underscores Vince Gill's touching ballad, "Kindly Keep It Country": Bb Bb Bb Bb7 Eb Eb Bb Bb. Looking at those chords, you might be tempted to think that they're dull or unimaginative. But when you listen to Gill's record, you encounter a rich, moving melody.

In the past, country chords rarely included major and minor sevenths. Today, with pop so much a part of hit country cuts, these chords are more acceptable. "For You I Will," sung by Aaron Tippin, features D Bm7 F#m7 A. "They're Gone," a smash for Diamond Rio, has a prominent major seventh with Am Fma7 G Em7 F F G G.

"They're Gone" also utilizes an augmented chord, a chord much more frequently employed in show songs than country tunes. It adds beauty and flavor to the melody, even though the use of this chord in country songs is still rare.

Here are other hit country chord progressions:

"Nothing But the Taillights": D7 C G G D7 C G G C C G G

"Husbands and Wives": F F/E Dm7 F/C F F/E Dm7 F/C Gm7 C7 Gm7 C7

"Keepin' Up": E B C#m C#m E B C#m C#m A A B B

"Then What?": A E B E A E B E

Keeping the Nashville Flavor

When you're writing country songs, try to keep a sound and an arrangement concept clearly in mind. Even though country and pop overlap somewhat today, the balance still has to retain its Nashville tone. Think of those steel guitars and fiddles. Imagine a country voice doing the song. It makes all the difference, because country phrasing is altogether different from pop. Madonna and Faith Hill are both blond and beautiful, but musically they have nothing in common beyond the fact that they sing.

Another little exercise has helped me through the years. I do more than imagine artists vocally; I close my eyes and picture them physically. How do they move? What are they wearing? What environment surrounds them? Seeing a country band with your mind's eye gives you a specific slant. This picture is your own, private form of MTV or VH1, a video you run in your mind to fuel your creative ideas and keep you on the right atmospheric track.

Recommended Listening

To get an overall feel for country, you must be familiar with a wide variety of artists. This sampling of CDs will make you an all-around connoisseur of the music:

Garth Brooks (contemporary country): *No Fences* (1990, Liberty)

Brooks and Dunn (contemporary country): *Brand New Man* (1991, Arista)

Buffalo Springfield (country and folk rock): *Buffalo Springfield Again* (1967, Atco)

Johnny Cash (traditional country/rockabilly): *The Sun Years* (1990, Rhino)

Floyd Cramer (instrumental, Nashville sound): *Essential Series* (1995, RCA)

Diamond Rio (bluegrass/contemporary country): *Diamond Rio* (1991, Arista)

Dixie Chicks (contemporary country): *Shouldn't a Told You That* (1993, Crystal Clear)

The Eagles (country rock): *Hotel California* (1976, Asylum)

Merle Haggard (Western swing): *Tribute to the Best Damn Fiddle Player* (1970, Koch)

Jerry Lee Lewis (honky-tonk): *18 Original Sun Greatest Hits* (1984, Rhino)

The Oak Ridge Boys (country pop/country gospel): *Y'All Come Back Soon* (1978, MCA)

Elvis Presley (rockabilly): *The Complete Sun Sessions* (1987, RCA)

Bonnie Raitt (country blues/rock): *Nick of Time* (1989, Capitol)

Linda Ronstadt (country rock/country folk): *Heart Like a Wheel* (1974, Capitol)

Merle Travis (traditional country): *The Merle Travis Story (24 Greatest Hits)* (1989, CMH)

Ernest Tubb (honky-tonk): *Country Music Hall of Fame* (1987, MCA)

Hank Williams (traditional country): *40 Greatest Hits* (1978, Polydor)

The pop world has become such a slave to technological advances that sounds and theatrics take precedence over many of the songs. Fortunately, country music has never succumbed to this trend. The attitude in Nashville is "song first." The guitars and drums may thunder more loudly than they used to, but the meaning of the lyrics and the tune predominate.

The Least You Need to Know

➤ If you write country music, avoid all pretension and slickness. Write with down-to-earth realism and deal in universal problems.

➤ Country lyrics are rhymed dialogue that blend street honesty with visual color.

➤ Country styles include honky-tonk, country gospel, bluegrass, hillbilly, Western swing, rockabilly, country rock, traditional country, and country pop.

➤ Chord progressions in country should be simple and uncluttered.

➤ Study all the country genres, from hillbilly and bluegrass to country pop.

Chapter 13

R&B and Rap

In This Chapter

➤ R&B roots

➤ Blues, gospel, and doo wop

➤ Soul, Motown, and funk

➤ Rap and hip-hop

Atlantic Records President Jerry Wexler coined the term "rhythm and blues," but the best definition of rhythm and blues is the one offered by Screamin' Jay Hawkins:

> "Rhythm and Blues is music about the pain you have suffered. It's about having a good time, feeling passion, experiencing humiliation. It's about your mother dying, your woman walking off, even a bottle of wine. Rhythm and Blues is a slave who picked cotton. It's a black man who ran from a lynch mob. It's something of pain, something of bliss, something of love, something of hate, revenge or laughter. Whatever the emotion, all great music is based on things you actually experience through living."
>
> —Gene Busnar, *The Rhythm and Blues Story,* Jules Messner, 1985

Rap/hip-hop is dance music, featuring singers who speak in rhyme to pulsating rhythms. It first caught on strongly in New York City's African American neighborhoods, developing in the early 1970s and heating up to an explosive point by the 1980s. Sex, partying, and political statements are recurrent rap themes. Rap records sample sections from other tracks, and edit pieces of different songs together as well.

Birth of the Blues

Heartache has always given life to great music, and the birth of the blues is a great example of this truth. Black people were taken by force from their tribes and brought over in chains to America. Many died; those who survived their ocean crossings were sold as slaves upon arrival. Blues began as a music of despair, of slaves crying out for liberation.

Music was the powerful bond that gave them strength to face their heavy burdens. The rhythms and chants of African music were a means for people to communicate with each other, a communication more eloquent than words. A call-and-response style evolved as one person sang lead against a chorus. Modern R&B owes its existence to these pain-soaked blues.

From a musical standpoint, blues are marked by a hammering beat and a melody built on flatted thirds, fifths, and sevenths. These slurred, flatted notes have built-in emotion, a sobbing, prayerful quality. The standard blues form is a *12-bar blues*.

Lyrical Lingo

A **12-bar blues** consists of four bars of tonic (first chord of the scale), two bars of subdominant (fourth), two bars of tonic, one bar of dominant (fifth), one of subdominant, and two of tonic. A modern example of 12-bar blues is Leiber and Stoller's "Kansas City": C (4 bars) F7 (2 bars) C (2 bars) and G7 (1 bar) F7 (1 bar) C (2 bars). The jazz of Count Basie focused on 12-bar blues.

A characteristic of all R&B music is hitting beats 2 and 4. Instrumentation generally includes a rhythm and horn section. The rhythm section has bass, piano, drums, and guitar. Trumpets and saxophones are staples of the horn section, with trombones participating every now and then. Strings became part of many R&B records in the 1960s.

Minstrel to Motown

In the 1800s, whites were attracted to black minstrel songs. These upbeat songs and upbeat tunes bore a resemblance to Anglo-American jigs and reels and utilized tambourines and fiddles. At the time of the Civil War, white minstrels gained great success in Europe and America playing these songs in a black style. White audiences reacted enthusiastically to the watered-down performances.

From the 1920s on, blues reached the masses through an ever-growing record industry. Jimmie Rodgers established his reputation as the singing brakeman from Meridian, Mississippi. The father of bluegrass, Bill Monroe, invested powerful blues feelings in his playing. Country and blues music were blended in the performances of Western swing bands.

Major labels rejected R&B, and newly formed independent companies such as Chess, Modern, Specialty, and Atlantic rushed in to fill the gap. R&B records first reached a large public in 1948 via WDIA, a radio station in Memphis.

The Johnson Influence

Singer, guitarist, and composer Robert Johnson was one of the greats of early R&B. His contemporaries of the 1920s and 1930s claimed that his vocals, guitar playing, and stomping feet had the power of an entire band. His early, primitive recordings (his first recording was in 1936) featured the tinkling piano fills, driving bass line, and powerful drum of a four-piece electric blues band. Following Johnson were Muddy Waters and blues singing great B. B. King.

Jordan's Jump

In the late 1930s, Decca Records got behind Louis Jordan and promoted his group, The Tympany Five. The Tympany Five specialized in a style that came to be called jump blues. Jordan's arrangements strongly emphasized horn riffs that repeated, and his hit songs such as "Choo Choo Ch'Boogie" found favor with black and white record buyers alike.

Crooner Nat Cole showed the world a more mellow blues form when he sang and played club blues. Club blues also reached a wide audience, as did the vocal sounds of The Ravens, The Ink Spots, and The Mills Brothers.

> **Backstage Banter**
>
> One-verse songs with a song structure of AAA (the verse repeated three times) caught on in the first quarter of the twentieth century. The AAA structure evolved into AAB structure (verse, verse, chorus), which was called the blues.

The Gospel Truth

God-fearing African Americans regarded blues as low class. The deeply religious were horrified when they heard "Honey Love" by The Drifters and "Work With Me, Annie" by The Midnights.

Gospel music took a controversial commercial turn when secular lyrics were attached to gospel melodies. In 1955, Ray Charles turned "This Little Light of Mine" into "This Little Girl of Mine." "I Got a Woman" was Ray's rewrite of "My Jesus Is All the World to Me."

Doo Wop

In the 1950s, R&B songs started centering on the lives and problems of teenagers. In "Charlie Brown," the Coasters expressed an adolescent sentiment, "Why is everybody always picking on me?"

The most popular form of R&B at this time was doo wop. The characteristics of doo wop are medium tempos and close harmonies. These songs are doo wop classics:

"Story Untold" by The Nutmegs

"Come Go with Me" by The Dell-Vikings

"Silhouettes" by The Rays

"You've Got the Magic Touch" by The Platters

"Barbara Ann" by The Regents

"Poison Ivy" by The Coasters

"Since I Don't Have You" by The Skyliners

"Stay" by Maurice Williams and the Zodiacs

"In the Still of the Night" by Five Satins

"Little Darlin'" by Diamonds

Backstage Banter

Ray Charles says, "The blues and gospel are pretty much the same. The main difference is that in the blues you're singing, 'Oh baby,' and in gospel you're singing, 'Oh, Lord.'"

Backstage Banter

Parents weren't sure that artists such as Chuck Berry provided appropriate music for their children, little dreaming that he would win a Kennedy Center Award for Lifetime Achievement in the year 2000. Berry's lyrics are found in such hits as "Roll Over Beethoven," "Maybellene," and "Lucille Were Witty and Clever." He also cut quarter notes into eighths, replacing the triplet that defined previous styles of blues.

Early R&B Hits

Listening to and studying early R&B classics, which were known as "race records," will give you a basic rhythm and blues background. All lovers of rhythm, blues, and gospel should know these Top 10 R&B hits:

"My Song" by Johnny Ace

"3 O'Clock Blues" by Ruth Brown

"Lawdy Miss Clawdy" by Lloyd Price

"Hound Dog" by Willie Mae Thornton

"Crying in the Chapel" by Orioles

"Baby Don't Do It" by 5 Royales

"The Things I Used to Do" by Guitar Slim

"Honey Love" by Clyde McPhatter and The Drifters

"Earth Angel" by Penguins

"Only You" and "The Great Pretender" by The Platters

"Long Tall Sally" by Little Richard

"Fever" by Little Willie John

"I'm in Love Again" by Fats Domino

"Rip It Up" by Frankie Lymon and the Teenagers

R&B's approach to sex and relationships was raw and direct, and these sentiments were reinforced by the blaringly sensual rhythm. Originally, the term "rock and roll" was a euphemism for sexual intercourse.

The Motown Sound

Sam Phillips of Sun Records visualized how R&B could be expanded when he said, "If I could find me a white boy with a black sound, I could make a million dollars." That boy turned out to be Elvis Presley.

Despite the fact that audiences were becoming more and more fascinated by R&B, the small independent labels that produced R&B records still felt that they were a minority enthusiasm. It took Atlantic Records and the *Motown sound* to change that thinking.

Lyrical Lingo

Rolling Stone's definition of the **Motown sound:** "While the vocalists provided emotion, the band mounted a nonstop percussive assault highlighted by a 'hot' mix, with shrill, hissing cymbals and a booming bass—anything to make the song jump out of the car radio. With tambourine rattling to a blistering 4/4 beat, the music came to epitomize what Motown called 'The Sound of Young America.'"

The Many Faces of R&B

Jump blues, club blues, and doo wop led to soul, funk, disco, and hip-hop.

The Sound of Young America

With his company Motown, Berry Gordy softened the harder blues and gospel edges of soul and made it accessible to everybody. The Holland Brothers, Eddie and Brian, and Lamont Dozier (a team later identified as HDH) turned out exactly the kind of records Gordy wanted, with such stars as Diana Ross and the Supremes, Marvin Gaye, Gladys Knight, Smokey Robinson, Martha and the Vandellas, Mary Wells, The Jackson Five, and Stevie Wonder.

These Motown classics are a must-listen for any aspiring R&B songwriter:

"Can I Get a Witness?" by Marvin Gaye

"Baby I Need Your Loving" by The Four Tops

"Come See About Me" by The Supremes

"Uptight" by Stevie Wonder

"Ain't Too Proud to Beg" by The Temptations

"What Becomes of the Brokenhearted?" by Jimmy Ruffin

"You Can't Hurry Love" by The Supremes

"Ain't No Mountain High Enough," "You're All I Need to Get By," and "Ain't Nothin' Like the Real Thing" by Marvin Gaye and Tammi Terrell

"I Heard It Through the Grapevine" by Gladys Knight

"My Girl" (The Temptations) by Smokey Robinson and the Miracles

"Twenty-Five Miles" by Edwin Starr

"ABC" by The Jackson Five

"If I Were Your Woman" by Gladys Knight

"Mercy Mercy Me (The Ecology)" by Marvin Gaye

"I Just Want to Celebrate" by Rare Earth

"Dancing in the Streets" by Martha and the Vandellas

Backstage Banter

Berry Gordy Jr. began as a prize-fighter and then became a hit songwriter, turning out Top 10 hits for Jackie Wilson such as "Reet Petit," "Lonely Teardrops," and "To Be Loved." But he had a bigger vision, a vision that led him to form Motown and become the most successful owner of a black label in record history.

Chicago Soul

Chicago soul was defined by a gentle, sensitive musician named Curtis Mayfield. Curtis and I wrote some songs in the early 1960s, and he confided his intention to write music that inspired people. He and his group, The Impressions, contributed such hits as "People Get Ready" and "Amen." The Impressions gained recognition for their memorable falsetto and for using strings on their records. As a solo artist in the 1970s, Curtis reflected the realities of inner-city life in such songs as "Freddie's Dead."

Southern Soul

Ray Charles was the king of southern soul, a style spotlighted on Stax and Atlantic Records. Isaac Hayes, Otis Redding, The Staple Singers, and Sam and Dave were major Stax artists. Here are some of the best examples of southern soul:

"Theme from Shaft" by Isaac Hayes

"Cold Feet" by Albert King

"Knock on Wood" by Eddie Floyd

"Sweet Soul Music" by Arthur Conley

"In the Midnight Hour" by Wilson Pickett

"Hold on, I'm Comin'" by Sam and Dave

"Respect Yourself" by The Staple Singers

"B-A-B-Y" by Carla Thomas

"Walking the Dog" by Rufus Thomas

"Your Good Thing (Is About to End)" by Mabel John

Funk: Forerunner of Rap

James Brown scraped away any sweetness from R&B and spearheaded the funk movement. Funk subtracted melody and played up rhythm. Chords virtually disappeared, and the rhythms became increasingly complex, knitting together a series of different instrumental parts.

Listen to these funk classics:

"Shining Star" by Earth, Wind and Fire

"Ladies' Night" by Kool and the Gang

"Flash Light" by Parliament

"I Wanna Testify" by Parliament

"Express Yourself" by Charlie Wright and the Watts 103rd Street Rhythm Band

"One Nation Under a Groove" by Funkadelic

"Funky Broadway" by Dyke and the Blazers

Disco and Dance

In the 1970s, disco went heavy on synthesizers and strings and was heartily embraced by African Americans, as well as Latino and gay audiences.

141

Listen to these disco classics:

"Staying Alive" by Bee Gees

"Dance, Dance, Dance (Yowsah, Yowsah, Yowsah)" by Chic

"Never Say Goodbye" by Gloria Gaynor

"Get Down Tonight" by K.C. and the Sunshine Band

"Love Train" by O'Jays

"Will It Go Round in Circles" by Billy Preston

"You'll Never Find Another Love Like Mine" by Lou Rawls

"Car Wash" by Rose Royce

"We Are Family" by Sister Sledge

"Hot Stuff" by Donna Summer

"Boogie Oogie Oogie" by Taste of Honey

"I'm Gonna Love Ya Just a Little More Baby" by Barry White

"Play That Funky Music" by Wild Cherry

Disco put dance in the limelight, but dance has always been a crucial element of R&B and rock. Who can forget kids on Dick Clark's American Bandstand saying, "But can you dance to it?" Now, videos have made danceability a must for most records; and Michael Jackson's MTV classics, "Beat It" and "Billie Jean," underscored this musical fact of life.

Rap and Hip-Hop

Like R&B, rap has taken the world by storm because it clearly conveys what African Americans are thinking and feeling. Rap was launched in the South Bronx, a dangerous neighborhood. Disc jockey DJ Kool Herc introduced the basic sound. As rock journalist Alan Light says ...

> "He would set up two or more turntables and mix only the hottest sections of several records together, switching back and forth between isolated, hyper-propulsive beats. The earliest *rapping* consisted of simple chants and call-and-response rhymes over the deejay's cutting and scratching, and it became one part of an emerging cultural phenomenon called 'hip-hop.'"
>
> —Anthony DeCurtis, James Henke, and Holly George-Warren, *The Rolling Stone Illustrated Story of Rock and Roll,* Random House, 1992

Bobby Robinson put it out on the grapevine that he was looking for the best rap acts. Right away he was contacted by the Funky Four out of the Bronx, what he calls "a dynamite little group," and became an instant rap hit.

Kids watched television, lusted after the better things in life shown on the screen, and used rap as a vehicle to make their emotions known. Synthesizers and drum machines made it easier and less expensive to do a rap record. No live musicians were necessary.

Hip-Hop to the Top

Hip-hop can be defined as a progression of events including deejaying, emceeing, break dancing, and graffiti that started in the early 1980s. Early exponents of the hip-hop form are Afrika Bambaataa and Grandmaster Flash, and the music's evolution, in the words of the *Chicago Tribune*'s Michael Kilian, "produced the remarkable rhyme schemes of Rakim and Slick Rick, the feminist flavor of Salt N' Pepa (endorsed by no less an intellectual than Pauline Kael), MC Lyte, Monie Love, and Queen Latifah; the agitprop poetry of Public Enemy and the gangsta sounding track of N.W.A."

Backstage Banter

Donna Summer is known as the female centerpiece of disco. A brilliantly gifted singer, she turned out hit after hit, including "Bad Girls," "MacArthur Park," and "On the Radio." Today, she's receiving equal acclaim as an artist.

Going to Extremes

Mos Def, age 26, a Brooklyn, New York rapper, told *Newsweek:* "Sex, violence, the underbelly, with junkies, prostitutes, alcoholics, gamblers … the new trend is depravity." Eminem's "Kim" tells a story in which he cuts his wife's throat and locks her in the trunk of a car. From the viewpoint of many, the form is going overboard.

Fortunately, rappers concur with this assessment, and there may well be some toning down to appease cries of outrage. But rap will survive because it reflects the longings and feelings of a culture, emotions that millions from different worlds also share. It is, as Public Enemy proclaims, "black America's CNN."

Lyrical Lingo

Legendary record executive Russ Regan defines **rapping** this way: "Rap depends on thinking at top speed. Most of all you need a breakneck, high-powered style. You also have to know when to forge ahead and when to keep cool."

Regan on Rap

Russ Regan did more than turn Elton John, Neil Diamond, Barry White, The Beach Boys, Olivia Newton-John, Alan Parsons Project, Irene Cara, and the DeFranco Family into stars. He operated a rap label (Quality Pecords) and became a devotee and expert on the form.

Lyrical Lingo

A **sample** is the reuse (in all or in part) of an already successful track to serve as the foundation for a rap vocal.

What Regan says about rap …

➤ "Beats. Great beats. Beats are the key to rap. That's why *samples* are so important."

➤ Then the message—whether it's a message about love, about violence, if it's real, it works.

There's a difference between rapping and rhyming. Rhyming guys don't make it. If you try to do rhymes, trying to be poets, it's phony rhyming. Rap is a real art. It's not something you can just do in a false way. I equate it to a lounge act and a recording act: a lounge act comes off plastic; a recording artist goes into the studio and comes off from the heart."

➤ "Delivery—how the rapper delivers his rap. I think Dr. Dre is incredible; Eminem is fabulous. Eminem is raw and real. I loved Tupac Shakur when he was alive. Snoop Dog, also brilliant. LL Cool J is excellent."

➤ "I think rap caught on because the urban community was ready for a new art form. Most of the great musical trends have started in the urban communities. The African Americans start the trends and are very creative. Now, 60 to 70 percent of the rap music buyers are white. The same thing happened when Motown hit in the 1960s. A lot of rap talks about a way of life, what they see every day."

Rapturous Albums

Here's a list of some of the best rap albums you can listen to:

Age Ain't Nothin' But a Number by Aaliyah

Mary by Mary J. Blige

Forever by Bobby Brown

Born Into the 90s by R. Kelly and Public Announcement

Finally by Blackstreet

Greatest Hits by Toni! Toni! Toni!

In His Own Words by Tupac Shakur

My Soul by Coolio

Here Come the Horns by Delinquent Habits

Life in 1472 by Jermaine Dupri

My Homies/Me and My Homies by Scarface

Recognize the Mob by 5th Ward Boys

Mutations by Beck

Significant Other by Limp Bizkit

Evil Empire by Rage Against the Machine

Order in the Court by Queen Latifah

360 Degrees of Power by Sister Souljah

Code Red by DJ Jazzy Jeff and the Fresh Prince

Big Willie Style by Will Smith

Hard to Swallow by Vanilla Ice

Rhythm and Rap

If you write R&B or rap, just keep in mind that these genres are the musical result of passion. The reason Fontella Bass's "Rescue Me" is played over and over again in motion pictures is because of its urgent emotional cry. "I Will Survive" is the ultimate survivor's stance, an announcement by Gloria Gaynor that she won't be destroyed.

The Least You Need to Know

➤ A 2/4 backbeat is the basis to rock; flatted thirds, fifths, and sevenths spell blues.

➤ R&B and rap are dance phenomena.

➤ Gospel tunes became hits when "Lord" was changed to "baby."

➤ Rappers think of their music as black America's CNN.

➤ R&B and rap is music of passion.

Chapter 14

Commercials and Children's Music

In This Chapter

➤ A songwriter's role in an ad campaign

➤ The importance of understanding the consumer's psychic needs

➤ How to write a successful jingle

➤ Children's music that adults will also enjoy

"Buy me! Buy me!" This cry, packaged in new jingles or classic hit songs, floods daily into millions of living rooms. Many of these pleas are ignored. But if the commercial has a memorable catch phrase, an unforgettable tune, or a captivating visual, we find ourselves hypnotically drawn in.

Good jingles are simple, but writing them isn't. Composers of commercials need an intuitive understanding of human psychology, of common desires and dreams.

Companies are spending increasingly huge sums on commercials targeted to children, knowing that if they can capture children's lifetime loyalty to their particular soft drink or toothpaste, the investment will pay tremendous dividends. More children's videos, CDs, and songbooks are also being sold every year, which means more work for songwriters.

Writing commercial jingles and writing children's songs are both areas rich with opportunity for songwriters who can master the brisk, compact style and uncomplicated lyrics and chords that work best in these forms.

Composing Commercials

Before an ad agency hires a composer for an ad campaign, much of the planning has already taken place. A typical national ad campaign includes the following steps:

➤ An advertiser contacts an ad agency to launch a national campaign for a new product.

➤ The creative director (with input from his or her staff) decides what the campaign's objectives are.

➤ A storyboard is worked out, and if the advertiser approves, the campaign moves ahead.

➤ Budget suggestions are presented, analyzed, and approved.

➤ The creative director puts out the word to production houses and asks to hear demo reels.

➤ The casting director alerts actors for upcoming auditions and starts examining videotapes.

➤ The composer is selected, and a recording date is chosen.

Getting Engaged

You're hired for the campaign. At the first meeting, you get a general sense of the product and what the client would like to put across to the public.

You make a bid, after ascertaining the following facts:

➤ How large an orchestra the client wants

➤ How much time you have to create and complete the spot

Even though you're a songwriter, you might be given the following things to work with:

➤ A complete lyric

➤ A concept for words written to a known melody

➤ A copy line and the concepts of the spots

➤ A description of the mood that the client and agency want to capture

Trouble Clef

Don't bother to send unsolicited material to ad agencies. You have to come in through a connection or an agent.

Like film directors trying to explain to scorers what they want in a scene, advertisers can't always convey ideas clearly. You have to be a detective and figure out their needs. Just because they're inarticulate doesn't mean they don't have a sense of what they want. They also know what they don't want, and you need to listen with an unprejudiced ear.

Hirschhorn's Hints

Have you already written a Top 10 hit or two? If so, submit them to advertising companies. The appetite for chart smashes from the 1960s on is at an all-time high, and your song may be just what they're looking for. On your own, you might take the initiative and write jingles about current, popular products; record the jingles and submit them. Creative directors may be drawn to your work if it has freshness and imagination.

Pressing the Right Buttons

The product may be a new dot.com company, perfume, soap, or cereal. The viewer may be a 35-year-old housewife, a high school senior, or a fourth-grader. There are countless millions of people, but only a few needs are common to all of them:

➤ **We need love, love, love.** Why do we need a new perfume? Why is a new car mandatory, when we still have a perfectly good one? Because television and radio tell us we have to be more attractive and more able to impress people in order to find love.

➤ **D'ya think I'm sexy?** As with love, we're never totally convinced we have enough sex appeal. But if we had the right shoes, the right earrings, the right suit, we would become, according to ads, irresistible to everyone who meets us. Buying someone the right drink will ensure a lifetime of happiness. It doesn't matter that the conscious mind questions this message. On a deeper level, we accept it—if the jingle is properly crafted.

➤ **A safe harbor.** No matter how much we pose and swagger, we know it's an act. Most of us are insecure, and commercials remind us that the right product can give us confidence. No social situation will be threatening if we wear designer jeans. If you tap into a person's fears, and subliminally let them know that these fears can be conquered, you've made your sale.

Backstage Banter

Former *New Yorker* magazine film critic Pauline Kael once asked the question, "What person, what creature, ever felt they were loved enough?" The answer is "No one." We have that space inside that never quite feels filled, and jingles rush to tell us that if we use a certain product, we'll find all the love we want.

➤ **I'm a big shot!** Give people a sense that they can be famous and important, and you have their attention and their dollars. If wearing an Armani suit will bring a $50,000 raise, the suit will find its way to many a closet. We crave recognition; we want a top job that will knock out our friends (and every woman or man who crosses our path).

➤ **What's in a name?** Whatever the product, whether it's Budweiser beer or Tommy Hilfiger shirts, keep repeating the name! Repetition is the key to popular songs, and the same is true of jingles. Your goal is to sell a product. Advertisers pay billions a year to induce customers into stores, and a subtle, indirect commercial won't do the trick.

Ready to Write

More and more, hit songs are being used to sell a product. To compete, your tune must be compulsively catchy and singable. It must be one of those "I can't get it out of my head" melodies, such as "It's a Small World" by Richard and Robert Sherman. Don't submit a melody to an ad company until you're convinced it has a memorable hook.

Hirschhorn's Hints

Don't think of jingles as a step-child of pop songs, something you're marking time with until your songwriting career explodes. Jingles and pop tunes are art forms in their own way. A patronizing approach to writing commercials dooms your efforts to failure.

Analyze the Objective

Before you start to write, analyze all the angles:

➤ What is the main theme of your commercial?

➤ What group of people is being targeted?

➤ What age are they?

➤ Where do they live?

Give Me "Yesterday"

Suppose the client gets an inspired idea: He or she wants to use a Beatles song. Fine, but the publisher sometimes won't allow those tunes to be cleared for commercials, and if it does, the price may be exorbitant. But the boss is mentally married to the idea. You'll probably be called upon to provide a melody that resembles the one the client favors.

Don't Be Obscure

Dig for that one clear idea and hammer it home. With attention spans at an all-time low (and remote-wielding viewers who click away from commercials whenever they can), you have to state your case instantly. Don't wander and don't make people guess or speculate about what you're conveying.

Personality

You want your jingle to sound unique and original. What good is a jingle if it's generic, bland, and similar to every other commercial on the air? You're fighting to be heard above the pack, and the way to achieve that is to offer a new sound, an offbeat way of touting the product.

Play with Words

One way to approach jingle lyrics is to find a well-known cliché and turn it inside out. When Al and I were hired to do our first commercial for Lloyd's Bank, we tested such phrases as "You'll Love Lloyd's," "You Can't Avoid Lloyd's," and "Lloyds—the Family Bank." Finally, we came up with "You Can Always Bank on Lloyd's," and it was enthusiastically accepted. With this one statement, we promised security, protection, and a family-type friendliness. We used the key word "bank" and found a way to merge it with a well-known expression.

Trouble Clef

You can't take a song such as "Ain't No Mountain High Enough" and alter the tune without permission from the company that owns the copyright.

Think Showtime!

If you have a sense of theater, think of your commercial as a small musical show. If the tone is comic, be playful with your piccolos and tubas. If it's funky and street-oriented, let your bass and drum explode. It's not enough to write the best jingle; you need to emphasize its qualities with a theatrical, flavorful arrangement. Every musician you hire should be thoroughly professional and able to play every rhythm and style. Make sure all of them are expert readers.

Don't Bury the Singer

In pop music, the "feeling" is what counts. How many people do you know who love a song and remember the lyric? Very few. The mix usually covers up half the words. In a jingle, every word counts. Let the singer be heard. This emphasis on the singer sometimes upsets arrangers and songwriters, who hate to lose a precious note, but if it's a contest between a guitar solo and a lead singer, the singer has to win.

Trouble Clef

Don't make the mistake of being too fancy. Use layman's language. Appeal to the guy on the street. Jingles are not the area for complex, show-off rhymes or complicated chords. Avoid gymnastic music leaps and keep the melody within a sensible range.

Trouble Clef

When a copywriter presents words that don't sing easily, you must, with tact and diplomacy, point out that the lyrics need changing. Tell that to the client right away; nobody likes surprises, even when your substitutions are an improvement.

Offer a Choice

Once you've worked out the idea and the jingle, do a recording of it. Offer three different versions. If you submit one, the client may love it, but like most people in show business, the client may be somewhat fearful of trusting his or her judgment. With three versions to pick from, the client feels more secure.

Don't Wing It

A lot of the work in pop music is spontaneous, even with an arrangement. Such creativity is not welcomed in the ad game. Pre-plan everything and get approval for everything, or your recording date could turn into a disaster.

What's the Deal?

Budgets vary widely in the jingle world, from a mere thousand dollars to seven figures. A deciding factor is whether the jingle is for cable, a local spot, or a national one. A television advertiser who wants to keep costs low will acquire music from a stock music house. These stock houses offer canned tracks for radio and television spots. Unlike the conservative expenditures for local broadcast spots, national agencies frequently spend lavishly.

Lyrical Lingo

A **package deal** is a fee paid by a company that hires you which covers all elements of a recording: composing, scoring, conducting, studio costs, mixing, and delivering the master tape to the client. You're totally responsible for accomplishing everything without exceeding that overall payment.

Publishing

When Al and I did commercials, we were allowed to keep the publishing rights. It was the late 1970s, and nobody even voiced a mild objection when we requested full ownership of the copyright. But publishing is now recognized, more than ever, as a huge source of income, and agencies aren't willing to automatically surrender copyright. If you can't get all the rights, negotiate for a split, but be prepared to give it up altogether in many cases.

Getting Paid

Most deals, whether for commercials, television, or film, involve part payment up front and the remainder when the project is completed. If you're fortunate, you may get the whole payment up front, but this kind of deal is rare. The agency may also want to divide your payment into thirds.

Package Deals and Their Drawbacks

Like many composers, I'm not crazy about *package deals* because you often end up with very little or no money at all. Say you receive $5,000 to handle everything: composing, scoring, conducting, studio costs, mixing, and delivering the master tape to the client. To walk away with more than artistic satisfaction, you have to budget down to the minutest detail. Your eye must be on the clock at all times so you don't go overtime.

Even if you keep on top of everything, changes may be suggested at the recording date. That's where your skill is most needed. You have to execute the changes instantly and be able to explain to the musicians what alterations you want without lengthy explanations.

Composers sometimes own music production houses. Their firms might offer a client overall services of orchestration, text, and composition.

The Market for Children's Songs

Opportunities to write for children are at an all-time high. Beyond writing for motion pictures and television, you can compose for direct-to-video productions, an outlet that continues to grow and surprise companies with its public acceptance. Videos featuring nursery rhymes, versions of classic stories, and sequels to hit films are racking up gigantic sales. Children's CDs and songbooks sell more each year.

Do Your Research

Check your local record stores and ask the salespeople which children's videos and CDs have recently sold the most. Buy them and study their form and structure. Then immerse yourself in Saturday morning shows. Videotape and watch each series at least three times. Note the fantasy and freedom of the programs on Disney, Nickelodeon, Cartoon Network, Fox Kids, and Kids WB.

Educational Productions

Audiovisual (AV) productions are now being utilized in organizations and schools for educational purposes. They take the form of videos, filmstrips, or slide shows and offer numerous employment opportunities for scorers and songwriters. Colleges, libraries, and industrial firms are just a few of the available outlets.

Demonstrate your skill by doing an educational film of your own and write music that shows off your abilities and highlights the key points of the subject under discussion. Let your local advertising agency see it. Connect with other educational outlets in your area and get your video around. Familiarize yourself with AV houses by combing the Yellow Pages.

Hirschhorn's Hints

Interpersonal relationships and agents are always vital ways to let people know your abilities. But those who create a Web site that attractively advertises their specialties have a distinct edge. A successful Web site does more than simply let clients know what you have to offer; the site must also be individual, offbeat, and eccentric. Study the competition, and make sure your Web site's visuals and catch phrases are different and memorable.

You won't get rich doing educational films, although your income may surprise you if you do several. Fees for audiovisual work are in the $300 to $3,000 range. As your reputation grows, the fees will become higher, and you'll have the choice of freelancing or taking a full-time job for one company.

Respecting the Minds of Children

When films and shows are tailored for adults, the creators treat them with respect. Why do kids deserve less? No one should write down to children or patronize them.

Three of my prime-time television family films, *The Original Top Ten*, *The Magic Paintbrush*, and *Dickens's David Copperfield* were presented on ABC. My children's feature films were all done for Disney: *The New Mickey Mouse Club*, *Pete's Dragon*, *Freaky Friday*, *Hot Lead and Cold Feet*, *The North Avenue Irregulars*, and *Happy Birthday Mickey Mouse*. When working on all of them, I kept a line by James Thurber in mind: "If a story is good, it can be enjoyed by adults as well as youngsters."

As a composer who has spent many years writing songs, shows, and films for people below the age of 10, I've always tried to follow this rule. I've often found that my own children and their friends catch on to the subtleties of a story or a lyric before the so-called adults around them do.

Make It Modern

No matter how young they are, kids are fully aware of Christina Aguilera, Britney Spears, the Dixie Chicks, 'N Sync, Toni Braxton, and Faith Hill. So don't write old-fashioned, generic melodies. Kids want to hear the musical sound of today.

Backstage Banter

Christina Aguilera and Britney Spears appeared on Walt Disney's *Mickey Mouse Club*, which gave them early training and put both on the road to stardom.

When Al and I did *The Original Top Ten* movie, we varied all the tempos, even including a rap chorus on Marilyn McCoo's "All God's Children." Billy Preston sang an R&B song, "Idols," and Frankie Valli sang "L-I-E-S," which was upbeat pop rock.

Keep It Moving

Would you write a ponderous, slow-moving musical for adults? Then don't move sluggishly when writing for children. Attention spans today are a quarter of what they were 30 years ago. If a song, no matter how well written, slows down the action, remove it.

Create Characters, Not Caricatures

Characters, whether they're animated or live action, should be real. If not completely real, they should have certain human characteristics everyone can identify with. Cartoon villains without dimension won't scare anyone, and cartoon heroes make kids yawn. When writing a children's show or song, think of the characters as flesh-and-blood people. Give them fears and frailties. No one is 100 percent courageous or 100 percent evil.

As a child, I remember a critic saying that Prince Charming in the Disney film *Cinderella* was a bore because he was a handsome Mr. Perfect. On the other hand, the zany, Disney-invented mice who loved and defended Cinderella walked away with the picture.

Thou Shalt Not Preach

One of my most enjoyable and challenging assignments was to write an animated musical of the Ten Commandments called *The Original Top Ten.* The 10 songs in the show had to have bite and a contemporary musical feeling, and they couldn't be preachy. No one, from toddlers to the elderly, will tolerate being preached to for long.

For example, Al and I didn't write a song called "Thou Shalt Not Covet." We translated the commandment into modern terms with an uptempo Billy Preston rocker, "The Grass Looks Greener in Your Neighbor's Yard." The commandment about "Honor Thy Mother and Father" became "Respect Your Mom and Dad" and was performed by Frankie Valli.

Backstage Banter

There's always a way to handle delicate material. In *The Original Top Ten,* adultery was the trickiest subject, and some network people were worried about bringing that commandment up at all. But that would have changed the Bible to nine commandments! We worked on it and finally devised, "Be Loyal to the One You Love," which makes the point without being heavy-handed.

Frame Your Story

In the case of *The Original Top Ten,* I knew that simply singing about virtue wasn't enough to create compelling drama. With the show's producer, Squire Rushnell, we worked out a plot in which three youngsters had to find the first Top 10 records ever made, records based on the Bible. Suspense was maintained when one of the kids started using devious, unfair means of acquiring the records. The show won the kind of accolades we had hoped for as an educational musical that entertained as well.

Match the Songs to the Story

Another of our prime-time animated musicals, *The Magic Paintbrush,* was based on a popular children's book and centered on a young boy with an ability to paint pictures that came to life. As in all animated songs, we made sure that every lyric line could be translated into a visual scene. We also wrote a song called "Keep on Believing" to express the theme of the show. It's important to know what overall point you're trying to make and include a song that clearly conveys that point.

Some people feel that songs, no matter how effective, interfere with the action. Disney's *Beauty and the Beast* proves otherwise. Every Manken/Ashman song in *Beauty and the Beast* propels the story forward. "Belle" defines the heroine's character, and "Gaston" comically points out the evil intentions of the villain. This movie has a perfect children's score; it's a textbook example to study when you're writing for young people. Nothing feels shoehorned in; the songs carry audiences along.

Don't Be Afraid to Be Dark

Seen today, one of our earliest musicals, *The Canterville Ghost,* demonstrates what can happen when children's shows are overly farcical and without enough humanity. When all the townspeople ran away from the Canterville Ghost, you wondered why. The songs we gave him needed more danger and tension.

Hirschhorn's Hints

As Disney has proved time and again, children don't mind being frightened, and an extreme effort to protect their sensibilities by being safe and cute will encourage a mass exodus to the popcorn stand.

When we did *Copperfield* on Broadway, we didn't shy away from the darker aspects of Dickens's drama. As a result, our score was nominated for a Tony award. But an animated television adaptation was less true to the piece and lost the Victorian flavor. For example, an eccentric supporting character, Mr. Dick, became Mr. Polly because the censors were afraid of the word "dick"!

Another point to remember: If you're doing a children's musical and basing it on a classic, resist altering elements that made the classic famous in the first place. It's highly improbable that you, as the composer or the librettist, can spin a better yarn than Dickens did. You can make small changes, subtract a character or two, but be sure the structure and the spirit of the original are preserved.

Free Your Mind

When you write for children, let your mind run loose. If you do, you'll hit upon zany, inspired titles, such as "I'm an Aardvark and I'm Proud" and "Captain Vegetable" from *Sesame Street*. Or an offbeat term may occur to you, such as the Turkish word "Pachalafaka." In "The Alligator King," by Donald Hadley and William Luckey, a typically madcap line refers to seven statues of girls with clocks where their stomachs should be. Children's tunes also lend themselves to audience participation and antics such as juggling, mime, and clowning.

Hirschhorn's Hints

When writing for children, think of yourself as eight years old. Let your beats be buoyant and your words have a playful spin. Concentrate on being funny whenever possible—whether you're doing "Supercalifragilistic Expialidocious" (from *Mary Poppins*) or "Passamashloddy" (from *Pete's Dragon*). When you're done, test the songs on children, and you'll immediately know if they work.

The beauty of writing music for children is the room this audience offers for creativity. Before long, it will seem natural to think of a dragon in someone's living room or a bird that turns into a lion. The joy of composing for kids is how completely it allows you to shed adulthood and be a child again.

The Least You Need to Know

➤ Jingles and children's music should be clear and direct, with a musical hook.

➤ Writing commercials is not demeaning work; it is a highly developed skill.

➤ To be successful at composing commercials, you must understand the consumer and be open and receptive to the client's ideas.

➤ Good children's music also appeals to adults.

➤ Writing for kids can be a creative and joyful experience.

Chapter 15

Movie Scoring and Songwriting

In This Chapter

➤ Scorers can become songwriters

➤ Early jobs that can get you where you want to go

➤ The director and other key players

➤ Music that fits the needs of the movie

➤ How to build your scoring knowledge and experience

Scoring and writing songs for movies are two of the most artistically challenging and commercially satisfying roads a composer can pursue. Sometimes, both score and songs are most effective when they stay in the background. But when they're the focal point and need to dominate, the composer must be willing to serve the film. The key to your success in motion pictures is knowing when you can be a star and when the effectiveness of the piece depends on your willingness to remain a supporting player.

Scorers as Songwriters

Legendary composers such as Max Steiner (*Casablanca, Gone with the Wind*), Erich Korngold (*Robin Hood*), Franz Waxman (*A Place in the Sun*), and Aaron Copland (*The Heiress*) handled only *underscoring* during the 1930s and 1940s.

On rare occasions, scorers crossed the line into songwriting. Alfred Newman's matchless melodic sense was utilized in such hit compositions as "The Best of Everything."

Lyrical Lingo

Underscoring is background music that is meant to support screen action. The purpose of it is to heighten dramatic and comedic sequences.

Backstage Banter

Max Steiner wanted to write his own song for *Casablanca*; Warner Brothers said no. "As Time Goes By," the song finally used in the film and performed by Dooley Wilson, was written by Herman Hupfield.

But in most of these cases, the songs became hits outside the movie after lyricists added words to the tunes.

The songs in MGM musicals such as *Easter Parade, An American in Paris,* and *Singing in the Rain* were written by Irving Berlin, George Gershwin, and Herb and Nacio Brown. Fred Astaire and Ginger Rogers also danced to Berlin, Gershwin, and a host of other musical hit-makers. Rodgers and Hammerstein, Jule Styne, Frank Loesser, Yip Harburg, Sammy Fain, Paul Francis Webster, and Livingston and Evans supplied the tunes; the scorer or orchestrator never did.

Henry Mancini, Michel Legrand, and Marvin Hamlisch brought about a permanent change. Their melodic flair was so extraordinary that they were allowed to compose songs for the picture in addition to their underscoring. Freelance songwriters found their positions threatened after studios decided that many scorers could handle both roles with equal skill.

As a songwriter, you have two alternatives to get your songs in the movies. If you have arranging talent, you can learn orchestration and scoring and thereby gain greater power to put your own music into the movie. The other thing you can do is to keep submitting your songs for consideration, because a truly good song will override politics and be recognized. In the end, producers are out to make money, and they'll choose material that best promotes their picture. The fact is that few scorers, no matter how well educated, have the commercial musical flair of a Mancini.

Make It Happen

You must make yourself known and heard. Perform your material everywhere or play your demos. Eventually, people will start to recognize you and admire your work.

Cut a CD of your best material and get it to all the producers in town. Heads of studios should be on your list, along with music supervisors and music publishers. Make sure your CD features a variety of moods so people see how versatile you are. And be a nuisance! The squeaky wheel gets the grease.

In addition, music agents are giving increasing attention to songwriters. These agents include the Carol Faith Agency, Gorfaine-Schwartz Agency, and the Kraft-Benjamin Agency.

Hirschhorn's Hints

Songwriters want more than hits; they also want to be acknowledged. That recognition will never happen if you don't make yourself visible. Harry Warren hated to attend parties, yet he expressed bitterness that no one knew him or credited him with his list of great songs, a list as long as Irving Berlin's. Warren wrote "The More I See You," "An Affair to Remember," "The Atchison, Topeka, and the Santa Fe," and "You'll Never Know." All his life, he lamented his anonymity without doing anything to change it.

Read the Hollywood Bibles

Daily Variety, which was launched in 1905, is the bible of show business activity. It lets writers know what pictures are being made, who the producers are, and which studios are doing them. The *Hollywood Reporter* does the same. Study both papers and make notes.

Memorize the names of every important person in the music and movie industry. You can be certain that your competition is thoroughly familiar with all aspects of motion picture production. *Variety* and the *Reporter* contain information about films that are in pre-production. At this early point, songwriters haven't been chosen yet, and you have a chance to jump in and volunteer your services. Everything depends on being the early bird, getting in on the ground floor before the job you covet has become general knowledge.

The Fat Spy—No Jurassic Park

When you're first making a name for yourself, it's unlikely that Steven Spielberg will call on you to score one of his films. I've done big films such as *The Poseidon Adventure* and *The Towering Inferno,* but my first endeavor was titled *The Fat Spy,* a disastrous "comedy" starring Jayne Mansfield, Jack E.

Hirschhorn's Hints

Pay particular attention to films done by independent filmmakers and other films being shot on a reasonable budget. The producers of these modest features would prefer to hire someone whose price hasn't reached stratospheric heights. If you're relatively new, your odds of being considered increase tremendously.

Leonard, Phyllis Diller, and a group called "The Wild Ones." The plot had something to do with finding the fountain of youth in Florida, and my collaborator, Al, and I wrote such numbers as "I'd Like to Be a Rose in Your Garden (but I'm Just a Thorn in Your Side)." Pretty embarrassing. But experience helps a songwriter to improve. *The Fat Spy* got us started. It gave us a chance to write 11 songs, and we were able to say we were professionals and had worked in movies.

Respect Your Material

No matter how unpromising the movie material looks at first, you must do the best possible job with it. Never slough off an assignment because it seems unimportant; don't treat anything as though you were slumming. You never know how the movie will turn out in the end. Hollywood history is packed with films everybody figured would fail, and these movies then turned into sleepers and won Academy Awards.

Our second film, *Who Killed Teddy Bear?* wasn't in that category, but it was much better than we expected it to be. The movie centered on a psychopathic killer, played by Sal Mineo, with a sister obsession. At first, we weren't going to do the film, but we then changed our minds. Despite the movie's sleazy subject matter, it had a fairly well-written script, and our five songs attracted some notice. The cast, which also included Juliet Prowse and Elaine Stritch, took ordinary lines and made them human and believable.

A Successful Disaster—on Spec

Unless you're a recording artist who can guarantee a single, producers must hear the songs for a movie in advance before they will hire you. Luckily, every time we tried for something without the guarantee of a salary and a job, the attempt turned out to be successful.

When a publisher friend of ours, Happy Goday, suggested we submit a theme for Irwin Allen's upcoming disaster blockbuster, *The Poseidon Adventure,* everyone we spoke to said, "Don't bother. They're turning down the biggest names in the business. If they don't want Henry Mancini, they're certainly not going to use a song by Kasha and Hirschhorn."

But as James Mason said to Judy Garland in *A Star Is Born,* a career isn't just talent, it's timing. It's knowing when to seize an opportunity. Something in my gut told me: Take the chance. And my advice to all writers is: Take the chance. What have you got to lose?

We showed up with dozens of other composers, and Irwin Allen said, "Go home and write a love song. We'll listen to it at eight tomorrow morning." Again, a friend (?) of ours commented, "Not enough time. You'll never be able to do a good job." But we obeyed our instincts, stayed up all night, and wrote "The Morning After." Maureen McGovern's magnificent rendition of the song became a worldwide number-one song, and it won an Oscar.

Hirschhorn's Hints

No matter what the circumstances are, perform. With *Pete's Dragon*, Al and I were handed an outline of the story and told to write five songs, without pay, for evaluation. Fate almost sabotaged us when I broke my arm while ice skating and had to play the score with one arm in a partial cast. But we performed for 40 people (employees were recruited from all over the Disney lot to give their opinions). Miraculously, the reaction was positive.

We also had to write four songs on spec for Jane Powell and Howard Keel when the touring stage version of *Seven Brides for Seven Brothers* first loomed as a possibility. These songs led to a Tony nomination and a show that has toured for over 15 years and is more popular now than when it began.

Taking a chance without firm promises is only one aspect of a writer's life. Another is simply this: Your job, your passion, is to write no matter what the circumstances. You write because you can't help it, because the desire to write is a relentless drive that won't let you rest.

Have a Strategy

Drive is essential, but so is working out a practical strategy. If you're a lyricist, it makes sense to link up with the composers who score films. I recognized the wisdom of this and made an effort to develop relationships with motion picture scorers. These efforts resulted in fruitful, creatively stimulating collaborations with Nelson Riddle, Marvin Hamlisch, Billy Goldenberg, Alex North, and many others.

Backstage Banter

Stephen King tells a story about his young son Owen. Owen studied the saxophone and learned to be a competent musician, yet King and his wife decided to stop his sax lessons. It became evident that the boy did only what his teacher expected of him, but had no sense of obsession about his music.

Underscoring

Many outstanding books have been written on the subject of underscoring. From my point of view, Henry Mancini's *Sounds and Scores* ranks at the very top. I learned to orchestrate almost entirely from this particular volume. Mancini supplies generous examples and explains things clearly. Best of all, his music is so tuneful and accessible that the instrumental parts are easy to absorb at the first lesson.

Another extraordinary orchestration book is *On the Track* by Fred Karlin and Raymond Wright. These books are also good:

The Techniques of Orchestration by Kent Wheeler Kennan, Prentice Hall, Inc., New Jersey, 1970

Music Arranging and Orchestration by John Cacavas, Bellwin-Mills Publishing Corp., New York, 1975

Scoring for Films by Earle Hagen, Criterion Music Corp., New York, 1971

Modern Harmonic Techniques by Gordon Delamont, Kendor Music, 1971

In the Scoring Game

When you're hired to write the score for a motion picture, you first have to understand the relationship between the score and the film. You also become part of a collaborative effort, which means that it's essential to develop a good working relationship with the film's director and music supervisor.

I asked Carole Bayer Sager, Oscar-winning lyricist for *Arthur,* and one of the screen's finest and most prolific wordsmiths, what she considered the first priority in writing for motion pictures: "Capturing the essence of the movie. If it's going anywhere in the body of the picture or the front, you have to be careful not to go ahead of the film and give the story away. You can't signal what's to come." She's right, yet song-writers often tell the entire plot in detail. Leave that to the script.

Follow the Right Leader

In his classic book, *The Season,* novelist/screenwriter William Goldman stressed the importance of finding the "muscle" in a production, the actual decision maker. That may be the director, the producer, the editor, the executive producer, or the music su-pervisor. If you pay close attention, you'll figure out quickly who has the final say; then make sure that this individual's desires are fulfilled.

Many directors have little or no musical knowledge and lack the vocabulary to convey what they want. You can't afford to be snobbish and tune them out because they're not educated musicians. They may still have an instinctively correct sense of how to heighten the scene with music, and it's your job to figure out what they mean.

Provide Reassurance

In the past, composers would write an entire score and neither director nor producer would hear it until the day of the recording. That's no longer true. Synthesizers have made it possible to make recordings of cues and try them out before final orchestra-tions are written.

Scorer David Shire says …

> "On *The Color Purple,* with Quincy Jones's army of synthesists and keyboard players and arrangers, Spielberg wanted a Synclavier mockup of every cue so that he could get a feel of exactly what the music was going to do … But one can get in trouble with them, I think, because the sound of a Synclavier imitating a symphony orchestra is still not an orchestra."

Nevertheless, this procedure protects against the disastrous possibility of a director disliking the music when it's too late to change it. The composer, too, can feel more relaxed, knowing that his or her work has been approved in advance and won't be thrown out, which has happened to even the best scorers.

Backstage Banter

This music business story has now become legend: A director, eager to capture the correct atmosphere for his film, told his arranger, "Use French horns so we can get a French background." That's about as sensible as using English horns for an English background.

Ask Questions and Do Your Research

Directors have many ideas, some of which they don't express. It's to your advantage to ask questions in order to pin down some of these ideas. Try to find out what instrumentation the director or producer favors. What does he or she want the music to say emotionally? Avoid technical queries, such as "Would you like the chords to go from C to E minor?" Such questions may only make the person feel uneasy or embarrassed and thus incur his or her resentment.

Marvin Hamlisch believes in research. When he was hired to score the James Bond thriller, *The Spy Who Loved Me,* he watched every prior James Bond picture. His score was totally original and representative of his delightful tongue-in-cheek approach, but doing the research gave him an understanding of what had worked with earlier Bond films.

Work Closely with the Music Supervisor

Music supervisors have gained tremendous power and influence in recent years. Their responsibilities include the following:

➤ Devise the budget

➤ Find composers and lyricists and recommend them to producers

➤ Seek out recording artists and record producers

➤ Negotiate soundtrack deals

➤ Coordinate artists' schedules with film release dates

➤ Attend dailies

➤ Attend screening of the film prior to spotting (Spotting is covered in detail in the following section.)

➤ Be present at spotting sessions

➤ Attend scoring sessions

➤ Function as liaison between composer and director

Hearing the phrase *temp track* upsets many a composer. Composers often dread them because directors fall in love with this temporary music and want it kept or reproduced. Director and producer become used to hearing these cues wedded to the scenes in their movie. Even when the cues are deleted and replaced with fine, fresh material, some regret often lingers about the loss of the temp themes. Producer Gerald Isenberg considers them counterproductive, but composer Charles Fox feels that temp tracks are a valuable way to learn about the movie and the potential score.

The best you, the composer, can do if the director loves the temp music, and you don't, is keep an open mind about it and still carefully integrate musical themes and thoughts of your own. If you've previously written music of your own that you can incorporate into the temp track, you can achieve a partial solution.

Talking About Titles

When you're hired to write a song for a motion picture, you have a choice: to use the film's exact title or to come up with something more singable and commercial. Certain titles present a challenge beyond the capabilities of any mere mortal: *The Rules of Engagement, Being John Malkovich, The Cider House Rules,* and *Drowning Mona* are just a few examples. Or going back a few years, how would one possibly incorporate *Death of a Salesman, Breaking the Sound Barrier,* or *The Brave Bulls* into a song title?

Suppose producer Irwin Allen had insisted our song be titled *The Poseidon Adventure*. It would have killed any chance for a hit. *The Towering Inferno* wouldn't have worked as a title either. *Breakfast at Tiffany's* is quite a mouthful, but Johnny Mercer and Henry Mancini came up with "Moon River" instead.

Spotting the Picture

Once the placement of music in a movie is decided upon, the music editor writes up a music breakdown, called *spotting* notes. He or she lists the cues and numbers them so that the first digit represents the reel number and the next digits offer the cue number within the reel. Therefore, 1M1 (or M11, or 1/1) means Reel 1, Cue 1. Composers should make their own notes as well.

Common spotting abbreviations include the following:

BG	Background
CU	Close-up
Cut	Direct cut from one shot to another
Dial	Dialogue
Ext	Exterior
FI	Fade in from black
FO	Fade out to black
Int	Interior
LS	Long shot
MS	Medium shot
MX	Music
O.S.	Off-screen (voice, sound)
Pan	Panorama shot, which means camera rotates, revealing sweep of scene
Pix	Picture
POV	From the point of view of named actor
Super	Superimposing one image over another (a double exposure)
2-Shot	Two subjects in frame
3-Shot	Three subjects in frame
V.O.	Voice over, a voice that doesn't lip sync with subject in frame
ECU	Extreme close-up
ELS	Extreme long shot
Zoom in	Effect of coming closer to a subject
Zoom out	Effect of subject receding

Lyrical Lingo

Spotting is watching the film and deciding where music should be placed.

Practical Scoring Tips

Beyond knowing the intricate techniques of scoring, a scorer must heed certain general rules when writing music:

➤ Concentrate, first and foremost, on the central character. What are that character's hopes, goals, and fears? Learn about the character until you understand him or her as completely as you understand a member of your own family.

➤ Certain scenes don't function well on their own. They may have undercurrents the director or writer failed to clarify for an audience. That's when a scorer should ride to the rescue. Suppose a character is shoveling snow or pumping gas. Your job is to get inside the person's mind and musically dramatize his or her emotions. The right cues can turn dead spots into exciting moments.

➤ Choosing the proper instrumentation is crucial. Insecure directors and producers may want you to go crazy with a huge, crashing orchestra. That kind of overkill can ruin a scene. If you sense that a three- or four-piece band or just a piano would accomplish the job more effectively, point it out. Be sure to have an explanation justifying your idea.

➤ A character might be pretending to feel one emotion when he or she is actually feeling another. If your hero is laughing but inwardly terrified, project that fear through your music. If the heroine is pretending to love someone but actually hates him, it might double the impact of the moment if you suggest it with your cues.

➤ Sometimes it helps to play against the events occurring onscreen. Happy music with bells and piccolos over a moment of horror can make the horror even more intense. You're skating on thin ice when you make these kinds of decisions, but they often heighten a scene's power.

Trouble Clef

When you score a love scene, guard against sentimentality. The right music can jerk tears, but the wrong music can make people feel manipulated and can turn off directors.

➤ Max Steiner, who scored *Casablanca* and *Gone with the Wind,* was a strong believer in writing individual themes for each character. Some directors favor that kind of musical emphasis. Others consider it corny. Check with your director before proceeding.

➤ Writing a single melody and playing it endlessly helps to sell the theme and frequently results in a hit record. This is again a case of seeing how your director and producer feel. They might prefer a score that catches a scene's every nuance. Requirements vary for each film. A love story usually benefits from a beautiful tune constantly featured with different instrumentation and rhythms. A thriller might suffer from the same treatment.

Hirschhorn's Hints

Will Jennings, lyricist for the Oscar-winning songs, "Up Where We Belong" (from *An Officer and a Gentleman*) and "My Heart Will Go On" (from *Titanic*) agrees with Carole Bayer Sager that a song should have an organic connection to the film, not just be placed there for exploitation purposes. He also approves of a song being utilized at the end, if the theme has been featured before. "That way it comes back with more emotional power than if you'd never heard the tune."

Get Into It

Learning orchestration is a combination of formal study and practical experience. The following are some valuable roads to follow in pursuit of that goal:

➤ Play classical works and follow along by reading the orchestral scores. Memorize every sound, color, and range. After you gain an overview with your first lesson, zero in on one instrument at a time. Go through the entire violin part, then switch to viola, cello, bass. Do this with each instrument involved. Copy the parts until they feel like second nature, until you're thoroughly familiar with each instrument's capabilities. Work with a copyist; learn to copy and transpose parts yourself and consider it a temporary (or possibly permanent) career.

➤ Find a private teacher to teach you orchestration, as I did, or if you prefer, attend a school like Juilliard. Pore over every arranging book you can get your hands on.

➤ Study conducting.

➤ Befriend film editors and watch them go through the process of editing a movie. It's the best education a potential scorer can have.

➤ Performing with an orchestra or band will help you to familiarize yourself with arrangements. You'll see what works and what doesn't. Some instruments move more quickly than others. You can't move as rapidly on a bassoon as you can on a piccolo. A bass isn't as flexible as a violin. As a musician, you'll automatically absorb this information.

If you want to become an all-around movie orchestrator, study every conceivable kind of score. Never restrict yourself to classical, jazz, or rock, or tell yourself that you're only good at certain kinds of things. If you decide, for example, that you can't do a rustic, country score because your specialty is sophisticated city arrangements, this attitude will become a self-fulfilling prophecy. Remember that John Williams did *Fiddler on the Roof, The Reivers,* and *Star Wars*—three scores that bear no ethnic resemblance to each other—and he did a brilliant job with each one.

The Least You Need to Know

➤ Do whatever it takes to gain experience and opportunities in writing songs for films and television.

➤ Bond with decision-makers.

➤ Learn to read the director's mind.

➤ Stay close to music supervisors.

➤ Study conducting and orchestration and learn about every instrument.

Live and Animated Musicals

In This Chapter

➤ Capitalize on your main animated character's unique characteristics

➤ Work with, not against, the book writer

➤ Create songs that nail your characters

➤ Place songs properly

➤ Look at the music from an arranger's and choreographer's point of view

As a two-time Tony nominee for Best Broadway musical and two-time Oscar nominee for Best Song and Score of a musical movie, I can testify from personal experience that creating a full musical is one of the most exciting and satisfying experiences a composer and/or lyricist can have. Emotionally, it's not too different from an intense love affair with its roller-coaster highs and lows, despair and joy. When a composer sees his or her words and music beautifully interpreted on a stage or on film, there is a sense of unmatchable triumph.

The process is not as mysterious as it may appear. Like every creative endeavor, musicals have their own set of rules and guidelines, as I learned while composing the Disney musical, *Pete's Dragon*. The first rule is: A musical has to have a strong, solid premise that can shoulder all the embellishments placed upon it.

In this chapter, I use *Pete's Dragon,* one of the earliest motion pictures to combine live and animated characters, to explore writing a musical score for a film genre that is today at its peak of popularity.

Not Eliza Doolittle, but a Dragon

When Al and I imagined writing a musical for film, we were stimulated by certain mental pictures: Gene Kelly dancing in the rain; Barbra Streisand belting out "Don't Rain on My Parade" on a tugboat; Leslie Caron in *Gigi,* dancing to "The Night They Invented Champagne"; or Kevin Bacon teaching his friend to dance in *Footloose.*

It never occurred to us that we'd be writing numbers for an animated dragon. In the late 1970s, when Disney gave us the assignment to provide the score for *Pete's Dragon,* we had no idea that by 1990, most movie musicals would take the form of animated features such as *The Little Mermaid, Beauty and the Beast,* and *The Lion King.* All we knew was that the personnel involved were superbly talented: choreographer Onna White (Oscar winner for *Oliver*), master orchestrator Irwin Kostal, and stars Mickey Rooney, Shelley Winters, Helen Reddy, Jim Dale, and Red Buttons.

Keeping Up with Current Styles

After the success of *Grease* in 1978 and *Fame* in 1980, the MGM-style film musical, in which characters sang songs onscreen rather than doing them through voiceover, started to lose popularity. People began to say, "The musical is gone forever." But I kept in mind the words Gene Kelly said to me, "Nothing ever disappears. It just resurfaces in a different form."

Animated musicals brought the musical back. In 1989, Disney released *The Little Mermaid* by Alan Menken and Howard Ashman, and it caused a sensation. Suddenly, the musical in animated form was bringing in record worldwide grosses. Characters still sang to each other, even though they were cartoons. The validity of the form was underlined when *Beauty and the Beast* and *The Lion King* went to Broadway and were immediately successful.

After 1989, all the guidelines that applied to the live musical became equally valid for animated musical films. If anything, animated replicas of live-action musicals were more popular than their counterparts. Soundtracks reached higher chart levels, selling in the tens of millions, and hit songs poured from all the Disney musical releases, as they continue to do.

Television Musicals

Television, according to current perception, is the new area for the musical, as exemplified by sky-high ratings for television remakes of *Annie* and *Gypsy.* The unpublicized truth is more encouraging. Television has always offered numerous opportunities for composers who write musicals.

Backstage Banter

Disney originally planned to go to Maine on location to film *Pete's Dragon.* It decided instead to build an entire city on its back lot. Cast and crew were disappointed, feeling that they couldn't capture the fantasy with artificial sets. When it was done, however, the city looked more magical than any location you could find in the real state of Maine.

Early in my career, somewhat intimidated by the prospect of Broadway, I trained my eye on television with the intention of developing and creating musicals. My first breakthrough was an ABC version of *The Canterville Ghost,* followed by another one called *Old Faithful,* which starred Zero Mostel and Burgess Meredith. Encouraged by the network reactions to these projects, I went on to do *The Magic Paintbrush, Charles Dickens's David Copperfield,* and *The Original Top Ten.* The first two were live-action movies; the next three were animated, in the manner of the contemporary Disney films.

Hirschhorn's Hints

People are always saying, "Television's only interested in doing classics. No one will do an original." I want to point out that three of my five television musicals were originals and so was *Pete's Dragon.*

Music Behind the Scenes

Saturday Night Fever, Footloose, and *Dirty Dancing* are definitive examples of the modern voiceover musical. *Saturday Night Fever* is the work of one writing group—the Bee Gees—and *Footloose* is the vision of Dean Pitchford, who did all the lyrics. Because both of these movies were conceived by one mind, they have more musical unity than *Dirty Dancing,* which recruited submissions from a dozen songwriters.

Dialogue vs. Music

Ideally, book writers want more dialogue, and songwriters want more music. In a musical, the book writer has to defer to the score, or the project won't succeed. Crisp, character-driven dialogue is needed to keep the action flowing and provide setups for the songs.

Musical book writers frequently resent this situation. They feel it renders them anonymous, and they're right. The more successfully they do their job, the more they'll be allowing a composer to shine at their own expense. You, as the composer or lyricist, must make every effort to work harmoniously with the librettist. Be open to his or her suggestions and avoid a competitive situation. At the same time, make sure your lyrics furnish as much information as possible, and don't duplicate points the dialogue has made.

Sometimes a generous book writer who looks at the overall show rather than at his or her own ego needs will encourage you to use lines of his or her dialogue as titles or incorporate them within the lyric. If you maintain an appreciative and responsive relationship with the book writer, a gift like that will occur more often. In the case of *Pete's Dragon,* book writer Malcolm Marmorstein had the same priority we did: to make our musical as fast-moving and enjoyable as possible. There were no ego clashes of any kind.

The Song's the Thing

Nothing is more tedious than a succession of numbers that all sound alike. In *Pete's Dragon*, we included a waltz, a ballad, pop songs, and a country rocker.

Hirschhorn's Hints

When devising characters, always consider the idea of giving them characteristics against type. We suggested that the songs about Elliott the Dragon make him lovable rather than menacing, with zany speech patterns and a language all his own. These eccentricities turned him into a more popular, less conventional character.

Trouble Clef

Opening numbers, with rare exceptions, have to grab viewers. Otherwise, you'll run into the popcorn problem, when children get up from their seats and rush out to the refreshment stand. Slow openings are a guarantee that you'll lose half your kid audience.

Nailing the Characters

What kind of numbers suit the different characters? You have to ask yourself this question over and over again. What defines each of the people (or the dragons) involved? Your job, as composer and lyricist, is to bring these characters alive, to let the audience see their dreams, desires, and goals.

Pete's Dragon centers around a young orphan who is battered and exploited by his illiterate foster family. Examining the villains, led by a monstrous Shelley Winters, we took into account that they lived in poor, rural surroundings. A country-flavored tune suggested their upbringing and background, and we made their signature song up-tempo.

The up-tempo drive conveyed the family's heartlessly aggressive behavior. A ballad would have been inappropriate for two reasons:

➤ It would have made the characters too sensitive and caring.

➤ The up-tempo song, titled "Happiest Home in the Hills," was our opening number.

Another character song in the movie painted a picture of medical con man Jim Dale. We made his phony miracle cures so outlandish and his claims for healing so transparent that children knew he was going to pose a danger to the dragon. With its barrage of eighth notes, the tempo of the song was therefore frenetic, to capture his fanatic personality.

Where Songs Belong

In the case of film musicals, songwriters are usually called after a script has been written. *Pete's Dragon* was an exception. We were handed a 75-page outline by author Malcolm Marmorstein. Frank Paris, head of Disney's story department, asked us to suggest where songs would work most effectively.

Placing songs properly is one of the first and most vital aspects of creating a musical. Numbers have to move the plot forward and not simply be tossed in at random.

They also need to move the story along. As Stephen Schwartz, composer of *Godspell* and Oscar winner for Disney's *Pocahontas,* says, "We all love our ballads, but sometimes they slow down the action." Deleting a tune you're attached to from a spot you've already chosen can be painful, but objectivity has to rule.

Easy Does It

The late Lehman Engel, who started the world-famous musical workshop at BMI (Broadcast Music, Inc.), always stressed the urgent need for what he called a "charm song." Charm songs are medium-tempo melodies that bridge the gap between gentle ballads and rip-roaring production numbers. These tunes are meant to please rather than electrify and induce a smile rather than uproarious laughter.

Hirschhorn's Hints

Rodgers and Hammerstein had a unique way of creating step-out songs that became hits on their own. They wrote opening verses to tell the story, and then moved on to a more general lyric. An excellent example of this technique is "Hello, Young Lovers," in which Anna, the heroine of *The King and I,* reminisces about her lost love before switching to a lyric that gives advice to every young lover in the world.

In *Pete's Dragon,* the charm song is "It's Not Easy," a number in which Pete tries to explain to a skeptical heroine (Helen Reddy) that his dragon friend exists. It's also a *step-out song.*

Our step-out song from *Pete's Dragon* was called "Candle on the Water," sung by Helen Reddy and later nominated for a Best Song Oscar. The words were deliberately chosen to work within the context of the story without being so specific that they made no sense outside the film.

Stand Up to Stars

When one of your stars requests a song that you know will prove injurious to the whole enterprise, you have to fight for the good of the show. Twice in my career, stars

Lyrical Lingo

Step-out songs are designed to work perfectly within the plot, but they also function on their own when lifted from the score. These songs are the ones with hit potential.

came to me, begging for songs that would "strengthen their character." The songs they wanted might have strengthened their characters, but they would have weakened the pace of the show and robbed the climax of impact. Opposing your leading players is difficult, and you have to do it with the utmost diplomacy. Sometimes the battle can't be won. But whenever possible, keep your focus trained on what will benefit the overall result.

The Performers and the Song

Often the composer has little say in the casting of a film. In the case of *Pete's Dragon*, producers Jerry Courtland and Ron Miller respected us and asked for our opinion, and then pursued actors we wanted for the roles. If you're asked at the start of casting to venture opinions, don't be shy or deferential. Make up a list of superior candidates.

For the leading parts, try to choose people who can sing. Many people feel performers without singing ability can "act" the songs, but nothing can match the pleasure of hearing melodies sung well. Aside from the aesthetic satisfaction, the tunes have a much greater chance of becoming hits. In today's Hollywood, where soundtracks are bigger business than ever, this consideration is tremendously important.

Trouble Clef

Richard Rodgers hated the fact that Gertrude Lawrence sang out of tune in *The King and I*, even though she acted the role convincingly. Sammy Cahn, who wrote the music for the Broadway musical *Look to the Lilies* in 1970, said, "We had Al Freeman Jr., and they kept telling us, 'He's an actor.' But I said, 'Can he sing?' Jule Styne answered, 'What good is a show if the book doesn't come off? He'll bring it off.' But I figured this way: Let the book writer handle the book, I'll handle the songs." Cahn was proved right when no successful songs emerged from the score. Conclusion: Get someone who can do both if possible.

Bring Out the Actor's Best Qualities

After the performers have been chosen, you as a composer should think of ways to capitalize on their unique characteristics. When Disney hired Mickey Rooney to play Helen Reddy's hard-drinking dad, we concentrated on writing a melody that packed the manic energy Rooney had as a singer. The result was "I Saw a Dragon," where Rooney sees the huge, horrifying dragon that is invisible to everyone else. The beat grows increasingly hysterical to convey the character's overwhelming terror.

Vocal Ranges That Match

Vocal ranges are always vital, and when writing a duet, a wrong choice can lead to disaster. Ask yourself right away: Who has the bulk of the number? In the case of "I Saw a Dragon," which teamed Mickey Rooney and Helen Reddy, Mickey sang the tune, and Helen spoke the lyrics. Their keys were incompatible, and it was dramatically necessary for Rooney to do most of the singing. Helen's singing voice was the logical one to feature, yet the choice had to be based on what best served the story. Helen had the better pop voice, but Mickey was the focal point of the scene.

Every Job Is Your Job

Never think: Choreography is her job; mine is to write songs. In writing a musical, visualizing yourself as choreographer, director, or actor helps you gain a creative overview that will make your songs come more brilliantly alive.

Arranger and Best Friend

When you work on a musical, the arranger is an incomparable ally. Songs are like people. No matter how handsome or beautiful people are, their beauty is tremendously enhanced with the right clothes and the right hairstyle. Many outstanding tunes have been distorted, weakened, or ruined by arrangers who don't understand how to do them justice or who have a concept that differs too widely from the composer's.

Meet with the arranger beforehand and establish a strong personal rapport. Tell him or her clearly what you're trying to do with your tunes. If you see a guitar and a harmonica, make it clear that 40 violins would be a major mistake. You also should be open to the arranger's suggestions. A guitar and a harmonica might be too sparse and might not give your song the emotional charge it requires.

Think Like a Choreographer

Another song from *Pete's Dragon*, "There's Room for Everyone," encouraged choreographer Onna White to create a huge dance, employing dozens of adults and children and spreading them out over an entire town. When you write songs for musicals, always check the lyrics afterward to see how danceable they are. An imaginative choreographer will do wonders with your material, but you can make the numbers twice as exciting by putting yourself in his or her place and saying to yourself, "How can I make this dance?"

Arranger Irwin Kostal, a close friend and a cherished mentor, once told me: "Give the choreographer visual aids to work with. You can make her job much easier and do your musical a world of good."

Backstage Banter

The late Irwin Kostal was one of the great unsung heroes of the musical world. He orchestrated *West Side Story, The Sound of Music,* and *Mary Poppins,* winning Oscars for the first two and a nomination for the third. He was also known in music circles as "the fastest pen in the world," because of his amazing speed in conceiving and finishing arrangements.

I Just Want This Small Change

Just when you think your show is in perfect shape, someone—the director, the star, the producer—will have ideas about how to change it. Your best song may be for a character that the director wants deleted; or the show-stopper has been given to a minor character who outshines the star.

In *Pete's Dragon*, we were given instructions to "avoid rock" and write something "timeless." This instruction was vague, but Al and I came up with something old-fashioned in a 1940s style. While congratulating ourselves on our ability to meet the producer's requirements, the order descended, "Make it a rock song." Thus, "Brazzle Dazzle Day" became perky rather than poignant, rollicking rather than romantic.

An even more towering change came about when the decision was made to eliminate Elliot, the dragon. The reasoning? "Kids will be happy to see Shelley Winters, Mickey Rooney, and Jim Dale. They won't care about a dragon. Let's do it like *Harvey,* in which the main character imagines, rather than sees, an invisible rabbit."

With no criticism intended of Winters, Rooney, and Dale, it struck us that an animated dragon would have far more appeal than a cast of adult live actors. We were devastated. It was obvious to us that the movie would have no chance of becoming one of Disney's classics if *Pete's Dragon* became just the story of Pete.

Backstage Banter

The Oscar-winning classic song "Over the Rainbow" at one point was deleted from *The Wizard of Oz.* Producer Arthur Freed threatened to quit unless it was put back in the picture.

We went to the head honchos and begged, pleaded. We played a duet written for Elliot and Pete that finally caused them to relent, a comedy number titled "Boo Bop Bop Bop (I Love You, Too)."

Once our animated hero was back in the ballgame, we gladly wrote songs to feature him. I regard the battle for the dragon as the most important artistic fight I've ever undertaken, no matter how much extra writing and rewriting it entailed. Be ready and eager to work around the clock and make any alterations necessary for the betterment of the show.

Monetary Rewards from a Musical

If the musical you write becomes a success, it can give you a lifelong income, the kind of income that provides a financial umbrella during lean times. Artists frequently cover (record a version) songs from musicals. Band arrangements, music folios, and choral arrangements also provide permanent income.

In the case of *Pete's Dragon*, Al and I were relatively new to Disney, and the remuneration was comparatively small. Fortunately, Sammy Cahn said to us, "Take it! Even if you have to pay them. It will put you on the map as musical writers, and besides, think of royalties."

Very soon after, the *Pete's Dragon* soundtrack was released, and we saw what Sammy meant. The album went gold, and the single received enormous airplay. The best part of the picture was yet to come. Through the years, songs from *Pete's Dragon* were placed in countless compilation albums, such as *Disney's Greatest Hits*, *Disney's Greatest Animal Songs*, and *Disney's Top Ten*. The sheet music also continued to sell and still does today.

Whether the songs are on voiceover or on camera, your goal in writing music for musicals should be to highlight character, move the story along, create a sense of drama, and deepen the emotional meanings of the story.

Hirschhorn's Hints

Gene Kelly once told me, "Nothing ever disappears. In show business, they write obituaries, and then the cycle turns, and everything old is new again. Never worry that a trend is gone for good—it's just taking a vacation."

179

The Least You Need to Know

➤ Cooperate, don't compete, with the book writer.

➤ The key to show writing is understanding the characters.

➤ Write at least one song that is general enough to stand outside of the show.

➤ Pick the best possible ranges and keys for your singers.

➤ Be sure that your tempos vary to keep audience interest.

➤ Factor in the choreography while you're writing your material.

Chapter 17

Musicals for the Stage

In This Chapter

➤ The illusion of reality in an abstract space

➤ Types of musicals

➤ Ways of getting your musical to the stage

➤ Special material for artists and performers

Most of the concepts that apply to film musicals are equally valid for the stage. But theater has differences a composer should keep in mind.

Creating an Illusion of Reality

On stage you don't have a camera moving freely around, capturing every detail of lavish locations. Julie Andrews can spin across the hills of Salzburg in Robert Wise's Oscar-winning film version of *The Sound of Music*. On stage, her movements would be comparatively restricted.

In the 1940s and 1950s, sets were large, often elephantine. They were usually opulent, with every detail spelled out. Going from one sequence to another was more a feat of heavy labor than a feat of the imagination. Today, such literal monstrosities arouse the ire of critics. Sets that zip in and out or revolve quickly are much preferred. They suggest a background or an atmosphere. So don't conceive your theater piece as a series of short scenes, each with elaborate set changes.

Backstage Banter

Illusions are in the eye of the beholder. While spinning around on the frigid Salzburg hills during the filming of *The Sound of Music*, Julie Andrews was suffering from a violent case of the flu and from dizziness caused by the medicine she was taking. But being a trouper, she made it all look easy. Gene Kelly had a temperature of 105 degrees when his memorable dance scene in *Singing in the Rain* was filmed.

Belting to the Balcony

Write songs that have energy, spirit, and that theater word commonly used today, an "edge." You have to reach viewers in the last row of theaters that are often huge.

Hollywood songwriters who set their sights on Broadway have been criticized for writing songs that were too sweet, too pleasant. This assertion has some truth to it; those who were used to the camera composed overly mellow music. After years of working in film, they were accustomed to the ever-present camera doing the work for them. Close-ups were able to furnish the necessary power, highlighting the tiniest expressions on the faces of the cast. That's why a movie can carry the weight of more ballads, whereas one or two are sufficient in a theatrical enterprise.

Lyrical Lingo

Minimalist refers to nondissonant, repetitive harmonies that rarely modulate and focus on simple scales and triads.

When Al and I wrote *Copperfield* for Broadway, José Ferrer and Otto Preminger encouraged us to compose music with a cutting edge that was outgoing rather than *minimalist*. Modern audiences want songs that dig deep and penetrate outer layers of personality. A score like *Rent* has a contemporary, powerful score. Stephen Sondheim writes music and lyrics that go for sharpness and truth.

Family shows such as *The Lion King, Aida,* and *Beauty and the Beast* reach out expansively. The rhythms have sweep and drive, and the music intervals allow a singer tremendous latitude. Small people inhabit a big stage, and they have to dominate through power and personality. Your music must have the expansive passion to make them larger-than-life figures.

Songs on Stage and Screen

In a film musical, songs are more sparingly utilized than in stage shows. Film is a realistic medium, and dozens of songs in a row produce boredom in your viewers. The stage has a fundamental fantasy element that makes it possible for listeners to enjoy one tune after another. That's why the movie version of *Evita,* a rock opera, did only luke-warm box office despite Madonna's presence. In a theater, *Evita* captivates almost everyone.

Important Musical Categories

Musicals have always fallen into certain categories. Some of the most well-known types are adult fairy tales, revues, historical musicals, musical fantasies, and musical biographies. Musical adaptations are also popular; novels, plays, movies, works of Shakespeare, and Bible stories have all been turned into successful musicals. Some of the most memorable musicals, however, have been complete originals.

Hirschhorn's Hints

Feel free to write as many songs as you consider necessary when composing for the stage. As you start working on a show, you'll keep some songs, eliminate some, and save some for re-evaluation at a later time. You'll be composing up to the last minute, because change and rewriting is the name of the game in theater.

Adult Fairy Tales: Love Heals

For the romantic, sentimental composer who loves happy endings, adult fairy tales are a fertile musical area.

➤ *Beauty and the Beast* (**Menken and Ashman**). Among Disney's most popular animated musical films, it is just as successful on the Broadway stage. A mismatched pair, a lovely young girl and a ferocious beast, discover that love transcends appearances and true beauty lies within.

➤ *The Unsinkable Molly Brown* (**Meredith Willson**). The road from rags to riches is always romantic, and in this backwoods fable, Molly Brown rises from uneducated tomboy to society belle. She even rescues people on the doomed *Titanic.*

➤ *Seven Brides for Seven Brothers* (**Hirschhorn, Kasha**). Two different points of view clash when a spunky waitress marries a chauvinistic mountain man and teaches him how to treat a woman with respect. (A new score was written for the stage version.)

➤ *Annie* (**Strouse/Charnin**). An orphan winds up as the cherished ward of a fabulously wealthy figure. This situation becomes plausible through Strouse and Charnin's buoyant, tuneful score and a need we all have to believe that love can triumph over any adversity.

A theme that links these adult fairy tales is personality transformation brought about by the miraculous powers of love. In *Seven Brides for Seven Brothers,* for instance, all seven men become courteous, considerate, well-mannered Prince Charmings.

Hirschhorn's Hints

Audiences can be counted on to cheer for a hero or heroine who rises to wealth, conquers snobs, and winds up with the love of her dreams. In *My Fair Lady,* a guttersnipe won over the shallow rich and married her professor. In Shaw's *Pygmalion,* the basis for *My Fair Lady,* Eliza didn't land Professor Higgins; but Alan Jay Lerner understood that audiences would reject the work if the two didn't get together. He went so far as to say that Shaw's ending was wrong.

Adult fairy tales are perfect properties for romantics. Within their wholesome borders, they have a core of realism. Consider the song "You've Got to Be Taught (to Hate and Fear)" from *South Pacific,* which features a romance between a naive American schoolteacher and worldly South Seas plantation owner. But an adult fairy tale must maintain its wide-eyed, optimistic viewpoint. The key to these beloved properties is that they make people feel good.

The Revue

Revues are generally composed of vignettes and skits with an overall theme, whether sexual, social, or political. Sometimes they're compilations that define the life work of a creative artist or a writer's literary contributions.

➤ *Cats* (**Andrew Lloyd Webber, T.S. Eliot**). The longest running musical in history, *Cats* is a series of T. S. Eliot poems set to Andrew Lloyd Webber's music. The story is just a slim excuse for Webber's tuneful score, which includes the standard, "Memory."

➤ *A Chorus Line* (**Marvin Hamlisch/Ed Kleban**). A ground-breaking musical documentary, this show utilized the lives, hopes, and dreams of Broadway dancers as a foundation for a Tony-winning musical revue.

➤ *Fosse.* Bob Fosse's choreography was the focal point of this revue, with excerpts from such shows as *Pajama Game, Pippin,* and *Chicago.*

Trouble Clef

If you're attracted to a set of stories or poems, you might find it enjoyable and lucrative to musicalize them as Webber did. Carole King's *Really Rosie* musicalized the works of children's writer Maurice Sendak. But remember: Before you decide to use a property owned by someone else, get the rights! Carol Hall, composer of *Best Little Whorehouse in Texas*, admitted that she never got rights to many properties she coveted early in her career. "I was totally ignorant," she says. "I mean I'd just do a musical I had no rights to, if it struck my fancy."

➤ *Jerome Robbins's Broadway.* This show features most of Robbins's dances from such masterpieces as *On the Town, A Funny Thing Happened on the Way to the Forum, Fiddler on the Roof, Peter Pan,* and *West Side Story.*

➤ *Smokey Joe's Café.* Jerry Leiber and Mike Stoller's hits provided the pulsing rock magic for this revue.

➤ *Ain't Misbehavin'.* This revue consists of 30 songs written or performed by Fats Waller.

➤ *Sophisticated Ladies.* This revue celebrates Duke Ellington's big band classics such as "Satin Doll" and "Mood Indigo."

The Historical Musical

The historical musical allows composers and lyricists a chance to musically portray an era and its people. When historical musicals succeed, they often become classics:

➤ *Titanic* (**Maury Yeston**). Maury Yeston's musical depicts the 1912 tragedy of an "unsinkable" ocean liner.

➤ *Cabaret* (**John Kander, Fred Ebb**). Pre-Hitler Germany, with its decadence and let's-live-as-though-there's-no-tomorrow attitudes; and the film *I Am a Camera* provided Kander and Ebb with the basis for a bitingly harsh, realistic musical drama.

➤ *Miss Saigon* (**Claude-Michel Schoenberg, Richard Maltby Jr., Alain Boublil**). This show reworks Puccini's *Madame Butterfly* as a Vietnam War drama.

➤ *Les Misérables* (**Claude-Michel Schoenberg, Claude Boublil**). Utilizing the French Revolution as background, *Les Misérables* (*Les Miz* for short), which was based on the classic novel by Victor Hugo, told the tale of escaped prisoner Jean

Valjean and the mercilessly moral policeman Javert who pursues him. *Les Miz* and *Miss Saigon* were two of the leading musicals to be *through-sung* and use *recitative* and *leitmotif* in a brilliant and commercially successful manner.

➤ *Pacific Overtures* (**Stephen Sondheim**). This musical of Japanese and Western relations is told in the traditional form of Japanese Kabuki theater.

The Musical Fantasy

Musical fantasies appeal to almost everyone, from children to the most jaded adults. Other genres come and go, but the commercial appeal of fantasies remains undiminished. If you're a writer with a rich imagination and a love of make-believe, this musical arena could be right for you.

➤ *The Lion King* (**Elton John, Tim Rice**). A combination of wizardly stagecraft and puppetry, this adaptation of the Disney film featured an Oscar-winning score by Elton John and Tim Rice.

➤ *The Little Shop of Horrors* (**Howard Ashman, Alan Menken**). Based on the 1960 low-budget film of the same name, this show pitted a nerdy hero against a man-eating plant and became the fifth longest running off-Broadway musical in history.

➤ *Starlight Express* (**Andrew Lloyd Webber, Richard Stilgoe**). This show anthropomorphized trains on a cross-country race that made unlikely, but effective subjects for Andrew Lloyd Webber's offbeat musical.

➤ *Nine* (**Maury Yeston**). Fellini's film *8½* furnishes the source material for Yeston's musical about a film director's fantasies.

➤ *Brigadoon* (**Alan Jay Lerner, Frederic Loewe**). This musical tells a romantic tale about two American tourists who discover a town that awakens only once every hundred years. The premise seems far-fetched, but Lerner and Loewe's memorable score ("The Heather on the Hill," "Come to Me, Bend to Me," and "Almost Like Being in Love") makes it believable and moving.

The Musical Biography

True-life heroes and heroines always make fascinating musical material. If you want to musicalize a colorful personality (and can obtain the rights), it often results in box office gold.

➤ *Gypsy* **(Stephen Sondheim).** In a daring, innovative approach that is typical of Sondheim, this show concentrated on a vicious, conniving stage mother named Rose who shoved her daughter (stripper Gypsy Rose Lee) into the limelight and then felt abandoned after Gypsy's success. In this case, the main character wasn't famous, although her children were. (Rose's other daughter evolved into actress June Havoc.)

➤ *Barnum* **(Cy Coleman, Michael Stewart).** This play about master showman Phineas Taylor Barnum featured juggling, tightrope walking, and trampoline feats by Jim Dale.

➤ *The Will Rogers Follies* **(Cy Coleman, Betty Comden, Adolph Green).** Beloved humorist Will Rogers provided the centerpiece for a lavish revue/biography with razzle-dazzle choreography by Tommy Tune and a glitzy production worthy of Florenz Ziegfeld himself.

➤ *Dreamgirls* **(Henry Krieger, Tom Eyen).** The Krieger/Eyen score didn't actually say the three heroines were the Supremes, but Supreme Mary Wilson has confirmed that director Michael Bennett based his play on Motown's most popular trio. The composers cleverly located the drama of this story by focusing on Florence Ballard, the tragic Supreme who died young after being ousted from the group. It's always preferable when you can take a known story and present it with a fresh twist, as composers Henry Krieger and Tom Eyen did here.

➤ *Evita* **(Andrew Lloyd Webber, Tim Rice).** Audiences love glamour, and *Evita* is one of the most glamorous of modern heroines. She's a woman who rose from poverty to become Juan Peron's wife and a powerful Argentinian figure in her own right. Her elegance and magnetism are emphasized when she tells a dress designer, "Christian Dior me, Lauren Bacall me."

Novel Adaptations

Shows based on classic novels are a Broadway staple. Al and I were nominated for a Best Score Tony for *Copperfield*, our Broadway version of Charles Dickens's *David Copperfield*. Lionel Bart turned another Dickens's classic, *Oliver Twist*, into the show *Oliver!* Rupert Holmes was inspired by an incomplete Dickens work to create *The Mystery of Edwin Drood*.

These great musicals all stem from classic books:

➤ *Ragtime* by Lynn Ahrens and Stephen Flaherty

➤ *The Scarlet Pimpernel* by Frank Wildhorn and Nan Knight

➤ *Jekyll and Hyde* by Frank Wildhorn and Leslie Bricusse

➤ *Phantom of the Opera* by Andrew Lloyd Webber, Charles Hart, and Richard Stilgoe

➤ *Big River* by Roger Miller

➤ *Candide* by Leonard Bernstein and Lillian Hellman

Play Adaptations

Dramatic plays or comedies are often changed into musicals:

➤ *Sweeney Todd* by Stephen Sondheim is based on Christopher Bond's *The Demon Barber of Fleet Street.*

➤ *Hello, Dolly!* by Jerry Herman is an adaptation of Thornton Wilder's *The Matchmaker.*

➤ The basis of *Do I Hear a Waltz?* by Stephen Sondheim and Richard Rodgers is *Time of the Cuckoo* by Arthur Laurents.

➤ Jerry Herman's *Mame* comes from *Auntie Mame* by Patrick Dennis.

➤ *110 in the Shade* by Harvey Schmidt and Tom Jones is a musical version of Richard Nash's play *The Rainmaker.*

Movie Adaptations

Movies have always been popular source material for composers, but now the trend is stronger than ever. For example, John Kander and Fred Ebb have created several shows from movies: *Woman of the Year* and *Kiss of the Spider Woman* are based on the movies of the same names, *Zorba* comes from the movie *Zorba the Greek,* and *Chicago* is based on the film *Roxie Hart.*

These musicals are also examples of movie adaptations:

➤ The film *Sunset Boulevard* inspired Andrew Lloyd Webber and Don Black to create the musical *Sunset Boulevard.*

➤ The film *Grand Hotel* became the musical *Grand Hotel* by Robert Wright and George Forrest, with additional music and lyrics by Maury Yeston.

➤ Frank Loesser's *The Most Happy Fella* is adapted from the film *They Knew What They Wanted.*

➤ *Promises, Promises* by Burt Bacharach and Hal David is based on the film *The Apartment.*

➤ *Applause* by Charles Strouse and Lee Adams is based on the film *All About Eve.*

➤ The musical *42nd Street* (music and lyrics by Harry Warren and Al Dubin, additional lyrics by Johnny Mercer and Mort Dixon) is based on the film *42nd Street.*

Backstage Banter

Frank Wildhorn is an established pop songwriter who composed Whitney Houston's "Where Do Broken Hearts Go?" Wildhorn makes certain his tunes have a life outside the musicals they're in by recording concept albums. In 1992, one of these concept albums, with songs from the upcoming *Scarlet Pimpernel,* featured Chuck Wagner, Dave Clemmons, Peabo Bryson, and Linda Eder.

Offbeat Adaptations

Ideas for musicals come from places as unexpected and diverse as cartoons, to famous art, to opera. *Annie* was a comic strip called *Little Orphan Annie*. The Stephen Sondheim musical *Sunday in the Park with George* was based on the pointillist art masterpiece *Sunday Afternoon on the Island of La Grande Jatte*. The rock musical *Rent* by Jonathan Larsen came from the opera *La Bohème*.

Shakespeare and the Bible

Shakespeare's plots are models of melodrama, action, and comedy, and songwriters have been turning to them for years:

➤ *Two Gentlemen from Verona* by Galt MacDermot and John Guare is a musical version of the Shakespearean play of the same name.

➤ *Your Own Thing* by Hal Hester and Danny Apolinar is their version of *Twelfth Night*.

➤ *The Boys from Syracuse* by Richard Rodgers and Lorenz Hart is an adaptation of *The Comedy of Errors*.

Backstage Banter

Sarah Jessica Parker of *Sex and the City* once played the lead in *Annie*.

Nothing beats the Bible for musical adaptation. Stephen Schwartz launched his career with *Godspell*. Andrew Lloyd Webber and Tim Rice have had much success with both *Jesus Christ Superstar* and *Joseph and the Amazing Technicolored Dreamcoat*.

Originals

Many composers would rather do musicals based on original stories than adapt proven properties. This approach is riskier, because producers usually seek protection from tried-and-true materials. Still, brilliant originals have achieved great success:

➤ *Falsettos* by William Finn

➤ *I'm Getting My Act Together* and *Taking It on the Road* by Gretchen Cryer and Nancy Ford

➤ *The Magic Show* and *Pippin* by Stephen Schwartz

➤ *Bells Are Ringing* by Jule Styne, Betty Comden, and Adolph Green

➤ *Into the Woods* by Stephen Sondheim

Get It on the Stage

Those who devote themselves to theater can't get enough of it. Theater people rush to see every possible production they can, musical or not. So should you. Don't attend just the highly publicized, expensive productions; see shows presented in 99-seat houses as well. College theater, community theater, high school and dinner theater can all provide exposure to a fine performance, an unusual orchestration, or a score you're not familiar with.

Once you've written a musical, you must get it on stage to analyze its virtues and weaknesses. Never mind where: a living room, a roof, or a restaurant will do. Only when you observe actors singing your words and music can you deepen your comprehension of lighting, costumes, scenery, and choreography. You'll then be able to rewrite without big money pressures and without temperamental stars to derail you.

Show Me the Money

Throughout theatrical history, composers have hired singers (or sung the material themselves) and put on a backer's audition. Sometimes studios or auditoriums are rented; other times the material is performed in a living room. Al and I raised money for both our Broadway shows by performing them in a director's home for different *angels*.

Lyrical Lingo

Angels, also known as backers, are those who write the checks for theater productions.

As a rule, however, you should hire a few other singers. It added extra tension to our presentation when we tried to play all the parts (especially with our Dickens piece, because Dickens is known as a writer with dozens of characters). The variety of voices makes everything much clearer to your listeners, all of whom are unfamiliar with your show.

Be sure you can explain the plot clearly and how your numbers fit into it, but don't interrupt the songs with overly lengthy explanations. Rehearse the presentation until it becomes second nature to avoid stuttering or stumbling. Finally, don't apologize for the lack of scenery or lighting. No one expects a full physical production. People can imagine a great deal, especially if your performance is simple, concise, clear, and to the point.

Hirschhorn's Hints

On the occasions when a show is not professionally done, you can sometimes learn more from the mistakes and avoid them in your own work. Try to pinpoint what the problems are and study why songs don't work and why certain lyrics slow up the action.

Do a Local Production

It's a mistake to think that local theater is consistently inferior to the highly budgeted productions. If you missed *Dreamgirls* the first time around, you'll still hear the songs and enjoy Michael Bennett's original concept in a converted garage. *A Chorus Line* in a relatively miniature format might gain intimacy that it lacked on Broadway.

Local theater is overflowing with talent. Exposure to it will inspire you, as a composer, and also give you a sense of how many modest avenues there are that provide launching pads for your own work.

Talk to theaters in your area and present your material. Find out if they're willing to put on a production of your show. If they will, you'll have access to a cast, musicians, director, and producer. Colleges, drama clubs, high schools, church groups, and dinner theaters are other outlets, and some of the shows they present are extraordinary.

Be a Talent Scout

Try your songs at parties and clubs. Work with singers who appear talented but haven't landed their first booking yet.

Trouble Clef

Never make the mistake of thinking that great talent is only on the Broadway stage. In doing a local production, you may discover a future star, someone who will excite high-level producers and turn your show into an appealing package.

When John Kander and Fred Ebb discovered Liza Minnelli, she was a novice, despite having Judy Garland and Vincente Minnelli as parents. Kander and Ebb created special songs for her, studied carefully what she did best, and helped her to spotlight her individuality and move out from the long shadows of her mother and father. With increasing fame, Oscars, and Tonys, Minnelli stayed with the composers who had seen her potential in the beginning.

Hold a Workshop

Organize a workshop. Gather actors together and develop your musical. Recently I workshopped a new show and was reminded again of how effective the process is. You can't get an accurate impression of the way the script plays or whether the songs and script are cohesively integrated until you watch it unfold before a live audience. Once you invite people to see the workshop production, you'll learn further what scores a bull's-eye and what needs correcting.

When you produce a workshop, watch for these common problems:

➤ Be alert for slow stretches when the audience begins to cough or squirm.

➤ Pay strict attention to a song that sounds beautiful on its own, but brings the story to a halt.

Trouble Clef

When a song doesn't fit, you can't make it fit. Irving Berlin wrote a song called "Mr. Monotony" for the movie *Easter Parade*. It slowed down the story. Then he put it in *Call Me Madam* and had to take it out when the show went on the road. Finally, it showed up in a compilation film, *That's Entertainment III*, and didn't work there either.

➤ Study your characters. Is one character too dominant, another too passive? Is a supporting player knocking out the audience with the best song, and your lead losing ground because he has the weaker numbers?

➤ Make sure your ending feels right. Is it too happy or too optimistic for the story that precedes it? Or is it too sad, leaving audiences depressed when they'd rather be elated? If you're honest with yourself, you'll feel those vibes.

➤ Is the show song-heavy? Or is it too "talky," in desperate need of a song or a dance sequence? Whatever the problem is, don't rationalize. Don't blame it on the actors or on a "bad" audience. Be open to problems and willing to fix them.

➤ Watch for second-act trouble. It usually means that the first act has failed to set up interesting plotlines that need resolving, or the second act may simply go on too long. Audiences grow more impatient as the evening wears on. Wind up the act fast.

Take It on the Road

If your show gains interest, be willing to take it to other towns and cities. In this video age, you should videotape all, or most of, the performances. Keep that video camera going, much the same way you keep your cassette recorder going when you compose. You may accidentally catch magic when one of your singers is practicing a number. Magic can't be predicted, so be ready to preserve it when it happens.

Cut a CD

Ideally, a well-produced CD of the musical's material will convey even more than live performance. You can do every song, but sometimes just recording the highlights is better. Include your big ballad, a couple of songs that establish your main characters, the opening of your show, and the closer. Make sure that your selections cover enough territory to make the basic story clear.

As in your commercial demos, be mercilessly strict with yourself about the choice of singers. This is not a time to let your friends participate (unless, of course, they're on a par with Audra McDonald or Brian Stokes Mitchell). Also, the singers should have acting ability and bear a resemblance to the character they're portraying.

Find Available Theaters

Theater Directory, published by Theater Communications Group, Inc., lists 335 not-for-profit professional theaters across the country. The listing includes address, business, and box office numbers, fax numbers, e-mail and Web site addresses, performance season, key personnel names (such as artists, management, and board members), and unit contract information. Underneath each listing is a heading, "Special Interests," which describes the kind of plays the theaters concentrate on. Target the ones that specialize in the type of show you've written and send them your music and synopsis.

The Producer's Viewpoint

Rob O'Neill, who has produced award-winning versions of *Sweeney Todd* and *A Little Night Music,* applies certain criteria when choosing a show to produce:

> "When I produced *A Little Night Music,* it was relatively easy to sell tickets, because the show had a specifically targeted audience, women who were going to see Dale Kristien and Amanda McBroom in the roles. I produced *Fiddler* knowing it would attract the whole family. I look for broad appeal, what the consumer is going to want in terms of tickets. The show doesn't always have to reach everyone, but it should appeal to one complete segment of the public."

Here is Marvin Hamlisch's opinion about the trend of today's theater:

> "Very family-oriented shows. A child will go to see *Beauty and the Beast* and want to see it again and again. So you're talking about two tickets and repeat business. But there's also room, and there's always been, for moving, important theater as well."

Hits from Shows

Broadway shows used to be an unending source of hit songs. *West Side Story* spawned "Maria" and "Tonight." Shows like *Guys and Dolls* ("I've Never Been In Love Before"), *Funny Girl* ("People"), *Gypsy* ("Small World"), *Oliver!* ("As Long As He Needs Me"), *The Bells Are Ringing* ("The Party's Over"), *Pajama Game* ("Steam Heat"), and dozens of other hits could be counted on to produce at least two or three chartbusters.

With the arrival of rock and roll, the kind of music included in Broadway shows of the past received less radio programming. But big hits can still emerge from today's Broadway musicals. *Cats* gave us "Memory." *Dreamgirls* produced "And I Am Telling You I'm Not Going." "Don't Cry for Me Argentina" came from *Evita.* "What I Did for Love"

Hirschhorn's Hints

Contact the Dramatist's Guild in New York for a list of important producers. Many of them will want your work to arrive through an agent, so focus your agent search with the same intensity. Two excellent sourcebooks to consult are *The New York Agent Book* and *The Los Angeles Agent Book* by K. Callan.

Hirschhorn's Hints

The road to Broadway is never easy, but the rewards are worth it. Marvin Hamlisch says, "There's a lot of money to be made from a hit show. In terms of a composer, tons more than a hit film. You get a percentage of the gross each and every week, in every town and country. You rarely, if ever, get percentages from movies."

was the showstopper in *A Chorus Line*. *A Little Night Music* introduced "Send in the Clowns," Stephen Sondheim's biggest hit as a solo composer/lyricist.

If you're writing a musical, try to create excitement about the score well in advance by releasing singles or a soundtrack before the musical is produced. The score for *Les Misérables* was first released as a best-selling double album. Andrew Lloyd Webber and Tim Rice offer an excellent example of using hit songs to garner interest in a musical. "Don't Cry for Me Argentina" and "High Flying Adored," two songs that later appeared in *Evita,* topped the charts before Webber and Rice approached Harold Prince to direct the musical. When the show opened in London and New York, the popularity of the songs helped *Evita* to become a hit.

Singles are only a small part of royalties a successful Broadway show can offer you. Hit soundtracks represent a lifetime annuity. Some recent hit soundtracks from Broadway shows include *Rent, The Phantom of the Opera, Les Misérables,* and *Big River.*

Special Material

Writing for popular in-person performers offers top training for the theater. Al's and my theatrical development was aided by writing special musical material for Zero Mostel, Charles Aznavour (including eight songs for Aznavour's one-man Broadway show), Ginger Rogers, Valerie Harper, and Liza Minnelli.

When you write such material, you'll quickly learn that you can't just string together a lot of tunes; your job is to develop an act that will capitalize attractively on every facet of the performer's personality. In other words, you're creating a character. You'll have to highlight their funny side, show their humanity, and give them numbers that express their emotional depth. You'll be forced to come up with specific, meticulously tailored lyrics and wean yourself of any tendency to turn out generalities.

Cleverness and wit are required. Once you've honed your ability to write humor, you're more than halfway home as far as theater is concerned. Sheldon Harnick of *Fiorello* and *Fiddler on the Roof* fame was told as a young struggling lyricist, "Don't worry about love songs or ballads. Anybody can write those. Write the special material, the comedy stuff, because that's hard to come by." Harnick heeded the advice, searching for offbeat ideas, and by the time he wrote his first Broadway musical, *The Body Beautiful,* he was a seasoned theatrical lyricist.

When you see stars in person or on television, get past the normal response of being dazzled by their personalities. Listen to what they're singing. Make note of the subject matter. Practice by writing tailored tunes and words for them.

If you know any local acts, submit your work. Up-and-coming performers desperately need good material, and they need an image. Maybe you can supply it.

The Least You Need to Know

➤ Songs for the stage have to create the illusion of reality, whereas songs for the screen have realistic settings.

➤ Musicals fall into 10 major categories.

➤ Showcase your musical at a local theater.

➤ Organize a workshop to learn where your musical needs improvement.

➤ Promote your musical with a CD, and take it on the road.

Part 4

Showing It Off

Learning how to make the right demo is just as important today as composing a smash song. You should cut demos so they have the impact of finished records.

Networking should be on your mind at all times. Everybody is a potential mentor, a potential contact, or a potential ally. Never offend the "little people" and save your charm for the people on top. Those little people are the ones who sometimes open the door to success.

Record production in someone else's studio or your own may seem mysterious and difficult at first, but it helps composers to become better at their craft.

Chapter 18

The Power of a Hit Demo

In This Chapter

➤ Piano-voice, guitar-voice, and other demo approaches

➤ Ways to locate the best vocalists and musicians

➤ How to make the most of your time in the studio

➤ Practical home equipment

➤ The demo package and presentation

Writing a song isn't enough. You have to convince others that it's a hit, and the only way to do that is by producing a strong demonstration record, or demo. A few composers still fight the idea of demos. They harbor the mistaken notion that they can present their songs in person to a publisher, producer, or artist. Unless you happen to be at a party or a social event and you have the opportunity to sit down at a piano and spontaneously showcase the material, in-person presentations won't yield desired results. Your chances of getting a record are much greater with demos than through in-person performances.

Even if an artist or producer listens to a personal performance of the song, that person will probably say, "I like it. Now do a demo so I can *really* hear it." In past decades, people trusted their ears. They had the imagination to envision a final record without every bit of musical and rhythmic detail spelled out. Few people have that sense of security anymore.

Publishers don't want the psychological discomfort of facing an eager songwriter and having to express their opinions directly. With a demo, they can play and replay the material, soaking it in and mentally working up production possibilities. From your point of view, a demo can also be a positive. You can embellish on your work in the studio and paint on the musical colors it needs.

Choosing Your Musical Approach

On the off chance that you *do* get to perform your songs in person, be well rehearsed. Don't stumble, say you have a cold, or clear your throat incessantly. Make sure the publisher, producer, or artist has a clear copy of the lyrics to read. Don't do more than three songs, preferably two. Don't try to force reactions before they're offered, and don't get defensive if the verdict is negative.

Hirschhorn's Hints

Remember, all responses are simply opinions, although some are more educated than others. Al and I performed a song called "Will You Be Staying After Sunday?" for a major publisher, and he said, "I'm sorry. It's definitely not a hit." After the song became a Top 10 record and sold a million copies, we ran into him on the street. He just shrugged and said, "We all make mistakes."

Demos can be sparse and simple or detailed enough to merit release as a master (a finished record). The kind of song you've written often dictates your demo approach.

Piano-Voice Demos

If you've written a beautiful ballad and hired a superb singer to perform it, the piano-voice demo will sometimes be enough. In a song of this kind, people want to hear the melody and words with complete clarity. Few ballads cry out for complicated production values. Remember, though, the piano has to be the whole orchestra. Whether you're doing the playing or you've recruited a studio pianist, the keyboard work must have as much body and dimension as possible.

Guitar-Voice Demos

Another simple demo approach is the guitar-voice demo. Again, this approach is best when you feel you've written an outstanding tune or lyric, and you want it to be strongly spotlighted. Guitars are naturally funkier than pianos; they convey a rhythm and blues or country feel more effectively than keyboards.

Voice with Piano, Guitar, Bass, and Drums

A guitarist, bassist, drummer, and pianist with a powerful lead vocalist and expert background singers are ideal for many demos. A setup of this kind offers clean, simple strength and will give you any groove you feel you need.

Cover Your Bases

When you make a demo, you want to be sure it has the broadest possible appeal. Yes, your main goal is to persuade Whitney Houston to do your tune, but Houston receives thousands of tunes, and your chances are slim. Why not open up new vistas in case she turns you down? One way to do that is to write a lyric that can be sung by both men and women. You can also use a solo singer for one version of the demo and a group of singers for another version.

Trouble Clef

A tastefully produced demo is preferable to an overproduced one. Don't get so caught up in the icing that you forget the cake. Your first priority is to show off the song, not to cloud it with too many instrumental figures or vocal parts.

Finding the Singer and Musicians

Everyone has a different idea of what matters most in a demo. To some, it's the orchestration; to others, it's the bass line. Drum parts are the lifeblood of demos to many. My feeling is that the singer must fit the tune and project what you hear, or the rest is irrelevant.

Choosing the Singer

Writers are remarkably careless when it comes to singers. Half the time they're considered as an afterthought. However, when we first presented our Oscar-winning "We May Never Love Like This Again" to the producer, he was so put off by the shrill Broadway-like interpretation of our singer that he nearly rejected the tune.

Fortunately, fate was on our side. He asked his secretary her opinion, and she said, "I think it's kind of pretty." He reluctantly accepted her evaluation and got the song in *The Towering Inferno*. This anonymous secretary rescued us and made our Oscar possible, but it was a close call.

➤ **Don't be fooled by a live performance.** Do not pick a singer on the basis of hearing him or her live. The visual impact of the singer's presentation may deafen you to how his or her voice sounds. Physical impact, expansive gestures, and personal charm can misguide you, no matter how keen an ear you have. Someone who prides himself or herself on holding big notes probably doesn't know how to let the microphone do the work. Insist on getting a tape or CD of your potential vocalist's voice.

➤ **Stars aren't everything.** Don't think you can have a hit only with stars. My own career is a case that proves the opposite. Two of our biggest hits were with unknowns. Our song, "Will You Be Staying After Sunday?" was composed with Gary Puckett in mind, and when Puckett turned us down, I was crushed. Shortly afterward, I was told that the Peppermint Rainbow was set to do the song. The Peppermint Rainbow? I mentally said good-bye to any success with the song, only to see it hit the Top 20 a few weeks later. Why? Because the record was superbly produced by Paul Leka, who later produced the number-one record, *Green Tambourine*.

Trouble Clef

Every singer excels in certain categories. A demo singer who specializes in country may not be able to rap or sing Latin-oriented rock with the authenticity of a Marc Anthony.

Picking the Right Musicians

The care you take in choosing a singer must be extended to musicians as well. As with vocalists, everyone has a specialty. Some musicians play brilliantly, but they can't read music. Others read parts at a glance, but they lack creative ideas and the ability to improvise. Some musicians want full lead sheets. The majority of musicians are content with just chords.

When possible, pick musicians who have played together in the past. You'll benefit immeasurably, both creatively and in terms of time saved, from the chemistry they've established and the unspoken communication and shorthand they've developed.

Locating the Best Players

If you're new to making demos and you need to connect with superior musicians, check out these places:

➤ **Your local musician's union.** The union will be more than happy to suggest people. In an era when live players are being supplanted by electronic music, the union is eager to get its members booked as often as possible.

Backstage Banter

Maureen McGovern had never cut a record when she did "The Morning After." Her version won an Oscar, went to Number One, and gave us the opportunity to compose a second Oscar-winning song. The key element to a hit song isn't getting a known star (although that can shorten the journey to chart status); it's having a great record to promote. And the route to a great record is a great demo that isn't so meticulously specific that any other performer is shut out.

➤ **Recording studios.** Get in touch with recording studios around town and learn whom they recommend. As you develop relationships with producers, studio owners, and engineers, ask them if you can sit in on their sessions. Not only will you become familiar with the finest players, you'll absorb invaluable studio procedure.

➤ **Visit clubs.** Speak to musicians and get their tapes.

➤ **Study CDs.** Comb the backs of CDs for musicians' names. All the players are listed there, with detailed information about their particular specialties. Look at the acknowledgements. In these sections, recording artists cite further useful information about guitarists, synthesizer players, drummers, or other individuals who have made a significant contribution to the record.

Backstage Banter

Garth Brooks started as a demo singer and is now one of the best-selling writers/artists we have. Bobby Darin's demo singing turned him into an international star, and Ronnie Dante (one of New York's busiest demo singers in the 1960s) became lead singer for the Archies and had a worldwide Number-One hit with "Sugar Sugar."

When You're the Artist

Many composers, such as the amazingly prolific Diane Warren, have no interest in becoming recording artists. Their main priority is writing the best possible songs with the greatest hit potential. You may be a freelancer like Warren, or you may have singer-songwriter aspirations. If so, demos are an excellent place to hone your skills and assemble a tape for presentation to a record label.

Figuring Costs

A few publishers exist who might like your work and be willing to foot the demo bill, but chances are more likely (unless you're already established and signed as a staff writer to a firm) that you'll have to invest in the demo yourself.

If demo costs are coming out of your own pocket, you'll probably be keeping close watch on what you spend. But if you're cutting a demo for a publisher who's paying for it, you need to watch costs as well. When you exceed the allotted budget the publisher has given you, the money you spend will be subtracted from your royalties if the song is eventually recorded.

Trouble Clef

I once worked with someone who felt that we should split the demo costs 30–70 because he had more experience in the business. Our collaboration didn't last very long. Be wary of suggestions like these. When you're writing a song together, 50–50 should be the split if the contributions are equal.

Royalties: Targeting Elvis

In the late 1960s, Al and I made up our minds to get a record by Elvis Presley. With consuming determination, we wrote song after song, submitting them to Elvis's publisher Hill and Range and gaining permission to do demos that Elvis and the Colonel would later evaluate. We spent freely, our minds trained on one thing: pleasing Elvis! We finally did it when Elvis came out with "Your Time Hasn't Come Yet Baby" and made it a worldwide hit. We waited for the royalties to pour in. Imagine our astonishment when the checks arrived, and a huge portion of our earnings had been subtracted to pay for the demo costs.

From that day forward, we watched our studio costs carefully. Every now and then we slipped because the studio atmosphere is hypnotic and seductive, but for the most part, we kept our demo budget within reasonable costs.

Prepare Now or Pay Later

Many writers prefer to "wing it," letting the creative process guide them when they get into the studio. Naturally, you'll fall upon fresh ideas and try new approaches when the session gets underway. But certain basics should be handled in advance to keep in-studio costs down:

➤ **The singer's key.** A surprising number of songwriters base the performer's key on his or her previous recordings, rather than making sure the key is absolutely perfect in the specific piece of material. Don't be satisfied if a singer says, "I'm always fine in the key of C." Each song is different.

Sometimes, when the sound isn't quite right, writers ask musicians to *transpose* the key. Many musicians are skilled at transposition, but others can do a good job only if the right chords are written out. That forces you, as the writer, to scribble out a new lead sheet with the altered key, and this process eats up studio time, which means money.

➤ **Nonprofessional vocalists.** When you have a limited budget, you may be tempted to compromise by using a friend or family member to sing your demos, but you have to be tough-minded. The reason why certain demo singers are repeatedly hired by successful songwriters is because these singers have studio savvy. They're quick, adaptable, and thoroughly professional, and they save time. Any money you save hiring a nonprofessional will be swallowed up by their lack of recording experience.

Lyrical Lingo

To **transpose** is to take a key and change it to another one; to take a song written in the key of C, for example, and write or play it in D.

Making the Demo

After you've planned the music for the demo, found the vocalist and musicians you'll be using, and figured your costs, you're ready to record your demo in a studio or at home. (If you have a home studio, see the section called "Demos at Home" later in the chapter.)

Choosing a Studio

Before picking a studio you haven't used before, ask for samples of other albums it has recorded. Analyze the sound it gets on its vocals. Sometimes, demos produced by the most highly praised studios can sound surprisingly thin or simply not right for the concept you have in mind.

Hirschhorn's Hints

A tiny studio without any reputation might give you exactly what you need. Ask for recommendations from friends and fellow songwriters.

Enlisting Creative Support

When you get the right musicians, you want to enlist their creative support. If possible, rehearse the singer beforehand. Never rule with an iron hand. Encourage a free, easygoing atmosphere. The record business is studded with instances in which a spontaneous solo turned the song into a smash.

As nervous or impatient as you may become, don't be overly critical. If someone makes a mistake, treat it lightly. Never go on the attack. If someone does a competent take that could still be improved, simply say, "That's terrific, but I'd like to give it one more try." When talented people are appreciated in the studio, they rise to unexpected heights. If they feel criticism, resentment will set in, and the results will be mediocre.

Staying Creatively Focused

In addition to being warm and open about suggestions, keep sharply focused on your own artistic vision. If you're new to making demos (and sometimes even when you're not), you can be swayed by experts into abandoning your original concept.

Remember that even experts are just volunteering opinions; nothing is written in stone. Even if you're recording your first demo, you may be on to something others don't grasp.

Holding Your Ground on Tempo

Never settle for a tolerably satisfying tempo. Don't accept a rhythmic pulse or groove because the engineer, the background singers, or even your own partner says it's okay. If you have that uneasy feeling in the pit of your stomach, listen to it. Otherwise, you'll find yourself at home a day later in a state of despair because the feel doesn't swing.

We once accepted a tempo that lost excitement, paradoxically, because it was too fast. Both the producer and the star were totally satisfied with it. The song was due for release a week later and represented a big opportunity for us. We pleaded, begged, cajoled. In the end, the producer agreed to try it our way, with the proviso that we were to shut up completely if the substitute tempo didn't work. It did, and the song was a Top 10 R&B hit.

We were taking a chance. By pressuring a producer we wanted to work with, we risked alienating him. But it's a worse risk to settle for something you know in your heart is a terrible mistake. If you believe in something, you'll never go wrong, in the long run, by fighting for it. So give the tempo your utmost attention whether you're making a demo or a *master*. The tempo is the lifeblood of commercial music.

Lyrical Lingo

A **master,** unlike a demo, is a completed record ready for release.

Handling Studio Disasters

Creative leadership in the studio means more than making proper artistic decisions. It means keeping your cool when problems arise.

Occasionally a musician you've hired won't show up. Stay calm. If it's a missing guitarist, the piano player might be able to fill in the part. A livelier bass line could compensate for the missing drums.

In this era of synthesizers, the absence of a musician is less serious, unless you're determined to do all the parts live. Of course, no synthesizer is going to replace a singer (at least not yet), so you might consider singing a temp track yourself until you can book someone to come in and do the part. Somehow, if you maintain a calm state of mind, the difficulty will resolve itself. With increasing expertise, you'll be surprised how capably you handle crises when they erupt.

Demos at Home

More and more, writers are purchasing their own equipment and recording songs at home. Obvious creative advantages include the luxury of working out parts by yourself by testing drum fills, guitar licks, or a piano line. You also have innumerable instruments at your disposal.

Suppose you're doing a rock record, but it suddenly occurs to you that a bassoon might lend something fresh and interesting: A lush woodwind section is one button away. Even if you decide to do the demo in a large studio later on (or finish it after recording basic tracks in your garage), you'll have a great head start, and you can test ideas without being stressed out by a ticking clock and escalating studio costs. For more about home studios, see Chapter 21, "Home Studio."

Upgrade Slowly

The trick with a home studio is to keep a sense of financial proportion, at least at the beginning. Once you enter the seductive synthesizer world, you'll want to continually upgrade your equipment. Countless composers have invested in machinery they can't afford, locking themselves further and further into debt.

Hirschhorn's Hints

Don't think that because a synth isn't new that it's not good. If you've done great things with your M-1, you don't have to give it away because something new is on the market. I still use most of my early equipment.

You don't need every state-of-the-art computer. You don't need to duplicate the setups of John Williams or Danny Elfman. Take it slow. As money and recognition trickle and, you hope, pour in, you can buy more synthesizers, sequencers, and drum machines.

Equipment changes with dizzying speed. Attend seminars, browse through stores, and ask questions. Study the equipment you see in studios or at the home studios of your friends.

Who Uses What

Gino Robair, journalist, author, musician, and specialist in setting up recording studios, points out that Roland's VS-1680 modular hard-disk recorder is capable of recording eight tracks simultaneously. "It can store 16-tracks of compressed audio or 8 tracks of uncompressed audio," says Robair, "and you can have up to 256 virtual tracks."

Hirschhorn's Hints

Let a day or two go by and listen to your mixes again minus the emotion of immediate recording. You'll know clearly at that time what needs to be subtracted or built up.

He also praises the following equipment:

➤ **The Yamaha EX5.** This keyboard waystation features 256 preset sounds, a 16-track sequencer, a 4-track arpeggiator, and reverb effects.

➤ **The Mackie 1-402-VLZ pro.** This unit features 14 input channels, as well as aux sends for effects and 3-band EQ on each channel strip.

➤ **Korg's D8 digital recording studio.** This 8-track, hard-disk recorder comes with a digital mixer and effects.

➤ **The Alesiss Q20 multieffects processor.** It includes four types of effects: EQ, reverb, pitch, and delay.

These descriptions are guidelines only. Equipment is a matter of taste and money. It's also a constant learning process.

Be a Maniac About the Mix

Once you mix a record, don't be immediately satisfied with it. The balance of ingredients in a studio, with the volume turned up to ear-splitting levels, can excite and fool you. Play a few different mixes in your car, on a boom box, or on a tiny tape player. You may suddenly notice that the vocal is buried or too loud, or the drums are overshadowing more delicate details such as a flute part.

Demo Presentation

When showing your demo to a publisher, producer, or artist, use these basic tips:

➤ Make sure your lead sheet looks professional. A sloppy, illegible lead sheet brands you as an amateur.

➤ Be meticulously careful in notating melody, chords, and rhythm. Don't write notes too close together, making lyrics crowded and unreadable.

➤ Never select a key that requires the use of numerous ledger lines. Making a reader follow the tune in C-sharp (which contains seven sharps) would be foolish.

➤ Write lyrics directly under the notes they belong to. Use a ruler and divide the measures evenly to prevent the possibility of mistakes.

➤ Use a dark pencil rather than a pen for the lead sheet.

➤ Always remember to include the key signature.

➤ If you feel insecure about writing the lead sheet, consult a copyist, musician, arranger, or friend who has the skill to do it right.

➤ Make sure you've included the copyright information.

➤ While the demo is playing, be quiet! Don't attempt to point out the song's virtues.

➤ If you're mailing the demo package, make sure you're sending the material to the right person at the company. Enclose a cover letter describing the songs. In the letter, let the producer or A&R person know your background, especially if you've had songs recorded.

➤ Label your CD or cassette properly.

➤ Target your material. Don't send the head of A&R a selection of your best work without including the singers the songs are for. Find out in advance which performers are heading to the studio and send them the songs prior to their sessions. It does no good to send a hit to Enrique Iglesias if he completed his album two weeks earlier and doesn't intend to record for another year.

➤ Make sure you enclose a stamped self-addressed envelope. Otherwise, the songs won't be returned.

➤ Include your name, address, telephone number, fax number, and e-mail address.

➤ If financially feasible, put the songs on CD rather than on cassette.

➤ Don't leave too much *leader* between songs, or your listener might get restless.

➤ In choosing the songs to spotlight, pick the ones you feel are the most powerful. Your first song should be the one you believe in most. It's no good if the third song is a hit; your listener won't get that far. Never include something you feel others "might like." You must be passionately convinced that each tune is the next big Grammy winner.

➤ Don't pressure your listener for an answer.

➤ Don't submit the only demo you have. Tapes are frequently misplaced or lost. Producers and artists expect you to have copies.

➤ Follow up a few weeks later. If you don't get an answer, wait two or three weeks more and then call again.

Lyrical Lingo

Leader is the word for empty stretches between songs on a cassette.

Songwriters of the past who presented their work on a piano or a guitar never had to dig deep into themselves to make a song more theatrical. They turned that responsibility over to an arranger. Today, you're required to be an arranger, a producer—a person who creates a whole musical canvas. Because you'll want to show off your song, you'll become more aware of rhythms, figures, vocal parts, and arrangements; and you'll learn more and more about how to put a song together. The exciting creative dividend of the modern music business is that it ensures that you will continue to grow as a composer and lyricist.

The Least You Need to Know

➤ Piano-voice and guitar-voice demos are often enough when the song is sufficiently strong.

➤ Budgeting carefully and preparing for studio time will save you heartache later.

➤ The best demos are made when a producer invites creative output from all participants.

➤ Making demos at home will give you extra time for producing, mixing, and experimenting with sounds.

Chapter 19

Becoming a Great Song Salesman

In This Chapter

➤ Write for attainable artists

➤ Understand the artist's personality

➤ Know what a good publisher does

➤ Choose whether to freelance or sign with a publisher

As a freelance songwriter who has made my living and my reputation writing for performers, I watched with dismay when singer/songwriters established dominance in the middle 1970s because freelancers found less and less opportunity to place their songs. But the pendulum swings back, and I'm delighted to say that freelance writers are regaining an enormous amount of the ground they lost.

To a great extent, this gain is due to the amazing efforts of one woman, Diane Warren. Warren is not a singer and has no interest in becoming one. She simply wants to have her material cut and to see her songs zoom to the top of the charts. Now on the verge of becoming the most successful songwriter in history, she has blazed a trail for freelancers everywhere.

Country outlets have always offered tremendous openings for freelance composers and lyricists (as Warren proved with "How Can I Live Without You?"). Now pop, R&B, and even rap are following suit. Whether you write freelance for artists or sign an exclusive contract with a publisher, you have more opportunities than ever before to sell your songs.

Casting Your Songs

Finding an artist to record your work can be complicated. Phil Collins is popular, but he's also a waste of time from a songwriter's standpoint because he records only his own songs. Madonna, who co-writes her material, is a remote possibility. If your material starts to circulate and gain acceptance, you might get a chance to write with her or with other stars who team up with writers they consider talented.

Trouble Clef

Do your homework and study available performers and the kinds of songs they're recording, or you're asking for rejection. Worse, once a producer sees that you've submitted illogical material to his or her artist, you can expect a pass on what you send later, even when it's ideal.

Your chance is best with an artist who takes outside material. Search *Billboard*'s Hot 100, and you'll come up with something like this entry:

> Lesson in Leavin'
> Jo Dee Messina
> Producers: B. Gallimore, T. McGraw
> Writers: R. Goodrum, B. Maher

The entry would tell you that Messina is an artist who's available to you if you have the right song.

Make sure any material you send artists is appropriate for their style. If you wanted a recording by country superstar Tim McGraw, for example, you wouldn't send him a rap song more suitable for Eminem. Seems obvious, doesn't it? But new writers send material to wildly inappropriate people. Half the time, they just ship it out to a dozen artists without regard to the artists' specific needs.

Ricky Martin Is on Tour

There's no point in writing for Ricky Martin if he's just finished an album and won't be cutting a new one for the next eight months. You have to investigate who's coming up for a date and needs material immediately by calling record companies and checking out tip sheets such as the following that announce this information:

➤ *New on the Charts*
  1501 Broadway
  New York, NY 10036
  212-921-0165

➤ *Parade of Stars*
  The Chellman Bldg.
  1201 16th Avenue South
  Nashville, TN 37212
  615-320-7270

➤ *Song Connection*
12390 Chandler Blvd. #C
N. Hollywood, CA 91607
818-763-1039

➤ *Song Placement Guide*
Marcia Singer
PO Box 189
Pacific Palisades, CA 90272
213-850-3606

➤ *Songwriter's Market*

➤ The Los Angeles Showcase *Musepaper*

➤ *Billboard*'s Talent and Touring Agency

➤ The National Academy of Songwriters Newsletter

➤ Nashville Songwriter's Association International

Combing *Billboard* with care will also give you a good idea of the artists' schedules. Meeting producers is another route to artists because producers frequently write for their artists and often collaborate.

Listen to the Artists' Records

After you've selected your artists, listen to at least three of their CDs and all of their singles. Try to find common denominators in their material. Are there intervals they always seem to favor? Octave leaps? Blues notes such as flatted thirds? What rhythms seem to predominate? Do their tastes run mostly to ballads?

As for personality, are they victims, or do they take over? Are the themes of their songs more often heartbreak, or are the songs about free spirits who don't get tied down? Once you make these determinations, you don't have to follow them with clinical precision, but they will give you a sense of what the artists are like, what they try to express, and what their musical capabilities are.

When you first listen to their songs, don't study them. Listen a second time and then a third. At that point, start your analysis. Without a single fact about an artist, without knowing where he or she was born or went to school or whether he or she has any sisters, you'll discover the essence of that person through his or her music. Music reveals just as much about individuals as facts do.

Personal Casting That Worked

My career has been amazingly diverse. I didn't plan it that way; I was a freelancer, and my success depended on getting many songs recorded, so I recognized the necessity of being versatile. The following is a list of artists who cut my songs and a description of how the recording happened.

My first approach was always to pretend I was the artist. Anyone with imagination can do it. No matter how superficially people may differ on the surface, all of us have universal needs, dreams, and feelings in common.

➤ **Taj Mahal:** "Give Your Woman What She Wants"

I knew that my lyrics had to have a raw, funky, bluesy edge. Slickness would have turned this artist off immediately. He also projects a natural sexuality, which I capitalized on with these lines:

> Give your woman what she wants
> and she'll never leave your side.
> Give your woman what she needs
> And she'll be satisfied.

➤ **The Chambers Brothers:** "Wake Up"

In 1970, when this song was recorded, the civil rights movement was at its height. Marvin Hamlisch and I felt that tapping into that problem was timely and important. Marvin wrote a gospel-oriented tune and I provided a lyric that urged everyone to wake up to society's injustice.

➤ **Julian Lennon:** "Is There Anyone?"

Julian, despite rock and roll aspirations and his father's image, has a soft, sensitive voice, and Al and I thought of him when writing this ballad. It was the kind of song we had a hunch he'd be drawn to, and he was. He recorded it in a television special, *David Copperfield*.

Backstage Banter

To our surprise, Al and I were told that Fred Astaire was planning to cut an album. We knew, as longtime fans of Astaire's movies, that he was smooth, polished, and elegant, and that any material we submitted would have to correlate with that persona. We submitted "The Old-Fashioned Way," an adult, romantic song we had co-written with Charles Aznavour, and we had the thrill of hearing Fred Astaire do it on his album, *Attitude Dancing*.

➤ **Maureen McGovern:** "We May Never Love Like This Again"

Maureen had just scored a number one with "The Morning After," and Al and I knew, without being told, that she would want to cut another big, passionate ballad.

➤ **David Allan Coe:** "You Can Count on Beer"

Anyone who could sing "Take This Job and Shove It" would, we felt, be receptive to a good-old-boy, tough-talking, hard-driving song, so we tailored one, and Coe sang about telling all his troubles to those bright golden bubbles.

As you can see, we didn't just send out tunes indiscriminately to *publishers*. We concentrated intently on who the artists were, what they represented to the public, and what message they were trying to convey.

Selling to a Publisher

A publisher who believes in you and has a passion for your music is worth his or her weight in gold. The fact that the publisher takes care of the business leaves you with time to do what you enjoy most: create.

The Right Publisher

Just because publishers are listed in books or trades, don't assume they can get records easily. Some publishers are extremely active in approaching artists and securing recordings, but many just acquire catalogues and let performers or film companies come to them for the use of the old material. Check to see what the publisher is doing with current songs written by others and whether any well-known composers and lyricists are on staff.

Staid, older, wealthier firms are unlikely to hustle the way that hungry new firms do. There's no point in allying yourself with a publisher who won't promote your work.

Lyrical Lingo

A **publisher** is the firm or individual you enlist to promote your song or song catalogue to record producers and artists. The publisher also handles synchronization licensing, which includes placing your material in films, on television, or in commercials. Publishers collect the money for songs they license and split the royalties with their writers. The split is generally 50–50.

Good publishers always know what's going on. Naturally, they're aware of when Shania Twain plans to record, but they also know about sessions with newcomers. These performers are the ones you might not notice in your zeal to get a cut by Enrique Iglesias. Remember, hit groups and artists were once beginners too, and they smashed through with talent, dedication, and promotion.

In our catalogue, we had our share of forgotten artists, such as Bobbe Norris, Rochelle, Wayne Rooks, Bob and Joe, and the Peppermint Trolley Company. We also had newcomers who hit it big like The Peppermint Rainbow and The Glories. Also keep in mind: Records released by new people, even when they don't make it, still garner airplay, and your BMI and ASCAP checks will reflect that.

Publishers with Production Companies

A publisher who also produces has a quicker, more direct route to getting records. Early in my career, I was a staff writer for Bob Crewe, producer of such Four Seasons hits as "Rag Doll," "Let's Hang On," and "Dawn." Bob had the power, if he liked something, to put it on the recording date. Within the first month, Al and I had a recording by Lesley Gore, and many others followed. We also worked with Phil Kahl and Joe Kolsky, publishers who produced Ronnie Dove. Phil and Joe cut "Let's Start All Over Again" and "One More Mountain to Climb" with Ronnie, and both became hits.

What Good Publishers Do for You

Publishers who get things done are tireless. They have a list of contacts, and they phone them constantly. When they're not shopping songs, they're having lunch with producers and forging relationships. They attend recording dates even when their own songs are not being cut, and they develop a street feel for what producers want.

A good publisher does these things for you:

Hirschhorn's Hints

Don't pay attention only to the publishers themselves; study the people they have working for them, such as their general professional manager and others on their staff. They may be the ones who cover the street and service your songs.

➤ **Picks the song.** The publisher's role, first and foremost, is to choose songs he or she feels can be recorded and turned into hits. You'll know fairly quickly if the individual you're meeting with has a particular enthusiasm for your material. If he or she says, "This stuff isn't for me, but bring me more," look upon that as a highly promising sign. Keep submitting. Listen to the publisher's viewpoints. Find out the type of material he or she prefers to promote. Keep your ear open for the kind of demos he or she considers effective. Good publishers meet with their staff at least once a week, go over the material in their catalogue, decide which songs are to be pushed, and then concentrate on those particular tunes.

➤ **Follows up on holds.** When artists and producers like a song, they ask for a *hold*. Publishers generally grant this request, but the hold has to be reasonable. After a few weeks or a month (or longer when the artist is exceptionally hot), publishers have to keep checking to see whether the song is going to be recorded. If no definite plans have been made, a publisher will ask for the tune back in order to send it to other singers. You want someone who will keep on top of the song and not drop the ball until all enthusiasm for the material has waned.

Lyrical Lingo

A **hold** is a period of time requested by the producer to consider the song, with the understanding that it will not be shown to anybody else during that period.

➤ **Nurtures contacts.** To be effective, publishers need a list of contacts, a list they're constantly adding names to. The best ones know that there are hundreds of outlets for songs beyond those that seem obvious. These lists are compiled through years of bonding with producers, artists, and arrangers. Hustling publishers will fly to Philadelphia or Miami or Rome on a moment's notice to hear an artist perform, if that artist has done the publisher's material in the past. Relationships are nurtured and tended. If an artist is demanding and has a habit of calling at 3 in the morning just to talk, your publisher must listen to the artist's nocturnal ramblings and express an interest, no matter how exhausted he or she may be.

➤ **Gets your song on the radio.** Say you have the record. Now you need to get it played. Publishers promote their songs with program directors, and after a record is on the air, publishers chart its progress. Often, they struggle to persuade stations to keep the records on because newer ones (possibly by bigger artists) are competing fiercely for a few choice slots.

➤ **Promotes covers.** Good publishers don't forget songs once they've been recorded. If your record by Mo McGuire doesn't hit, your publisher will take the song to another artist, and if that cut doesn't score, and he or she truly believes in the song, the publisher will shop it to a third artist. Some publishers get a dozen recordings of a tune before the right record catapults it to the top.

➤ **Handles subpublishing.** Rarely does a writer think beyond the United States, but good publishers do. They have subpublishing deals with other firms in England, France, Germany, and Japan. They'll work a song until cuts start showing up in other languages. Their efforts will lead to printed editions of your work where the sheet music is released individually or as part of a songbook.

➤ **Shows you the money!** Through contacts and experience, publishers are able to collect the *mechanicals* due you (and them). This collections expertise is an important consideration, because record companies would always rather pay later rather than right away; a good publisher has the clout to speed up the process.

Should a publisher choose to accept your song, he or she may either pay for a demo, give you an advance, or both. When Al and I began, we lived off advances of $200 here, $300 there. To be able to live off our advances, we had to write three or four songs a week. Poverty makes a writer prolific.

Lyrical Lingo

Mechanicals are royalties that come from the record company and are for record sales only, not for performances.

Working for a Publisher

I'm a speed typist and former court reporter. I didn't want to make that my life's work, but the skills came in handy when I got a job as assistant/writer for Ivan Mogull Music. Between my clerical responsibilities, I turned out such tunes as "You'd Better Know What You're Getting Into," an early record for Patti Austen. I had an opportunity to study the business firsthand and see how it worked, and I was able to pay my bills.

You don't have to be an assistant. If you have the right assertiveness and personality, you can be a professional manager, taking songs around to artists and producers. You won't necessarily be promoting your own material, but you'll meet everybody who counts in the business.

Sign with a Publisher or Freelance?

Security is attractive, and if a publisher offers to sign you to an exclusive contract, you might be tempted to grab it. "Just think," you may say to yourself, "with no money worries I'll be able to create in a relaxed, pressure-free atmosphere." Yet publishing your songs yourself also has advantages.

Signing Up

Signing with a publisher sounds good, but before you put your name on the dotted line, examine the long-range implications of the arrangement, good and not-so-good:

➤ **R-E-S-P-E-C-T.** You don't have to love your publisher, but you do have to respect him or her. Is the person in tune with the current tastes and trends of the market? You don't want a publisher to say, as one did to me when I was considering an exclusive contract, "These kids today are just making noise. Give me Jerry Vale."

➤ **Your own headquarters.** Being signed gets you off the street. You have an office of your own and access to musical instruments, computers, stationery, phones, fax machines, and e-mail. That's a tremendous advantage, if it doesn't offer so much structure that you lose your cutting edge. If you do accept such a setup, be sure you get out where your fellow writers are. When you're building a career, stability isn't your prime goal.

➤ **Musical siblings.** When Carole King, Gerry Goffin, Barry Mann, Cynthia Weil, Howie Greenfield, and Neil Sedaka were signed to Don Kirshner at Screen Gems Music, an atmosphere of friendly rivalry existed. It was a rivalry Kirshner did nothing to discourage. This competition drove everyone in the office to greater heights. The presence of other songwriters pursuing the same artists will give you extra incentive.

➤ **Who gets the publishing?** A conflict may arise when someone offers you a movie job but tells you that they have to have all the publishing. Motion picture companies are always reluctant to surrender a piece of their copyright, and the same goes for television. The publisher who pays your salary certainly isn't going to let you do a project that doesn't bring the firm any revenue. So you'll very likely be forced to turn down the opportunity. Factor this potential conflict into your decision before signing any exclusive agreement.

➤ **Typical deals.** When a new writer is signed, $200 to $400 is a typical weekly stipend offered. Hit songwriters earn a good deal more. This money is not a salary, but an advance against future earnings. If you do write a hit record while you're signed with a firm, the advances will be subtracted from record sales (not BMI or ASCAP airplay), and you'll be paid the remainder.

Trouble Clef

In what area has your publisher had success? If most of his or her contacts are with middle-of-the-road artists and you're interested in country, it won't make sense to sign with that publisher. Make certain your priorities are the same.

Backstage Banter

Publisher Michael Brettler of Shapiro, Bernstein, and Company says that he looks for quality, someone who's prolific, and someone who's aggressive and will make additional connections.

If you've signed a song over to a publisher, don't sit back and decide that it's the publisher's job to sell the song and there's no need for you to pitch in. Writers have to help themselves. There's never a time when you should place total responsibility on someone else when you have the energy and resources to push your material. Try to imagine the assertive Diane Warren taking a back seat and giving all the power to someone else. Publishers, in general, appreciate your help, but you should be in constant touch with them so you don't see the same people they do and create confusion.

Doing Your Own Publishing

Hirschhorn's Hints

Once a producer or artist makes a firm commitment to record the song, it's customary to take the song out of circulation until after the record has run its course.

If you're a good promoter, with a talent for casting and pitching, you may not need a publisher. Many songwriters find they have the ability to get records on their own steam. If that's the case, you're in a far stronger financial position than songwriters who are signed to publishers.

As your own publisher, you have a perfect right to show your song to as many people as you choose to. You also get to keep your publishing rights, which doubles your income. It places you in a far more flexible position. A major artist usually wants a piece of the publishing, and if you own it yourself, you're in a position to give it to the artist or at least negotiate a split that's mutually agreed upon.

Creative Selling

Paul Jabara, who wrote the Donna Summer/Barbra Streisand number-one duet "Enough Is Enough" and Streisand's "The Main Event," was determined to sell his songs. When ordinary routes failed, he went to extremes. Reputed to have locked Donna Summer in the bathroom so he could play her a song, he also said, "You have to have a plan of action. That may mean finding out what plane he (the producer) is flying on and booking yourself on that flight. If you're that aggressively into wanting to make it, you'll pursue that moment and find it."

Whether you sign with a publisher or freelance, if you believe in a song, keep pitching it. The Everly Brothers' "Bye Bye Love" was turned down by 30 people before the duo cut it.

The Least You Need to Know

➤ Target artists who are available.

➤ Study every facet of the artist's records.

➤ You must respect the publisher you sign with.

➤ Choose a publisher with wide and varied contacts.

➤ Self-publishing is fine if you're a good promoter.

Chapter 20

The Singer/
Songwriter

In This Chapter

➤ What to look for in an agent, manager, and entertainment lawyer

➤ A legendary record executive's view of what makes a successful singer/
songwriter

➤ Ways to get the media behind you

➤ Major and minor record labels

➤ A career in cabaret

Do you have singing talent along with a gift for writing? If so, it's worth developing. Freelance songwriters, even writers as prolific and successful as Diane Warren, always have to depend on others to cut their material.

The Elton Johns and Billy Joels of the world have the luxury of writing and enjoying a guaranteed outlet for the work. Even though their labels or their producers might voice objections from time to time, these singer/songwriters basically hold the power to immediately put new songs on CDs and take pleasure in guaranteed releases.

If you're convinced that you can be a successful singer/songwriter, and you're ready to dedicate yourself to a recording career, start lining up a support system that will help you reach the top. You may not find the right agent or manager immediately. While searching, book yourself as many gigs as you can. It will give you a chance to work out the kinks in your act, polish your presentation, and find out which songs work best with an audience. By the time agents or managers see you, you'll be the kind of total professional they're eager to sign.

What Makes a Good Agent?

When you sign with an agent, be sure that agent's commitment to your career is total. A half-hearted representative who pushes you only when others have already expressed excitement is no asset.

Trouble Clef

If you suspect that your singing talent is minimal, don't push yourself as an artist simply because you want an outlet for your songs. Be committed to singing for its own sake. Not all songwriters are star vocalists. Observe with as much objectivity as possible the reactions of those around you. Ask yourself: Do I have what it takes to be a singing star? Am I willing to make the required sacrifices?

There's a cliché that says "Don't depend on an agent to get you a job." I don't buy that. Nor do I buy the old bromide "Agents don't get you work, but they can negotiate a deal for you." When you're starting out, you need someone to hustle and land you gigs. You can help, of course, and you should help. But you shouldn't have to do it alone, not if you're shelling out 10 percent of your earnings. After you've gained recognition, there will always be people who can negotiate contracts. You can be sure that Marty Erlichman, Barbra Streisand's representative of over 35 years, didn't get that position without working up a sweat to help his client. Nor did he sit back after she made it.

Whether you go with a small or a big agent, make sure your agent won't be insecure and undersell you so that you're knocking yourself out for practically nothing. If the agent accepts jobs that pay too little, there should be a specific reason. Possibly the exposure is important, and people who count will see you. You also want somebody who knows how to pace your career without burning you out by overbooking you. Your agent has to view you as a human being, not a machine he or she can use to make a few extra bucks.

Small Agencies

The advantage in signing with a small agency is that its client list is not so extensive that you get lost in the shuffle. If you're heckling your agent and so is Will Smith, who will be listened to first? Your agent might be just as new and hungry as you are, and even though he or she hasn't established all the contacts in the world, a powerful desire to promote you will compensate.

The Big Enchiladas

The large, major agencies have more contacts, more money, and more power. Major agencies represent artists in every field: films, television, commercials, concerts, and records. They have close relationships with record labels, and a single call from them can get you the attention you need.

Managers

Personal managers handle different functions than agents. Unlike the agent who books you, a manager isn't expected or legally permitted to get you jobs. Only your agent can do that. But the manager handles just about everything else: contracts and promotion, the shopping of CDs and cassettes, and a marketing strategy. Above all, a good manager should supply an overall approach to your career. You'll have ideas of your own, of course, but you and your manager should work together to conceive and act on a workable plan.

Hirschhorn's Hints

Try to find a manager who's good at discovering your various other gifts and wants to develop them. Many singers and writers can also act, write scripts, produce, direct. A manager should never be shortsighted. You want a person who pulls things out of you that you never even knew were there.

Mutual Obsession

If a manager has sufficient belief in you, you could literally become his or her life and vice versa. An intense bond based on the mutual need to succeed could form. These relationships are a combination of friendship, desire, and a dedication that obliterates everything else in your lives. A manager who makes you such a top priority will attend performances he or she considers crucial to the building of your reputation. Count yourself lucky if you find someone with a drive that matches your own, a drive that centers on you.

I Just Want to Be Your Everything

Daylle Deanna Schwartz, author of *The Real Deal*, quotes an excellent definition of managerial participation by Peter Ciaccia (PC Management):

> "A manager winds up being everything to the acts ... the A&R person, the publicist. A manager has to make good judgment calls for the band. He is the liaison between the artist and the record company. When a band is unsigned, he works with them from the beginning to find a home for them. He's out there selling the band, selling the image and music of the band. He has to have a good sense of what the market calls for, what would interest people, and how to get to the people. He creates a realistic buzz about the band ... he has to be tied to the street."

A Lawyer You Can Trust

Although the multitudes of lawyer jokes would have you believe otherwise, many hardworking, honest, effective attorneys exist. Just don't jump for the first one you meet. Attorneys are necessary because they have more information and experience than you do, and the old saw "A man who represents himself has a fool for a client" is still valid.

Backstage Banter

For total involvement in advancing your career, managers usually earn between 15 and 25 percent. Contracts are often for 3 years, but they may run for as long as 5 or even 10.

You Gotta Shop Around

Even if you meet an attorney who impresses you and whose expertise is in entertainment law, check him or her out (just as you would a doctor). Find out how much the attorney knows about the following areas:

➤ Publishing

➤ Performance rights, foreign rights, and recording

➤ Current copyright laws

Don't Be Frightened by Fees

When I started in the music business, I met an attorney who quoted me fees that almost provoked cardiac arrest. But the attorney saw potential in me. I had just signed a contract with RCA as a recording artist, and four of my songs were about to be recorded. This situation was no guarantee of a Beatles-type explosion, but it indicated the possibility of an enduring future.

He and I decided on a percentage of future earnings. My records sold minimally at first. Yes, I could have made 10 million and given away a huge chunk of income, but it was just as likely (or more so) that I wouldn't even get on the charts at all. Settling on a percentage was a gamble, but it removed my initial anxieties about costs and made it possible for me to have good representation when I needed it. He also had strong industry contacts and arranged introductions that furthered my career.

Do You Have What It Takes?

Do you have a target audience? A certain style? Charisma? Enough songs to attract a top record label?

Who Are Your Future Fans?

Are your targeted audiences made up of 13-year-olds? Do you covet the college crowd? Or is your music tailored to 30-somethings? It's not enough to say, "I want to appeal to everyone." Dr. Dre has his public, just as Clint Black, Christina Aguilera, and the Dixie Chicks have theirs. They're not the same.

You may have a clear, fully formed concept of how you want to be perceived. If not, you have to invent yourself. Bruce Springsteen was a more passive, folk-oriented performer before he became a forceful, physical, sexual "boss."

What Do You Look Like?

In today's visually oriented music world, appearances count. You don't have to be handsome or beautiful in the classic movie star sense, but you do need an individual look, an offbeat style of dressing. Depending on the audience you hope to attract, you might want to wear big hats or suspenders. Or you might wear dark glasses, green eye shadow, or a nose ring. Regardless of how conservative or far-out your garb is, you need a look to distinguish you from your competitors.

Hirschhorn's Hints

When you make a video, think it through carefully. You must come across as colorful, fascinating, and idiosyncratic. If you're an excellent dancer, work that in. Find a unifying theme, rather than just going through a bunch of unrelated images.

Russ Regan's Rules

Producer/record label president Russ Regan discovered and promoted Elton John, Neil Diamond, and The Beach Boys to super stardom. Regan has the following to say about the careers of singers/songwriters:

> "Singers/songwriters have to have charisma. And intelligence! I love an artist who has charisma and is smart, because if he's smart, he can handle success. Those qualities were obvious in Elton John. He was electrifying on stage, a combination of great songs and a fantastic stage presence.

> "When you're just a songwriter and you go to a publisher, you don't want to overwhelm him with songs. You're selling the music, not yourself. But a singer/songwriter is different, because you're being judged as a potential album artist. When a singer/songwriter comes to me, I want to hear at least five songs. You can't really judge an artist on one or two anymore, you've got to hear five.

> "And the other thing is, the more you write—if you have talent in the first place—the better you become. As for demos, I personally don't mind piano-voice. I can hear a song, because I'm a song person. But a lot of people like full-blown demos. I'm an exception. It would be wiser and safer for a new singer/songwriter to do a demo that gives a complete idea of what the record will be like."

Feed the Media Monster

Certain singers/songwriters have an innate sense of how to handle the press. They know when to be outrageous, when to be humble, and when to be controversial. Madonna went from sexual shock tactics to spirituality and motherhood. Elvis was a master in his day, doing raunchy bumps and grinds on stage and talking offstage about his beloved mom and his ties to the church.

Until you become the next Elvis or Madonna, though, you'll have to continually feed the media:

➤ **Do interviews.** Prior to any performance, advance pieces should be set up to tout club or concert appearances. These pieces are often more effective than reviews at drawing public interest, especially if the reviews don't turn out to be raves. Meeting journalists face to face is preferable, but most of the time you'll be doing *phoners,* telephone interviews that rarely last more than 15 minutes. As you grow more adept at phoners, you'll become skilled at packing in the relevant information. Pertinent facts will roll off the tip of your tongue.

Hirschhorn's Hints

Utilize theatricality in your press releases and press kits. Demos, videotapes, articles, reviews, and pictures should be included. All newspapers and magazines, as well as deejays and heads of radio programming, expect these materials.

➤ **Use exclusives.** Depending on how far along you are in your career, you might land an exclusive, a highly visible spot in *The New York Times,* for example, or one of the other major newspapers. Press conferences also have value, although they generally only allow for sound bites and provide sketches of a performer's personality, rather than a full portrait.

➤ **Hire a publicist.** Good publicists are expensive and hard to find. You can't judge one by all the coverage he or she secured for the Backstreet Boys. A publicist once proudly told me (with a straight face) that he had gotten layouts all over the country for Paul McCartney. This is no achievement. When publicists are able to take relative unknowns (or just-rising singers) and get them impressive spreads, it shows that they have clout with the press.

➤ **Go national.** Don't discount the need for publicity, however, if you can't afford to hire a PR person or firm. Don't just don't settle for the *Podunk Herald* or a television station in a small Nebraska community. Unless you're seen and promoted in the big cities, publicity won't do a thing for your profile.

➤ **Try for top billing.** Your manager will always fight for better billing, and should. People do raise their estimation of your worth as your billing escalates. But don't insist on being a headliner right away; being an opening act for a major star also reflects favorably on you.

Backstage Banter

Elvis Presley was asked to do *A Star Is Born* and he refused because he couldn't bear to be billed second to Barbra Streisand. At the time, his film career was foundering. As the burnt-out rock star, he would have been superb and would have given the picture a hot, gritty realism. Always ask yourself: How good is the gig, how big is the booking, how instrumental will it be to your career?

Signing with a Label

There's no doubt that a singer/songwriter gets less personal attention from a major label than from a minor one. The major label compensates by having more resources at its disposal. The obvious one is large amounts of money to spend on promotion. Their distributors are more powerful. Staffs are larger, and video budgets are handsome by comparison with the independents.

The Majors

A major-league label has many advantages to offer:

➤ **Marketing department.** Publicity, promotional videos, in-store displays and album cover artwork are the responsibilities of this department.

➤ **A&R department.** This group decides which artists to sign after listening to their demos or seeing them in person. They supervise record projects and suggest or select producers for their acts.

➤ **Sales department.** This department's job is to get records into stores.

➤ **Promotion department.** This department follows the record when it's released and makes sure that it has maximum airplay.

➤ **Business affairs.** Their priority is contracts between the singer/songwriter and record label, but also with record clubs and foreign distributors.

Hirschhorn's Hints

Make extensive use of the Internet by visiting Web sites and getting information about the labels you're interested in signing with. Be sure you know the names of the A&R people responsible for acquiring new artists.

Even if you prefer to sign with a large company, though, that company may not be eager to sign you before they see early signs of success. Local hits or hits stemming from smaller labels will attract them.

The Minors

A minor label will see you as more of an individual human being. The purse strings will be tighter, but it's entirely possible that the financial output, though more selective, can accomplish just as much.

Suppose your manager gets an offer from one of the lesser labels and tries to talk you into signing. Receiving the offer might thrill you so much that you want to sign that afternoon. Think twice. Is your manager suggesting this deal because he or she has contacts with this company, and the negotiation is easy? If you have dreams of being with Columbia, take your time before committing to Nobody Records.

Come to the Cabaret

When we think of singer/songwriters, rockers are generally the images that come to mind. But other singer/songwriters represent a fast-growing and hugely popular genre. They don't get mentioned in *Billboard,* but they have die-hard fans in small clubs around the country. They are cabaret artists.

Backstage Banter

Michael Feinstein's career demonstrates what going the cabaret route can achieve. Feinstein became an assistant and personal confidante of Ira Gershwin and a protégé of Rosemary Clooney, establishing himself as a highly admired inter–preter of the Gershwin classics. A worldwide cabaret performer, he has now opened his own cabaret club, Feinstein's, in New York.

Cabaret performers appeal to the more sophisticated segment of the population. They do Cole Porter, Lorenz Hart, Noel Coward, and Stephen Sondheim. Very often they write their own witty and brilliant material.

Amanda McBroom, who wrote the million-selling standard and Golden Globe winner "The Rose" for Bette Midler, has become one of the key cabaret performers of the new millennium. She starred in *Jacques Brel Is Alive and Well and Living in Paris* at New York's Village Gate and has seen her songs recorded by Judy Collins, Anne Murray, Harry Belafonte, The Manhattan Transfer, and Betty Buckley. McBroom's CD, *Portraits,* contains such beautiful and definitive cabaret songs as "Best Friend," "Errol Flynn," "Whoever You Are," and "Ship in a Bottle."

The progression of McBroom's career is a textbook example of a cabaret singer's/songwriter's climb to fame, as you'll see by the following interview I did with her:

Q. How did you become a cabaret artist?

A. I had been a theater singer, done a lot of musicals, folk singing throughout high school and college. I wanted to do songs that would express my personal feelings and have them performed. A friend of mine who had an act at the Bla Bla Café sang some of my material, and I got it into my head to do a nightclub act.

Q. How would you define a cabaret singer?

A. There are two different kinds. One is a preserver of the tradition, which is the people who sing Jerome Kern, George Gershwin, people like Julie Wilson. Then there are the others, like me, those that write for the theater, or intend to, and find the cabaret a perfect forum for their work. The modern sophisticated balladeers are cabaret songwriters.

Q. How do you feel about rock and roll?

A. I love it, but I feel cabaret suits me better. Cabaret material is what I write best.

Q. Do you play an instrument?

A. I play three: piano, drums, and guitar.

Q. What's the advantage of being a cabaret singer/songwriter?

A. It's very spiritually rewarding. If you're a cabaret singer, my advice is, "Don't put a label on yourself." Write what your heart believes. It will find its niche, whether cabaret, rock, garage metal.

Q. What's your writing process?

A. Carry around a pencil and a piece of paper. Write down what comes to you at any time. Don't ignore things and wait for them to come back to you later.

Q. Does your work have a theme?

A. My life is my theme. I write about all my feelings. And remember, there are many places open to a cabaret performer. There's the Cinegrill in Los Angeles, Davenports in Chicago, Arci's Place in New York.

Performing your songs in a cabaret forum helps you to become a better actor. McBroom drew rave reviews for playing the demanding role of Mrs. Lovett in Stephen Sondheim's *Sweeney Todd*.

In addition to McBroom, if you listen to the highly regarded team of Karen Benjamin and Alan Chapman, you can learn a tremendous amount about cabaret writing. Chapman's hilarious satire, *Everybody Wants to Be Sondheim (But Me)*, is cabaret at its best. Anyone interested in learning how to write humor will gain immeasurably from exposure to McBroom, Benjamin, and Chapman.

Cabaret writing is show writing, and it's an ideal way to improve your skills and eventually arrive on Broadway. At their best, cabaret lyrics are clever and witty. But they also have tremendous emotional depth.

The Least You Need to Know

➤ Agents, managers, and lawyers are necessities for becoming successful as a singer/songwriter.

➤ You must have, or develop, an audience concept and a look to advance your singing career.

➤ A carefully orchestrated publicity campaign helps build your audience and attract the best professional support.

➤ It's not the size of your record label that counts; it's the promotion they do for your album.

➤ A cabaret career can take you to Broadway.

Chapter 21

Home Studio

In This Chapter

➤ Key synthesizer definitions

➤ The impact of sequencers

➤ Computers and music

➤ Basic home–studio setups that won't break the bank

➤ The magic of mixing

Home studios are an ideal environment for you to create songs and demos. In the privacy of your own world, you can spend days and nights developing tunes and arrangements without the pressure of mounting hourly costs. The majority of composers today opt for this solution.

Writing songs and recording them may remain your sole objective in having a home studio. But for many composers, the home studio is a starting point on the road to a career as a record producer. The productions can be your songs with you as the artist. Or, as your equipment expands and improves technologically, you might wind up recording other artists.

One of the most inspiring record industry stories centers around LaRock Sound, a successful studio that started in a tiny bedroom with a few pieces of primitive equipment. The composer/engineer was a young Canadian-born drummer named Roger LaRocque. Roger was one of the industry's leading percussionists, until he saw that live drums were being replaced by drum machines. Faced with the threat of drastically diminished wages, Roger purchased a Linn drum machine and the Linn 9000 and put them in his bedroom. That was the beginning. Within a few years, such stars as Julian Lennon, James Ingram, Frankie Valli, Billy Preston, Nell Carter, Quincy Jones, Tony Orlando, Irene Cara, ZZ Top, Sheena Easton, and hundreds of others were recording albums, television shows, and feature films in his studio.

Embracing the Technology

Some people feel that digital doesn't sound as warm as analog did in the past. Possibly not, but nobody has huge rooms like the old Capitol Studios did with $15,000 microphones. Analog sound means having soundproof control audio rooms with padding, a feature most composers don't have in their living rooms. Control rooms cost $100,000 to $300,000 when they're built properly, so go digital. You can achieve your goal to record music, write songs, and get your compositions across with quality good enough to serve your purposes.

Equipment Choices

Equipment alternatives change as quickly as the weather. The trick is not to feel you have to buy the latest gadget as soon as it hits the market. Advertising will make you insecure if you let it; the message advertisers convey is always: You'll lag behind; you won't be able to come up with great material unless it's composed on one of our state-of-the-art keyboards. Just remember this: No one cares what kind of equipment the song was written on. No one is interested in whether a bridge was composed on a synthesizer costing $1,000 or $100,000. The key is still a great song.

Trouble Clef

Avoid buying equipment that puts you in tremendous debt. Young composers have bankrupted themselves in their rush to acquire the latest gear, and the mental strain of the debt makes it impossible for them to concentrate on writing.

Roger LaRocque's Experience

Roger LaRocque remembers when electronic keyboards first showed him the future of the music business:

➤ **Vintage keyboards.** "Certain ones, like the M-1, were creating excitement," he recalls. "The DX7 when it first started. The GX8P and D-50. They're vintage keyboards, and we still use them today."

➤ **Sequencers.** Roger explains the impact of the sequencer on his home studio and the power of experimentation that led him to sell a song and get an important record:

"I moved from 4 to 8 to 16 tracks, but I didn't do it quickly. I got a bigger mixing board and more outboard gear until I was able to reproduce the full quality of the orchestra. It's not just a question of overextending myself to buy equipment. It's learning what you have, understanding it all thoroughly. You have no time to learn the simpler equipment if you rush to add new things before you're ready."

As it was with Roger, the M-1 was my keyboard of choice, and it served me well. Suddenly I had strings, bass, drums, woodwinds, brass, and an organ at my fingertips. I composed a score for a primetime musical special on the M-1, and when I presented the cues to the network, the reaction was wonderful. I still use my M-1 even though so many new keyboards are in fashion. I also blend my M-1 with other keyboards to make it sound bigger.

In common with many engineers/producers who have made a success by operating a home studio, Roger accepted the value of experimenting. We all want a tried-and-true roadmap so we can avoid mistakes, but the beauty of technology is the opportunity it gives you to try new things. Don't be afraid to turn knobs or move faders.

Hirschhorn's Hints

Embracing manuals, rather than resisting them, was Roger's first lesson. At first glance, manuals seem incomprehensible. The temptation is to rip them up and toss them in the trash. Don't do it. The answers are there if you don't panic.

Ease into the Manual

The trick is to read your manual for your equipment the first time without any attempt to learn it. Your first reading is an overview. Absorb the language and make a passing note of general information, without forcing yourself to grasp specifics. Take time out, perhaps a day, before reading it again. This time, pay closer attention. It won't seem so strange and terrifying. If you have to pore over individual chapters three or four times, be open to the idea. You'll be startled, after a while, to realize how clear the information becomes.

Equipment Terms

You must know a few terms before getting your feet wet in the home studio arena.

➤ **Analog.** Machines made with analog electronics controlled by linear voltage.

➤ **Assign switches.** Controls that route signals to various locations.

➤ **Bouncing tracks.** A procedure by which tracks are combined on the multitrack. This way, you can open up tracks on the tape machine.

➤ **Chorus.** A stereo effect that can be created with a delay unit.

➤ **Compressor.** A piece of outboard gear that controls level.

➤ **Delay.** An outboard unit that creates time-dependent effects. These effects include multiple hits, chorus, and such effects as flanging.

➤ **Digital.** A system controlled by numbers (digits).

➤ **EQ (equalization).** A process by which frequencies are cut or boosted, influencing the timbre of the sound.

➤ **Frequency.** A term that defines cycles per second. The higher the frequency of a sound, the higher its pitch will become.

➤ **Interface.** A general term describing how different pieces of equipment are working together.

➤ **Input.** Where signals go into a piece of equipment.

➤ **Internal sync.** A sequencer mode in which the sequencer is being driven by its own internal timing pulse.

➤ **Level.** Volume.

➤ **Limiter.** A device that controls level.

➤ **Monitor.** Anything you use to listen with.

➤ **Monitor amp.** An amplifier used to drive a speaker system.

➤ **MIDI (musical instrument digital interface).** A system in which sounds generated by a group of keyboards can be combined and recorded into a keyboard/sequencer/controller.

➤ **Mixer.** The audio command center that processes incoming signals for tone and level. It takes signals, whether they are instruments or voices, and blends them cohesively to create a good overall sound.

➤ **Output.** Where signals come out of a piece of equipment.

➤ **Patch bay.** A device used to bring all inputs and outputs in a studio to one central location.

➤ **Sampler.** Sounds created by a digital recording system, including instruments and sound effects.

➤ **Saturation.** A point at which a tape won't accept any more level. Above the saturation point, tape gets distorted.

➤ **Sequencer.** A device that records MIDI information.

➤ **Signal.** An audio source flowing through a system.

➤ **Signal processors.** Equalizers, limiters, compressors, echoes, reverbs, and amplifiers that alter timbre and tone.

➤ **Sync mode.** A mode of operation on a tape machine in which the machine is reproducing what is on the tape at the record head.

➤ **Sync track.** The track on a multitrack machine where the sync pulse is recorded.

➤ **Synchronizer.** A device that locks two machines together.

➤ **Synthesizer.** A machine, such as a sampler or a digital piano, that gives you all the existing orchestral and pop sounds.

236

Where to Buy

Retail stores are an obvious place, but you can find excellent second-hand equipment in the *Recycler* or in your local edition of *The New York Times,* which has a special section on equipment that can be purchased. Friends in the same business may have suggestions or may be selling off some of their equipment at a reasonable price. Also check bulletin boards at music schools.

Computer Software

One of the best ways to go is with a computer, whether a Macintosh or a PC. After you've bought your computer, you'll want software. Cubase is popular. I recommend it because it allows you to manipulate and edit your performance. It comes complete with digital mixing boards and effects. Cubase also possesses a live, human feeling on playback and *quantizes* well.

Cubase allows editing, which is also a feature of other programs such as Vision, Performer, and Logic. You can go into the performance itself and change notes and correct poor pitch. If you want to add a seventh to your chord, you can do it.

The cost for Cubase is in the neighborhood of $500 to $700, depending on the options, and it contains everything. It offers plug-ins, such as digital reverbs, delay, chorus, processing effects, EQ, doubler, compressors, and full automation. You also can purchase independent plug-ins to add to your collection. It includes free MIDI synths (synthesizers). All you need to purchase is one keyboard/controller.

Lyrical Lingo

Quantizing is computer auto-correction of musical performances and rhythm mistakes.

Equipment Recommendations

There's a dazzling range of equipment you can buy to set up a home studio, and new items are being added every day. This section provides some advice to help you make sense of it all.

Roger's Picks

Roger LaRoque gives the following advice on what basic equipment to buy:

➤ "You can buy a synth, say a Kurzweil 2000, a Roland JV 80 or JV 90, or a D 50—any of these. One keyboard, one computer, either PC or Mac. I recommend a Mac for music—it's simpler to use."

➤ "You'll need to purchase a mixer, as well as an audio card if you want to record more than two channels at a time in the computer. The Motu 2408 Mark of the

Unicorn has a lot of great equipment and is MIDI interface, so you can record MIDI in your computer. The audio interface records analog to digital, like guitars, vocals, drums, through a microphone or through line-in inputs or XLR inputs."

➤ "There are other sound cards in addition to the Motu on the market. Local music stores will recommend alternatives. Some programs and some computers already have them."

➤ "Self-powered speakers are the next priority. They're modestly priced (only a few hundred dollars each), and you have a lot of good products from Yamaha, Fostex, Tascam, Mackie, Alesis to choose from. Now you've got the computer, music program, card interface, MIDI interface, audio interface, audio mixer. You have your speakers. As for microphones, Shure is one of the best, an SM57 or 58."

➤ "You must have a little mixer to make DAT copies and cassette copies, return audio into the computer, and control levels. You'll also need them for mixdown."

Memory

The entire setup Roger described is in the range of $1,500, without the synthesizer, which is amazingly reasonable when you realize the far-reaching implications of what you can do. But the more tracks you use on the computer, the more memory your computer must have. You'll need extra storage room to record more audio files, which take a great deal of computer space. I have 512K of RAM in my G-4 with a 500 megahertz processor. You'll need 350 to 500, but most current computers have that. You'll also need a hard drive of about 30 to 50 gigabytes. Keep a separate hard drive for your music files; you need one that is anywhere between 10 to 30 gigabytes.

Hirschhorn's Hints

Spend a little more money on microphones if you can afford it. AKG has fine mikes for $200 or $300, as does Alesis, Shure, Electrovoice, Audiotechnica, or Rhodes.

Workstation

Machines are continually improving. An example is a digital music workstation with 8 or 16 tracks. It contains digital tracks and digital editing. You don't need a DAT player, because you can mix inside the machine. The workstation also has a mixing board. Unlike the past, when items were separated, today everything is included in one box, except the microphone. All you need to do is get a microphone, speakers, and a set of headphones. Get two headsets, because you'll need a couple when you're recording a singer.

Other Inexpensive Approaches

Another inexpensive approach is to buy a Fostex 16-track, half-inch tape machine. I recommend half-inch

30 IPS. These machines usually operate at 15 and 30 IPS. You'll get less noise at 30 IPS, although it will take double the tape. But the speed really improves the quality of the recording. You can buy one of these machines for $500. (They used to cost $5,000.)

Many M-1s and Kurzweil 2000s come with internal sequencers. Most Roland and Yamaha dealers have keyboards with sequencers. All you need is a keyboard and an old 16-track machine and a synchronizer, monitor, and mixer. You can shop around for old analog boards, although I have a digital board that is much more compact and has several other features: *automation* on each channel and compressors and gates on each channel that are also automated.

If you'd rather go the warmer analog route, check the market for older analog machines. They're still available. The problem with old analog machines is the possibility that some of the recording heads will be worn out. If you don't know how to evaluate them, bring someone in who knows how to analyze recording heads or playback heads.

Once you've purchased your gear for your home studio, close your mind to technological improvements and create! There's time enough to expand on your basics as you go along.

Making Music

Because synths sound infinitely better than they did in the past, the music world has become a blend of both live and synthesized orchestration, sparking a wave of fresh creativity. Mixing is a tricky business, but you can avoid some common pitfalls by following the advice in this section.

> ## Lyrical Lingo
>
> **Automation** is a system that records all your moves. You can put more vocals on the chorus, feature an instrument, or ride vocals among limitless other possibilities.

Live vs. Synthesizers: No Conflict!

When MIDI exploded onto the music scene, it had immediate opposition. Live musicians, the protests rang out, would never be used again. For a while, this danger seemed real. Now producers want to utilize both, so synths and live players are combined. This arrangement satisfies both sides of the argument: There's nothing as beautiful as a live sound, and it enhances whatever orchestrations you've conceived for your synthesizer. On the other hand, electronic sounds are improving daily. Furthermore, the synthesizer is able to do more than contribute literal reproductions of acoustic instruments. It offers creative mixes of sound that often don't resemble anything the public is familiar with.

Economically, the blending of live and electronic music is a logical solution for producers. They get the reality of a live trumpet without having to pay for a full trumpet section. They may request a cello solo against synthesized string accompaniment. In any case, this kind of integration produces beautiful results.

Keep It Short

Some composers, enjoying the luxury of limitless recording time and experimentation, cut demos and masters in their home studios that drone on for six or seven minutes. Don't fool yourself that your material is so brilliant that no one will care about the length. Overlong tunes are also impractical. You can do two songs in place of one that runs on and on. The short song is easier to mix, costs less when you hire musicians, and doesn't burn out your singer. Also, long songs take up twice the space on your hard drive.

Trouble Clef

Don't overuse strange sounds and combine them with your track just because they intrigue you. What you choose has to make sense and integrate properly with your overall track and concept. The sound of wind rustling delicately through the trees would probably be odd in a hard-driving rap song.

Hirschhorn's Hints

If you've written a song for Madonna, and you've matched your mix to the songs on her album, you're approaching the situation logically. But suppose Madonna doesn't take the song you've submitted. With a home studio, you can remix it to suit someone else, whether it be Enrique Iglesias or Whitney Houston.

Mixing

Roger LaRocque offers this basic advice on mixing:

"If you don't experiment with simple gear, you won't have a basis for what comes later. The important priority is learning how instruments work together, how rhythm sections blend. In mixing, you have to be able to divide your frequency so everything doesn't land in the extreme low end, high end, or mid range. Some of this information can be taught, but much of it is the result of moving faders, trying things out."

Trusting the first mix you hear in your headphones is a mistake. Mixes always sound better in headphones, but the only true way to evaluate them is to hear the music on your speakers.

Mixing for yourself is an easier matter than mixing a record for others. If your studio turns into a paying proposition and you have a stream of artists cutting demos or masters, study their previous records carefully. Try to match their sound. If your singer has done records that feature bass, drum, and guitar, you can't give him or her too much keyboard or horns. That might be your taste, but it's not the singer's.

Keep an ear out for these potential pitfalls when you're mixing:

➤ **Just because you're a drummer ...** If you're a drummer, your temptation in the mix will be to feature drums. If you're a pianist, you'll often get keyboard-heavy. Keep an overall perspective.

A mix is like a painting. Impressionists use millions of colors, but they know where to put them to create one overall effect.

➤ **Rhythm overboard.** I'm a keyboard player, and I pride myself on having an impeccable sense of rhythm. But nobody is so tight rhythmically that they don't go over the rails from time to time. Don't settle for an imperfect rhythm. It may sound like a minor glitch at first, but rhythmic mistakes magnify and become intolerable the more you listen back later on. Let MIDI rescue you immediately with quantization.

Old vs. New Arranging

When I started arranging, I had to write out the orchestration, go to the recording date, and pray. If it worked, I breathed a sigh of relief. If it didn't, there was no way to make major changes, and I would have to face a disgruntled producer or director. The beauty of today's technology is hearing your work in advance. The downside, of course, is being expected to show every cue as it's written. When you have producers, directors, or artists who can't make up their minds, you'll find yourself rewriting these cues over and over again. However, this method is still preferable to showing up at a date and not having the power to make major changes because the clock is ticking loudly, expanding a budget everyone thought was too high in the first place.

All instruments have specific characteristics. As a keyboard player, I had to learn not to write guitar parts that were keyboard in nature. Don't forget that a flute doesn't possess the range your piano does. Trumpets sound terribly peculiar three octaves below middle C. Make sure a live instrument can play the part you've written for it on your synthesizer, or the results will be artificial and annoying.

Engineering a Session

Plan carefully for recording sessions. I've assumed many times that my equipment was fine and have been shocked to discover that one thing or another wasn't working properly. Think of the 16-year-old who checks his car incessantly, even neurotically. Adopt his mindset. You don't want mishaps during a session, especially if you've hired other people.

Write up a questionnaire and ask yourself before the date if all the pertinent points, such as the following, have been covered:

➤ Will your master be mono or stereo?

➤ How many tracks do you want to use?

➤ Are all your instruments in perfect working order?

➤ Do you have sufficient head cleaner?

➤ Do you have enough tape and the right kind of tape available?

➤ Do you have extra cables?

241

Last, organize your tapes. Nothing is worse than needing a tape and not being able to find it. Multiply that dismay when an artist or a publisher has paid you to engineer a session, and you don't have the tape to give them. Or you've written a song that a publisher suddenly shows interest in, and you can't find the demo. Label everything! And put a date on it, too. Make copies of everything you send out.

One last psychological point: A home studio is totally yours. Your emotions are deeply invested in it. Going to other studios, even ones you trust, is a less powerful commitment. The home studio becomes an extension of your creative self. You live in it; you stay up all night trying new things; you rush to get there in the morning. For this reason alone, consider establishing your own private recording domain. It could give you great personal satisfaction along with topflight creative results.

The Least You Need to Know

➤ Manuals are your friends, not your enemies.

➤ You don't have to get into debt for years to come to set up a fully functioning home studio.

➤ Synthesizers and live instruments blended together make a beautiful arrangement.

➤ Mixing is the most important part of production.

➤ Advance preparation is essential for a productive recording session.

Chapter 22

Producing Your Own Hit Songs

In This Chapter

➤ Learn about producing

➤ Choose the right material

➤ Cut the best track

➤ Try a different musical approach

➤ Have a productive attitude in the studio

Songwriters may enjoy the triumph of having their work recorded by major artists, but they rarely retain artistic control over the final product. However, if you produce your own material, you can shape it to your vision.

From the time you make your first few demos, you'll be able to sense whether you have the talent for record production. You won't be satisfied with an acceptable demo. You'll keep reworking it, making sure it competes favorably with records you hear on the air. If you feel you have the gift, my advice is to pursue it. You'll enjoy increased financial rewards as well as the satisfaction of hearing your songs exactly as you conceived them.

How Do You Learn to Produce?

Some people love the studio and would live in one if they could. Others are impatient and eager for rapid results. The nuts and bolts of record production strike them as tedious and time-consuming. Unless you absolutely adore every intricate phase of studio work, don't consider being a record producer simply because you want to control how your songs are done. You won't do as capable a job as a producer who is totally committed to every facet of the process.

Record producing isn't something you generally learn in school. You learn it only by watching and doing. Go to every session you possibly can and study producers in action. You'll decide by observation what you want to emulate or avoid. Listen to records of every kind. Set aside your personal tastes and prejudices. No one ever learned a craft selectively. Many movie directors had to do low-budget horror movies before they did high-budget epics. Absorb everything.

Backstage Banter

Burt Bacharach began producing out of self-defense to protect his songs. As he puts it, "I just thought that my songs were getting changed from the way I heard them ... there was a really good song that had a three-bar phrase, instead of the standard four-bar phrase, and the A&R man convinced me that it would be better with a four-bar phrase, making that song out of proportion and ruining it. I didn't want that to happen again."

—Eric Olsen, *The Encyclopedia of Record Producers*, Billboard Books, 1999

Producer Mike Clink (Guns n' Roses, Sammy Hagar) says, "I used to spend all my money on records. I'd read the backs of album covers, listen to the music, and try to figure out how they were made." If you don't have much cash, save it for CDs rather than extra shoes or clothes (Anastasia Pantsios, *The Encyclopedia of Record Producers*). To learn by listening, see the list of recommended records in the "Top Producers" section at the end of this chapter.

Ask for help, especially at the beginning. Don't be ashamed of not knowing something. Only fools pretend to be brilliant when they don't understand important facts. Many producers have a mentor side to their personality and are glad to answer your questions.

Every person alive starts out with a sense of insecurity. Some are just better at hiding it. Keep telling yourself that you'll gain more and more confidence as you go along.

After you've gained some skill as a producer, you may be offered the opportunity to work for a record company as part of its production staff. Being a staff producer offers the security of a weekly salary and projects that are directly assigned to you by an

A&R man at the record company. As a staff producer, you have to accept the fact that you won't have much input about which artists are signed and which you'll be expected to produce for the company. An executive producer finances the session and provides the final word on when he or she feels it's completed.

As you build your reputation, you have the choice of being an independent producer who doesn't work for a record label. If you're a maverick who doesn't want to function under strict conditions, this is the better way to go.

A Producer's Job

A record producer chooses the artist, finds the material, supervises the recording, and mixes the final product.

Backstage Banter

Producer Rhett Davies (Brian Eno, The B-52's) advises getting to work early:

"I would get to the studio about 10 in the morning and I would set rhythms up—get interesting grooves going, weird things happening, and have a keyboard hooked in, ready to go. Bryan (Ferry) would saunter through the door at about one o'clock, and this vibe would be happening already."

—Eric Olsen and Dawn Darling, *The Encyclopedia of Record Producers*

Techno or No?

Some producers love every facet of technology. Others feel it inhibits them. Either approach is fine if it works for you. All that matters is the result, no matter how it's accomplished.

Neil Kernon (Jon Anderson, Kansas) starts his day this way:

"The first thing I do in the morning is switch on my computer, clean my teeth, and put on coffee. Computing is integral to everything I do. I've been on e-mail for 14 years. Before the Internet, I was on IMC, a music industry e-mail system. In the studio, I've worked with SSL or Neve computerized boards. I do sequencing work with a Mac."

—Anastasia Pantsios, *The Encyclopedia of Record Producers*

How Involved Will You Be?

People sometimes look critically at creators who want to assume huge responsibility. The assumption is, "He's an egotist … he's taking too much on … it'll never work." Only you know, in your heart, how much responsibility you're capable of assuming. In movies, Woody Allen tackles all phases of his films. On records, Walter Afanasieff (Mariah Carey, Celine Dion) does the same. Afanasieff creates the arrangements, writes the songs, and records all the backing tracks.

Be a Director

When you produce, be decisive, but don't try to do everyone else's job. Don Cook (Brooks & Dunn, Lonestar) claims he wouldn't "dare touch a knob" of the engineer's, although he makes suggestions about mixes. "He's so good I wouldn't tell him how to do what he does anymore than he would tell me how to do what I do."

On the other hand, you must express yourself with clarity. You've chosen to handle three or four roles, and your personnel will look to you for final answers. Even if you're not absolutely positive about something, don't seem nervous and doubtful. You don't necessarily have to run a "totalitarian dictatorship," as Snuff Garrett defines it, but you should always be perceived as a leader.

You have to see the whole picture and visualize the end result. But don't become impatient with details. As Michael Cuscuna (Dave Brubeck, Dexter Gordon) says, "Most of the fun is in the details, whether it's horn obbligatos, a very tasteful slide guitar part, or a wonderful organ chord."

Planning a Recording Date

Whether you're recording a solo singer, a group, or yourself, you need to follow certain organizational steps. Most vital is picking the right material.

What Are the Songs?

Even when the songs to be recorded are yours, you need to be ruthless about your choices. Unless you feel the song is one of your masterpieces, don't include it in the session. Of course, objectivity is harder to achieve when you're assuming the multiple responsibilities of writing, producing, and possibly singing.

Consider everything from the record company's point of view (the people who have to promote the record) as well as your own. Yet if the record company expresses a preference for some of your songs, and you feel that you've written better material, fight for your point of view. You won't always win, but if you feel passionate about it, you have to try.

Try Different Studios

You may love a certain studio, such as a studio you've built and assembled yourself. Remember, though, studios offer uniquely different sounds. David Z. (Sheila E. and Jody Watley) favors recording in different studios because you work a lot harder. There are a lot of records out there that sound the same because they're done in the same room. David likes to stretch a little by using closets, bathrooms, and hallways.

Backstage Banter

Andy Johns (Bon Jovi, Van Halen) has this to say about studios:

"The room where the instruments are has to sound good. The mixer is not important as long as it's not horrible and doesn't break down. The monitors have to be good. Tape machines can be analog or digital. As years go by, I find that stuff is less and less important. I don't use drum machines or samplers. I get the sound from the room. If the sound isn't right, the guy's got the wrong gear—wrong guitar, wrong amps, wrong drums."

—Anastasia Pantsios, *The Encyclopedia of Record Producers*

The Engineer

Make sure your engineer sees things the way you do. Sometimes engineers are aspiring record producers, and they can have a strong sense of the final artistic goal that may clash with yours. The engineer you work with is a crucial ally. Be sure you communicate well with the engineer, both artistically and personally. Above all, make certain the engineer excels at mixing.

Up-Front Budgeting

When you're working on an independent master and the studio is your own, you can afford more freedom with time. But if you've been hired by a record label to produce, work out your budget

Hirschhorn's Hints

Try to know as much about engineering as the engineer does, even if you don't do the engineering yourself. Ask questions. That way, you'll have a stronger grasp of the overall process.

247

carefully right from the beginning and adhere to it. Your budget will include prices for the amount of session time needed, musicians, your engineer, an arranger, and background vocalists.

Earnings

Producers work for the love of music, but they also have to eat. The best way to ensure that you earn some income from producing is not to allow *cross collateralization*.

Ask for increases in points for your production contributions as sales escalate. Be sure after advances have been recouped that you get royalties from the first record sold.

Rehearsal

To save time during the recording session, rehearse your material as thoroughly as possible beforehand. Make sure the singers' keys are perfect and try out several, rather than taking your artist's word for it. Even if you're the artist, don't quickly pick a key that seems comfortable. Often, comfortable keys don't offer the maximum impact. Stretching for a high note, pushing, or wailing might be more effective. When deciding on that final key, the depth and power of emotion should be your overriding priority.

Mike Stoller, one half of the legendary Leiber and Stoller partnership, describes a regimen worth remembering when he discusses rehearsing the Coasters:

> "The most important time was the weeks of rehearsal before the recording session. I would sit at the piano and work with them on setting background harmonies. Jerry would work with the lead singers. We would outline the general concept and the ideas for the arrangement would come. I would write out the charts and play piano on the sessions."

—Carlo Wolff, *The Encyclopedia of Record Producers*

In the Studio

Before you think of performance, train your eye on the track. Zero in on vocals, percussion, and guitar. Work on your drum sound until it's just right; the main goal is to find a drum sound that matches up well with the other instruments.

Be sure your groove falls right in the pocket—not too fast, not too slow. Keep in mind that excessive speed doesn't guarantee excitement. Don't work out a tempo by intellectual means. Just because another, similar hit with a similar groove uses a certain metronome beat doesn't mean that same beat will work perfectly on your tune. Each number has highly individual rhythmic requirements.

One Hundred Ways to Confuse Yourself

The Beatles recorded "Sergeant Pepper's Lonely Hearts Club Band" on four tracks, with no loss of artistic quality. Today, you can easily work with a hundred. Even though you're confronted with so many possibilities, try to decide what you want to feature in the beginning. You can test other alternatives after you do the basics, but be aware that the amount of available tracks can be a trap. Some producers become so overwhelmed by choices that they don't finish the record on time, and if they do, they're still not sure they made the right decisions.

Engineer Jeffrey Norman recalls that Creedence Clearwater Revival's John Fogerty knew where every part was going to be. For example, in the thirteenth bar on the seventh eighth note, he knew there was going to be a little "yeah," and it sounded completely spontaneous, but it was all planned.

Artists Are Only Human

If your singer starts to flub notes and lyrics and looks exhausted during the recording session, don't come on like a Simon Legree. The same goes for your engineer and any other personnel. If you drive people too hard, you'll get diminishing results. Curb your anxiety and all-consuming desire to get things finished. When the personnel you're working with get the breaks they need, they'll give you much better work.

Musical Approaches

There are as many musical approaches as there are producers, but they all have the same object: to capture the attention and imagination of the audience.

Soul Power

"As a producer," says Jim Dickinson (Frankie Paul, Sanchez), "what I'm looking for is soul. The cliché about the natives in the jungle is they won't let you take their pictures because you're capturing their soul. Capturing the soul of the moment, the spirit of the performance is exactly what you're doing as a producer" (Carlo Wolff).

Potent Performances

Without an emotional, exciting vocal, your record won't soar. As Rod Argent (Nanci Griffith, The Zombies) says …

> "The performance is everything. If you're recording a singer, then everything should stem from that. We try to get the master vocal at an early stage so that everything being played reacts to the vocal as in a live situation."
>
> —Ben Cromer, *The Encyclopedia of Record Producers*

What you don't want is to write a smash song and then ruin it with an uninspired vocal, either your own or the artist's you're producing.

When analyzing takes of a performance, you may find that one take is technically astonishing and another is flawed but more dramatically affecting. Go with the one that moves you and the other people listening. Dozens of singers have expressed regret that they went for technical perfection at the expense of a certain feeling. Some performances tap into emotions and can't be duplicated; they're just one-time miracles. Don't let any of those get away.

Good Goofs

Musicians and singers are human, and they make mistakes. I can't tell you how many times a guitarist or a singer hit a supposedly wrong note and started rushing to correct it when I called out, "Wait! That's terrific. Can you do it again?" Turns out their goof was much better than what I'd originally written. Don't be so focused on your original concept that your mind is closed. It could cost you a hit.

Experiment

In pre-synth days when acoustic orchestras and bands reigned supreme, experimenting and coming up with new, offbeat sounds was a minor priority for artista, writers, and musicians. Today, with electronic access to so many sounds, noises, and iinstrumental combinations, experimentation is a key factor in hit recording.

Be Weird If It Works

David Z. says …

> "The theory was to do anything we needed to sound different. We even talked about putting guitars under water at one point, just to see what it would sound like. We just did all kinds of weird things—multiple source recordings, which I still do a lot of—especially with guitars. I take it from one amp and split it into another one; that way you can basically make sandwiches of sound."
>
> —John Farinella, *The Encyclopedia of Record Producers*

Play with the Atmosphere

Kurt Bloch (Fastbacks, Sicko) likes to set up, as he calls it, an "artistic vibe":

> "Sometimes it might be appropriate to have incense and candles burning and the lights down. Sometimes it works better to have all the lights on and have everybody going 'eahhrrgghh' and drink a lot of coffee and be screaming at each other and all revved up so they rip through their songs or whatever. Everybody is different. Every session is different."
>
> —Dennis Dikek, *The Encyclopedia of Record Producers*

Vary Your Themes

When you're in the studio and you want to sell yourself as a songwriter and producer, make sure the songs you pick are highly varied. Utilize different rhythms. Follow a ballad with something up-tempo. Lenny Kaye (Patti Smith, Suzanne Vega) likes to have many different styles within an album because that gives an artist a chance to move into whatever his or her next album will be, and it will make sense. He doesn't believe in monochromatic records. He will, for example, place a song with a little string quartet next to a piece of avant-garde noise. Kaye has never been one for pure music. He likes mongrel music, "where styles copulate with each other and form some weird child that sounds different."

Voice First

Never mind how other record producers do things. We all have a unique way of hearing.

Jack Clement (Johnny Cash, Charley Pride) views his role of producer as orchestrator. He finds a voice, and then finds out what works with that voice, what instrumentation. "Sometimes it's heavy with piano, sometimes it's heavy with guitars, and sometimes it's heavy with fiddles and steel guitars (Deborah Evans Price, *The Encyclopedia of Record Producers*).

Trouble Clef

Dave Bascombe (Depeche Mode, Tears for Fears) advises against mixing a track so much that you lose perspective. He feels that it's hard to mix your own work if you've lived with it a long time and you've pushed the fader up every day, over and over again. Retaining freshness is vitally important.

Trouble Clef

Songwriters frequently have a compulsion to change the demo that got everybody excited in the first place. They tinker and embellish to a point where the charm and specialness of the original is lost. If the demo worked beautifully without a mass of strings, keep the strings out. If it was magical with acoustic guitar, don't substitute an electric one. Maintain that original magic.

You *Have to Love It, Too*

When you're getting close to the end of a recording date, you may tell yourself, "I don't love it, but the people will." This thought is a recipe for disaster. Unless you love the record and it satisfies you in every conceivable way, the public will probably not respond. If you don't love the record, try to figure out why. Is there something in the lead performance or the arrangement that seems lacking? Have you talked yourself into something that you don't really feel? Search for clues. Ask those around you, but don't show something unless you're convinced of its worth.

You can labor over a production until it becomes overcrowded. Too many ideas cancel each other out. Hearing a superb guitar solo, a brilliant piano lick, and a wonderful vocal note simultaneously is a waste. Choose your spots and feature them so that they stand out and count for something.

Top Producers

The following producers are among the best in their field. This list provides a small sample of their records as a guideline to expert producing talent.

➤ **Walter Afanasieff**

Michael Bolton: *Time, Love, and Tenderness* (Columbia, 1991)

Mariah Carey: *Emotions* (Columbia, 1991), *Hero* (Columbia, 1993)

Natalie Cole: *A Smile Like Yours* (Elektra, 1997)

Barbra Streisand: *Higher Ground* (Sony, 1997)

➤ **Brian Ahern**

Johnny Cash: *Ghost Riders in the Sky* (Columbia, 1979), *The Essential Johnny Cash (1955–1983)* (Legacy, 1992)

Emmylou Harris: *Portraits* (Warner Bros., 1996)

Anne Murray: *The Best … So Far* (EMI, 1994)

➤ **Rod Argent**

Nanci Griffith: *MCA Years: A Retrospective* (MCA, 1993)

The Zombies: *Time of the Season* (Date, 1969)

➤ **Burt Bacharach**

Patti LaBelle: *On My Own* (MCA, 1986)

Dionne Warwick: *Greatest Hits—1979–1990* (Arista, 1989)

Dionne Warwick: *Golden Hits Part 1* (Scepter, 1967)

➤ **Dave Bascombe**

Depeche Mode: *Music for the Masses* (Sire, 1987)

Erasure: *Pop, the First 20 Hits* (Sire, 1992)

➤ **Howard Benson**

Blue Meanies: *Pave the World* (Beach, 1996)

Pretty Boy Floyd: *Leather Boyz with Electric Toyz* (MCA, 1990)

➤ **Tchad Blake**

Crowded House: *The Very Best Of* (Capitol, 1996)

S.E. Rogie: *Dead Men Don't Smoke Marijuana* (Realworld/Caroline, 1994)

➤ **Joe Chiccarelli**

Lone Justice: *Shelter* (Geffen, 1986)

Oingo Boingo: *Nothing to Fear* (A&M, 1982)

➤ **Robert Clivilles and David Cole**

James Brown: *Universal James* (Scotti Brothers, 1992)

Aretha Franklin: *Greatest Hits, 1980–1984* (Arista, 1994)

➤ **Michael Cuscuna**

Luther Allison: *The Motown Years—1972–1976* (Motown, 1996)

Dave Brubeck: *Time Signatures: A Career Retrospective* (Columbia, 1992)

➤ **David Z.**

Fine Young Cannibals: *Finest* (MCA, 1996)

Jody Watley: *Greatest Hits* (MCA 1996)

➤ **Rhett Davies**

Legend Soundtrack (MCA, 1986)

King Crimson: *Three of a Perfect Pair* (EG, 1984)

➤ **John Fogerty**

John Fogerty: *Willy and the Poor Boys* (Fantasy, 1969)

John Fogerty: *Blue Moon Swamp* (Warner Bros., 1997)

➤ **Snuff Garrett**

Cher: *Gypsies, Tramps, and Thieves* (MCA, 1971)

The Brill Building Sound: Singers and Songwriters Who Rocked the Sixties (Era, 1993)

➤ **Andy Johns**

Van Halen: *Best Of—Volume 1* (Warner Bros., 1996)

Rod Stewart: *Storyteller: The Complete Anthology* (Warner Bros., 1989)

➤ **Quincy Jones**

Michael Jackson: *Thriller* (Epic, 1982)

Michael Jackson: *Bad* (Epic, 1987)

253

➤ **Lenny Kaye**

Patti Smith: *Masters* (Arista, 1996)

Suzanne Vega: *Solitude Standing* (A&M, 1987)

➤ **Robert John "Mutt" Lange**

Shania Twain: *The Woman in Me* (Mercury, 1995)

Billy Ocean: *Greatest Hits* (Jive, 1989)

The Least You Need to Know

➤ The way to learn producing is to study every hit record.

➤ Cut only the songs you truly believe in.

➤ Figure out which instruments you want to feature.

➤ Be confident about learning new technology.

➤ Always experiment.

Part 5

Finishing Touches

When you write a hit song, you want to be paid fairly, and ASCAP, BMI, SESAC, and the Songwriter's Guild of America will help you collect every dollar you've earned. You'll also want to utilize the vast resources of the Internet. Read about some inspiring success stories that the Internet made possible; these stories show what you can accomplish with creative use of this powerful new tool. Finally, look at imaginary lists of songs in several of 2001's major Grammy categories. They point to the fluidity of genres and the inclusiveness of today's popular music, signaling an era of unparalleled opportunity for songwriters.

Chapter 23

Royalties and Guilds

In This Chapter

➤ The history of ASCAP, BMI, and SESAC

➤ Royalties and payment procedures

➤ How guilds log performances

➤ Copyright basics and caveats

➤ The Songwriter's Guild of America

Songs are an art form, but sooner or later, you'll want to get paid. Royalties are aptly named because it can be a royal pain if you don't receive them, or you can feel like financial royalty when they show up in your mailbox. The beauty of royalties can be summed up in the words of a dancer friend of mine: "When songwriters get old, they have an annuity whether they work or not. I don't."

Assuming you've built a songwriting catalogue that contains compositions that are continually replayed, you'll be able to live (moderately or handsomely, depending on the case) on checks you receive every three months. This is a goal well worth striving for. BMI, ASCAP, and SESAC monitor performances of your songs in all media and make sure that you get the royalties due you.

SGA (the Songwriter's Guild of America) offers a completely fair writer's contract, reviews the publishing contracts of its members, supplies a copyright renewal service, helps writers to find collaborators, and campaigns in Washington, D.C., for its members' rights.

The Big Three: ASCAP, BMI, and SESAC

From the point of view of any songwriter who has had hit songs or songs recorded by important artists, ASCAP (the American Society of Composers, Authors, and Publishers), BMI (Broadcast Music, Inc.), and SESAC (Society of European Stage Authors and Composers) are the most important organizations in the music business. Recorded material doesn't always enjoy large sales, but the songs show up often on radio and television just the same. BMI, ASCAP, and SESAC collect those monies and send them to members every three months.

Hirschhorn's Hints

New writers who feel alone, who haven't quite found their bearings, should know that the societies are their second homes. All three are endlessly helpful in making calls for writers, pairing them up with collaborators, or suggesting them for projects.

BMI, ASCAP, and SESAC are sympathetic and supportive of songwriters and publishers. I can state quite simply, as a long-time insider, that I might not have had the satisfying career I've experienced without BMI. Friends of mine from ASCAP confirm the importance of their ASCAP affiliation.

By offering a brief background on my evolution as a BMI composer/lyricist, I can clearly point out many encouraging facts to newcomers in the music business. Two wonderful BMI executives, Stanley Catron and Ron Anton, first made me feel special by inviting me to lunch and agreeing to give me advances when I desperately needed them. Although my early records were recorded by such people as Anthony Newley, Buddy Greco, and Nancy Ames, they didn't get on the charts, and no airplay income was garnered.

Ron Anton and Stanley Catron helped me financially anyway, because they believed in my ability and fully expected me to have hit singles. In return, I worked like a madman to justify their expectations, and the breakthroughs did come with singles by Jay and the Americans, Ronnie Dove, Clyde McPhatter, and Elvis Presley.

Later in my career, I co-wrote a musical that I intended for Broadway, *Copperfield,* and BMI gave me a theater advance against future royalties from the show. I was also privileged to attend a workshop they funded, conducted by the late, brilliant Broadway musical director Lehman Engel.

Ron and Stanley eventually left BMI, and I received the same backing from Doreen Ringer Ross, Del Bryant, Paige Sober, and BMI's superbly effective President Frances Preston, a woman who understands songwriters and is driven by a desire to help them achieve their due, artistically and monetarily.

Basic Functions

BMI, ASCAP (the two largest, with the majority of songwriter membership), and SESAC license songs for performance on radio, television (broadcasting networks as well as cable), and the Internet. Nonbroadcast sources of revenue include restaurants, colleges, orchestras, airlines, skating rinks, theme and amusement parks, arenas, and anywhere music is publicly performed.

Clubs and hotels generally sign a one-year blanket license. The agreed-upon rate is predicated on the following:

➤ Live music weekly budget

➤ Seating capacity

➤ Whether the venue charges admission

The greatest amount of performance income stems from radio and television, with approximately 15 percent coming from hotels, clubs, and arenas.

Backstage Banter

Esquire magazine singled out BMI President Frances Preston as "the most influential and powerful person in the country music business." *Ladies Home Journal* cited her as one of the 50 most powerful women in America.

Distribution of Royalties

It has become increasingly common for writers from different societies to collaborate, and the royalty amounts often differ. In the case of Al and I, Al belonged to ASCAP, and I was a BMI member. Fortunately, when we compared checks, we found that both societies were totally fair, and the amounts, over a period of time, were roughly equal.

ASCAP

ASCAP, a nonprofit organization formed in 1914, made it clear that musical works were copyrighted and owned, and anyone who wanted to use the songs had to obtain the owner's permission. This organization was formed in reaction to the unjust treatment received by Stephen Foster, who wrote so prolifically and died without a penny to his name.

Music users objected violently in the beginning, and there is, even today, reluctance by some clubs, hotels, and restaurants to pay for use of music. That they do is a tribute to Frances Preston, president of BMI; Marilyn Bergman, president of ASCAP; former presidents Ed Cramer (BMI) and Hal David (ASCAP); BMI senior vice president Thea Zavin, and a host of others that preceded them.

Backstage Banter

A small group of writers, including Irving Berlin, Victor Herbert, John Philip Sousa, and James Weldon Johnson, formed ASCAP in 1914 with the intent of collecting public performance fees and dispersing these payments as royalties to the society's members.

Works registered with ASCAP (and BMI) become part of their repertory. The process of collecting your performance money is done through a blanket license. Most users of ASCAP pay a yearly blanket license fee for the right to use any song or cue in the organization's catalogue. Operating expenses are deducted, and all the rest of the money received is sent to members.

Approximately 25 percent of ASCAP's income comes from agreements with foreign licensing societies. Roughly one half is the result of performances from networks and television stations. Radio accounts for 25 percent of total royalty collections.

ASCAP collects from these organizations:

Backstage Banter

Many of the ASCAP board members are songwriters or scorers. Along with Marilyn Bergman, a three-time Oscar-winning lyricist, they include John Bettis, Cy Coleman, Arthur Hamilton, Hal David, James "Jimmy Jam" Harris III, John Mandel, David Raksin, and Jimmy Webb.

ABC, CBS, and NBC television networks

PBS (public television)

Cable television

Other commercial television networks: Warner Brothers (WB), Fox, and Paramount (UPN)

Background music services (Muzak, airlines)

Local commercial radio stations

NPR (National Public Radio) and college stations

Over 2,000 colleges and universities

Over 1,000 symphony orchestras

Nearly 6,000 concert presenters

Theme parks, Internet service providers, restaurants, hotels, bars, skating rinks, and circuses

Membership

Until the 1940s, ASCAP's members were principally Broadway, film, and pop composers. Today, members are accepted on the basis of one published song or a song that has been commercially recorded. The society has a board of 12 writers and 12 publishers, which is voted in by its membership.

Showcases and Awards

In addition to collecting and distributing royalties, ASCAP presents film scoring workshops and workshops in R&B, pop, country, musical theater, jazz, Latin, and concert music. The organization also provides sponsorship for showcases, giving members the chance to show their talents before important industry people. The ASCAP Foundation offers scholarships, awards, and grants to composers.

Payment Procedure

To track down what musical works are receiving performances, ASCAP utilizes cue sheets furnished to them by broadcasters or directors of programming. In addition, they take computer-based program schedules and network or station logs into account.

The major television networks submit program logs, as well as cue sheets. Nonnetwork television surveys encompass *TV Guide* and cue sheets and information provided by *TV Data* and Tribune Media Services. Cable television's performance data is derived from program guides and contributed to by cue sheets and cable services.

ASCAP's surveys consist of a random sampling of local commercial television airplay; a sample of local commercial radio airplay; a complete count of performances on the major television networks; a sample of performances on airlines, ice skating shows, and some circuses; and a sample of performances on wired music performances (Muzak).

Cue sheets contain specific information about the writers, composers, and publishers who contribute music to a show and the type of music usage. A music cue sheet includes the following information:

Title of musical composition

Timing of music used

Type of usage

Names of composers/lyricists

Publisher

Affiliation

Payment System

Payments are sent to members every three months. Writer royalties are sent out in October, January, April, and July. Publishers receive their checks in September, December, March, and June.

Hirschhorn's Hints

Annual dues of $10 for writers and $50 for publishers were established in 1914. These dues are still the same. You can obtain membership applications, sample contracts, and other information by writing or phoning any of the ASCAP offices listed at the end of this section or visiting the Web site at www.ascap.com.

Hirschhorn's Hints

Try to help fellow writers whenever you can. You're in a fraternity where that help will come back to you when you need it. Composers are almost always supportive of their own. Bequests have been contributed to ASCAP by such successful composers as Michael Masser, Jerry Leiber, Mike Stoller, and the estates of Yip Harburg and Richard Rodgers.

The majority of publishers and writers are paid on what ASCAP calls the 100 percent current performance plan. This means that they receive 100 percent of their royalties in the distribution of all performances in a specific performance quarter. You can get more information about this plan by calling Member Services at 1-800-95-ASCAP or by e-mailing MemberServices@ascap.com.

ASCAP Locations

ASCAP has the following offices:

Los Angeles
7920 W. Sunset Boulevard,
Third Floor
Los Angeles, CA 90046
Phone: 323-883-1000
Fax: 323-883-1049

New York
One Lincoln Plaza
New York, NY 10023
Phone: 212-621-6000
Fax: 212-724-9064

Nashville
Two Music Square West
Nashville, TN 37203
Phone: 615-742-5000
Fax: 615-742-5020

Puerto Rico
510 Royal Bank Center
255 Ponce de Leon Avenue
Hato Rey, PR 00917
Phone: 787-281-0782
Fax: 787-767-2805

London
8 Cork Street
London W1X1PB
Phone: 011-44-207-439-0909
Fax: 011-44-207-434-0073

Chicago
1608 West Belmont Avenue,
Suite 200
Chicago, IL 60657
Phone: 773-472-1157
Fax: 773-472-1158

Miami
844 Alton Road, Suite 1
Miami Beach, FL 33139
Phone: 305-673-3446
Fax: 305-673-2446

BMI

BMI, also a nonprofit organization, was formed in 1940 by 480 broadcasters. BMI's stockholders comprise its board of directors. The company's president and executive committee devise company strategy and handle daily decisions. Stockholders receive no dividends.

BMI was formed in reaction to ASCAP's closed-door policy against composers who wrote R&B, country, gospel, jazz, and folk music. Today, no such prejudice exists, and ASCAP is welcoming of all genres, as BMI is.

Like ASCAP, BMI utilizes a blanket license system. It collects license fees from each user of music that BMI licenses and distributes to its writers and publishers all the money collected. Through cue sheets and computerized data, BMI pays its members for all performances on network, syndicated, and cable television on a true census basis, keeping track of over 6,000,000 hours of programming annually. BMI operates on a nonprofit basis. Aside from operating expenses, every penny is sent directly to its writers and publishers.

Backstage Banter

BMI has 175,000 writers and more than 75,000 publishers who receive earnings when their works are performed.

Membership

After you get something recorded, it's vital that you join one of the societies. Tracking airplay on your own is virtually impossible and you'll lose income if you don't affiliate. For BMI information, sample contracts, or a membership application, go to their Web site, www.BMI.com, or write or phone one of the BMI offices listed at the end of this section.

Seminars, Workshops, and Showcases

BMI's seminars and workshops to help songwriters include the following:

The BMI-Lehman Engel Musical Theater Workshop

Sundance Composer's Lab

BMI TV/Film Composer's Conducting Workshop

Film and Television Composer's Workshop

BMI Jazz Composer's Workshop

BMI showcases include the following:

New Music Nights. A showcase series held every other month, featuring the best emerging bands and artists. Most often held in Los Angeles, but sometimes produced in San Francisco, Portland, Seattle, Arizona, and Colorado.

R&B Showcase. Held in Los Angeles and Oakland. Unsigned talent showcase in R&B music genre.

BMI Music Connection Showcase. Nashville. A weekly music showcase held at the legendary Exit-In. Features today's hit songwriters, as well as the hit writers and stars of tomorrow. Contact BMI Writer/Publisher Relations.

Collaborator's Connection. Held at BMI offices on the second Wednesday of every other month from 6:30 to 8:30 P.M., this is a forum for songwriters to network. Contact Samantha Cox at scox@bmi.com.

Pitch-A-Thon. New York City. Songs being pitched to an A&R representative. Held every other month at Eureka Joe (168 Fifth Avenue, between 21st and 22nd streets).

Payment Procedure

Monitored stations send BMI all the information about the music performed. Known as logs, this information is put through an elaborate computer system that multiplies each performance listed by a factor that reflects the ratio of the number of stations logged to the number licensed. BMI monitors approximately 500,000 hours of commercial radio programming annually.

In addition, 50,000 hours of noncommercial college radio programming are tracked, and separate payments are made for these performances. Television feature, theme, and cue music performed on networks, cable television stations, and local television stations are reported to BMI on music cue sheets, which list all music performed on a program. Performances are logged using such sources as *TV Data*, cable program guides, and local television station logging reports.

BMI has constructed a sampling procedure. Once a year, individual stations are sampled for three days. This technique adds up to 440,000 sample hours from commercial stations and 50,000 sample hours from college stations annually. The stations are not told when they're being logged.

ABC, CBS, and NBC Network Television Rates

Performance Type	Primetime (7:00 p.m. to 10:59 p.m.)	Late Night (11:00 p.m. to 1:59 a.m.)	Overnight (2:00 a.m. to 5:59 a.m.)	Morning-Day (6:00 a.m. to 6:59 p.m.)
Full feature (45 sec. minimum)	$11.50	$9.00	$5.00	$6.00
Theme (per show)	$5.00	$3.32	$0.58	$1.00
Background (per minute)	$1.10	$0.72	$0.52	$0.60
Logo (per show)	$0.30	$0.24	$0.22	$0.28

© Joel Hirschhorn

Local Television Rates

Performance Type	Daypart A (4:00 P.M. to 10:59 P.M.)	Daypart B (All Other Times)
Full feature (45 sec. minimum)	$3.00	$1.50
Theme (per show)	$1.60	$1.00
Background (per minute)	$0.76	$0.42
Logo (per show)	$0.18	$0.16

© *Joel Hirschhorn*

Networks send BMI cue sheets of all the music they use, which includes scoring cues, theme music, and songs. With the rise of performances, bonuses begin to accrue, from 25 percent to 100 percent. All works that have had more than 25,000 logged U.S. feature performances are paid at bonus rates.

The bonus rate has four levels:

➤ **Super (S) Bonus Payment rate.** This rate is four times the base rate. It is given for those works with the highest cumulative history whose current quarter's performances together constitute approximately 10 percent of the current quarter's radio feature performances of all BMI works.

➤ **Upper-Level (U) Bonus Payment rate.** This rate of two-and-a-half times the base rate is given to those works with the next lower cumulative history whose current quarter's performances together constitute approximately 15 percent of the current quarter's radio feature performances of all BMI works.

➤ **Mid-Level (M) Bonus Payment rate.** Two times the base rate. Those works with the next lower cumulative history whose current quarter's performances together constitute approximately 25 percent of the current quarter's radio feature performances of all BMI works.

➤ **Entry-Level (E) Bonus Payment rate.** All other works with a history of 25,000 or more performances receive one-and-a-half times the base rate.

Hirschhorn's Hints

Keep in mind how valuable it is to aim for motion pictures and television. A "film work" written for a full-length motion picture or a made-for-television movie receives BMI's Upper-Level Bonus Payment rate if it's utilized as a featured work of not less than 45 consecutive seconds or as the main title theme or closing credits work.

Payment System

BMI Royalty payments are sent out in January, April, July, and October. Live concert royalties are distributed every six months in April and October for pop concerts and annually in July for classical concerts.

The payment procedures for radio, public television, and cable television are as follows:

➤ **Radio.** Payment is made for a local commercial radio performance based on the license fee paid to BMI by the station broadcasting the performance. If the station's BMI license fee is among the top 25 percent of license fees paid by radio stations in the previous year, each performance of a popular song on that station will be paid no less than 12 cents total for all participants. Two songwriters will receive three cents a performance (six cents if they wrote the song alone), and the publisher will receive the other six cents. If the station's BMI license fee is among the bottom 75 percent of license fees paid by radio stations in the previous year, each performance of a popular song on that station will be paid at the rate of at least 6 cents total for all participants.

➤ **Public television.** BMI receives compulsory license fees for performances of music on public television broadcasting stations and distributes the fees from this source to those songwriters, composers, and publishers whose music is broadcast on public television stations. Rates vary from quarter to quarter, depending on the amount of the license fee collected and the base value of BMI performances tabulated during a quarter.

➤ **Cable television.** BMI collects license fees from both pay cable networks (for example, HBO, Cinemax, and Showtime) and basic cable networks (for example, MTV, USA Network, Lifetime, Discovery Network, VH1, TNN, and so on). The list of cable licensees changes from quarter to quarter.

BMI Locations

BMI has offices in the following locations:

Los Angeles
8730 Sunset Boulevard,
3rd Floor West
West Hollywood, CA 90069-2211
310-659-9109

Miami
5201 Blue Lagoon Drive,
Suite 310
Miami, FL 33126
305-266-3636

Nashville
10 Music Square East
Nashville, TN 37203-4399
615-401-2000

Atlanta
PO Box 19199
Atlanta, GA 31126
404-261-5151

New York
320 West 57th Street
New York, NY 10019-3790
212-586-2000

London
84 Harley House
Marylebone Road
London NW1 5HN, England
011-44171-486-2036

Puerto Rico
255 Ponce de Leon
East Wing, Suite A-262
Royal Bank Center
Hato Rey, PR 00917
787-754-6490

SESAC

The Society of European Stage Authors and Composers (SESAC) was founded by Paul Heinecke in 1930. SESAC, unlike BMI and ASCAP, is a for-profit organization. The corporation's owners, Freddie Gershon, Ira Smith, Stephen Swid, and the merchant banking house of Allen and Company, distribute 50 percent of the firm's income and retain the other half.

Backstage Banter

When people thought of SESAC's catalogue in the past, they thought of gospel and Christian music only. It now includes Latin, new age, television and film themes, jazz, and pop.

SESAC consults music trade publications, such as *Billboard, Radio and Records, The Gavin Report,* and *College Music Journal* to determine how much music is being played. It also gathers information from affiliates. Its major sources of information are radio playlists, the *Billboard* information network, network and cable programming service logs, regional editions of *TV Guide,* program syndicators, and a census of movie performances from *TV Data.*

SESAC offices have two locations:

New York
421 West 54th Street
New York, NY 10019
212-586-3450

Nashville
55 Music Square East
Nashville, TN 37203
615-320-0055

Copyright Basics

The duration of copyright protection is for the life of the author plus 70 years. It may be extended if you have a co-author who outlives you; in that case, the copyright lasts until he or she dies. Lyrics and melody are the items covered; rhythm and harmony by themselves are not.

When two or more songwriters collaborate, all the writers own the copyright equally unless specific contractual stipulations are made to the contrary. In states with community property laws, rights to the song are divided between the writer and his or her spouse.

Trouble Clef

When I first started taking my songs around the Brill Building, one publisher made an offer to publish a song of mine for $200. In my anxiety to be a professional and get my career going, I almost agreed. This arrangement is not acceptable under any circumstances. You don't pay a publisher to take your song.

Copyright Registration

A composer and/or lyricist should obtain the proper form from the Copyright Office in Washington, D.C. Send it with the filing fee ($30) and submit a copy of the work for registration. If the song is unpublished, one copy is sufficient; if the song is published, two copies are expected. Although the Copyright Office doesn't demand them, it's a good security measure to send lead sheets and cassettes or CDs.

For information and forms, contact the Copyright Office:

> **Copyright Office, Library of Congress**
> Washington, DC 20559-6000
> 202-707-3000
> lcweb./loc.gov/copyright

Watch Out!

When you make a deal with a publisher to assign copyright of a song, be aware of the following:

➤ Make sure there's a reversion clause. Possibly you'll be willing to grant a publisher two, three, or even five years of ownership, but somewhere down the line, the song should revert back to you if no records have been attained.

➤ Don't accept a contract that doesn't have an organized royalty schedule, preferably payment every three months. Six months is maximum.

➤ Don't leave the issue of "future advances" up in the air. A publisher once told me, "I believe in a handshake arrangement. Don't you trust me?" Questions like that are pure intimidation. Business is business. The publisher may seem like the most honest person in the world, but if so, why should he or she be reluctant to verify specific terms by signing an agreement?

➤ Ask for 50 percent of the publisher's income on all licenses the company issues.

The Songwriter's Guild of America

The Songwriter's Guild was formed in 1931 by writers Billy Rose, George M. Meyer, and Edgar Leslie to rectify a system of payment that often omitted royalties or paid them on only 1 percent of sheet music sold. The rate for *mechanical royalty rights*, from 16.66 to 25 percent on piano rolls and records, was equally unjust.

The Guild's Creed

Since 1976, the Guild has taken firm stands on source licensing, home taping, derivative rights, author's moral rights, the deductibility of business expenses, and compulsory license and copyright registration fees. In their words …

> "Our president and board members spend considerable time and energy talking to the media, lobbying, negotiating, and coordinating with other industry groups and raising the funds needed to get the songwriter's message through. The Guild maintains its efforts to advance, promote, and benefit the profession of songwriting."

Lyrical Lingo

Mechanical royalty rights (those pertaining to sales rather than royalties for airplay) allow usage of your material by others on records or CDs, as long as they give notice to the copyright owners and pay them.

The Popular Songwriter's Contract

The Guild's contract provides maximum protection for songwriters assigning copyrights to publishers, and it is not necessary to be a member of the SGA to use one. If you're signing any publishing contract other than the one supplied by the Songwriter's Guild of America, take it to an attorney. Granted, the fee may be a rough pill to swallow, but if your song goes Top 10 and you find yourself with barely enough money for lunch, you'll regret not having an expert look the papers over in advance.

To obtain an SGA membership application, sample contract, or other information, contact one of the following offices:

New York
1560 Broadway, Suite 1306
New York, NY 10036
212-786-7902

Hollywood
6430 Sunset Boulevard, Suite 705
Hollywood, CA 90028
323-462-1108

Copyright Act of 1976

Known as the "author's bill," the Copyright Act of 1976 offered writers the following:

➤ **Term of copyright.** Unlike the old act, which required songwriters to obtain copyright renewal after an initial term of 28 years in order to get a second 28 years of protection, this one offers a single term: the author's lifetime plus 70 years. The writer of any song composed after January 1, 1978 can rest assured that his or her work will not fall into the public domain until the copyright expires.

➤ **Contract termination.** A contract can now be terminated as to United States rights after a specific period of years (usually 35).

➤ **Statutory mechanical rate.** The new rate structure, which began January 1, 1998, is as follows:

January 1, 1998	7.1 cents
January 1, 2000	7.55 cents
January 1, 2002	8.0 cents
January 1, 2004	8.5 cents
January 1, 2006	9.1 cents

The Least You Need to Know

➤ ASCAP, BMI, and SESAC collect royalties for your airplay performances.

➤ ASCAP and BMI have showcases and other services for their writers.

➤ ASCAP and BMI pay songwriters four times a year.

➤ If you don't use the SGA's Popular Songwriter's Contract, be sure to get legal advice before you make a deal with a publisher.

➤ Publisher contracts should provide for payment every three months, six months maximum.

Chapter 24

What's Happening in Songwriting?

In This Chapter

➤ The Internet miracle

➤ The ups and downs of Napster

➤ Ways to make the Internet work for you

➤ What the Grammys reveal about songwriting's future

When rock came in, many pop songwriters dropped out. When synthesizers and sequencers made their initial impact, nervous devotees of the acoustic world let their careers fall apart. Now the Web site world has taken over, and the same resistance is being expressed.

Don't be part of the group that retreats at the first sign of change; there are always those who protest, "It's a fad." In motion pictures, talkies were pronounced a passing fad, too. History keeps proving that some fads have a way of sticking around. If you look at the Web in a positive light, you'll find an amazing new world that can further your career.

To keep on top of what's happening in songwriting, study the songs that are nominated for and win Grammy awards. They clearly spell out what top producers, artists, and executives like and want to hear, but they do more than exemplify current public taste. The Grammys tell the observant songwriter what musical and rhythmic trends are on the way.

The Good New Days

Are you one of those people who asks, "Why not go back to the good old days, when times were simple?" The "good old days" is an illusion; times were never simple, love was never without problems, high school was frequently torture, and being part of a teen rock band posed as many problems as being a professional on a session does later on. Doing a first demo certainly causes novices as much anxiety as professionals have when they're arranging for a full CD.

Hirschhorn's Hints

Get a laptop and immediately adopt it as a friend, your writing alter ego. You can write in the car, in an airplane, or on vacation. Carry a spare battery.

If you're uncomfortable with computer technology or have lingering doubts about whether the Web is a good thing, try to put your feelings aside and read on. This chapter is full of information about the many ways the Web can help songwriters, beginning with how it changed composer Steve Schalchlin's life.

Steve Schalchlin's Internet Miracle

Perhaps the most inspiring and instructive story the Web has ever produced centers on composer Steve Schalchlin. He wrote the songs for a Broadway musical, *The Last Session,* which drew raves across the country.

In 1996, before the success of *The Last Session,* Steve had been diagnosed with AIDS and told he had very little time to live. He began an online diary as a good-bye letter to the world, and he channeled all his feelings into *The Last Session,* which he co-wrote with life partner Jim Brochu. It told the tale of a songwriter who plans to cut his final album and then commit suicide. This story reflected Steve's mindset, but he defied all medical authorities and began to recover, aided by experimental medicines and the surging creative drive to share his dramatic experiences with the world.

According to Steve ...

> "The biggest hurdle for any new theatrical production, especially in a crowded market like New York City, is attracting publicity. When our musical *The Last Session* debuted off-Broadway in 1997, it was during the busiest theatrical season in 25 years. Hundreds of new works—*The Lion King* and *Ragtime* among them—were jostling for attention.
>
> "Yet *The Last Session* landed an impossible-to-obtain full-page story in *The Sunday New York Times* "Arts and Leisure" section, became the world's first major production to be broadcast over the Net, and got me an invitation to speak at Harvard University. The Internet helped our production complete a successful New York run with subsequent productions all over the country, including a Los Angeles production that garnered Best Musical, Best Book, and Best Music and Lyrics

awards from the L.A. Drama Critics' Circle, Backstage West Garland Awards, and many others."

The AIDS Crisis and the Internet

When Steve began his Web site in March of 1996, most of the people he knew didn't even have e-mail addresses, and the word Internet was met with a puzzled response. But he was immediately intrigued with the idea of having a page that could be accessed by anyone on earth.

"The AIDS turned deadly at this time," Steve recalls. His decision was to keep an AIDS diary online. He confided all his pain and comfort on the Internet. One month after going online with the Steve Schalchlin Survival Site, www.bonusround.com, he received an e-mail naming it "Cool Site of the Day." His hit counter suddenly registered in the thousands. E-mails flooded in from all over the world from students, doctors, nurses, other patients with various diseases, teachers, and from theater enthusiasts who had become deeply involved in his struggle and in the positive way he chose to battle the disease.

"But I was dying," Steve said. Everything turned around for him when he was given a new, experimental drug called Crixivan:

> "Diary readers went from mourning my death to celebrating with me. I changed the name of the site to Living in the Bonus Round. I started dividing the diary into chapters and books because what had been the journal of a man dying was now a journal of a man coming back from the grave, relearning how to live, and making miracles happen."

Backstage Banter

In 2000, another show, *Bare*, gained increased awareness through e-mail and chat groups. Some of the show's songs were being played on the Web site www.barethemusical.com, and Napster featured a bootleg version of the score.

Backstage Banter

Steve was offered a chance to do a small workshop production in Los Angeles. The Internet changed his life again when a diary reader from El Paso named Don Kirkpatrick came to see the show and contributed $10,000 for a staged reading in New York. This reading turned into an off-off Broadway production down on 29th Street at the Currican Theatre.

An online arts reporter for *The New York Times*, Matt Mirapaul, had been monitoring Steve's site, looking for a story angle. He had become a fan and an admirer based solely on the Internet site without hearing one note of Steve's music. When the show was in rehearsal, Mirapaul sent a photographer, saw the production, and wrote a flattering feature online in his arts@large column at nytimes.com, comparing it to *Rent* and *Angels in America*.

More Online Miracles

"The diary affected people in New York and across the country," says Steve. "Today we have a fanbase that stretches across the country. I created e-mail lists at egroups.com (all free), where fans of the musical and readers of the diary interact with each other. I have stayed involved in all the discussions, and when new people stumble onto the site, I direct them to the lists where they become a part of the community."

"Example: A producer at a theater in Baltimore wrote me and said they were interested in a small production of *The Last Session*. So I was able to encourage him to join the fan list where he promoted his production and interacted with *Last Session* fans. When he started his local version of the show, we organized a weekend where fans flew in from all over the country and supported it."

Schalchlin says, "The Internet allows me freedom to write anything I want, stay involved with my fanbase, promote new works, and support local productions by bringing much needed publicity to cash-starved theaters."

Hirschhorn's Hints

Steve's story should open your mind to the vast possibilities stemming from the Internet. Songwriting communities are being created all over the Internet on Web sites, chat rooms, e-mail lists, IRC, and newsgroups. The Internet is a communication device that gives the songwriter more power than ever before in history. An additional measure of the Internet's influence comes from an English instructor in Norfolk, Virginia, who says, "[The Steve Schalchlin diary's] message has, to put it bluntly, made me want to be a better person."

As Steve concludes ...

"At one point in my life, I was managing director of the National Academy of Songwriters, where my job was to help young or aspiring writers break into the business. The one thing I learned was that the ones who really made it were the ones who integrated their art into every facet of their lives."

Napster

Napster offers people the chance to trade copyrighted music without having to pay for it. This controversial music miracle (or monster, depending on your point of view) was created by 19-year-old Shawn Fanning.

Fanning's background conforms to Hollywood legend. Raised in Brockton, Massachusetts, he lived on welfare and had no biological father at home. Fortunately, John Fanning, his loving uncle, bought Shawn a computer when he was a high school sophomore and hired him as an intern during summer vacations. Shawn learned how to program computers while working at NetGames, John Fanning's online-gaming site.

As soon as Shawn Fanning began work on the Napster software, he and his uncle saw the far-reaching possibilities. In January 1999, Shawn left college to give Napster his complete attention. He alerted his friends in chat rooms, and they were hooked.

Fund-Raising

Yosi Amram, a Harvard University MBA, was the first Napster investor, contributing $250,000; and $100,000 came afterward from tech entrepreneur Bill Bales. Bales was hired as vice president of business development. When students across the country developed a Napster obsession, the funders' faith in the enterprise was justified. It rapidly passed the 1 million download mark, and many colleges banned it. At Grinnell College in Iowa, networking specialist Michael Pifer complained that Napster was eating up all available bandwidth.

The inevitable RIAA (Recording Industry of America) lawsuit came on December 7, 2000. Heavy metal stars Metallica also sued for copyright infringement. John Fanning expected a positive verdict for his company and was horrified when the U.S. District Court in San Francisco ruled against him, ordering all copyright-infringing musical content removed.

The Future of Music Downloading

Just when it looked as though Napster was down for the count, it formed an alliance with Bertelsmann, a globally formidable company as well as the owner of BMG music. As a representative says, "Over time, and as we gain industry support, we'll work to transform Napster into a membership-based service that preserves the Napster experience. There will always be a free, promotional file-sharing element to Napster."

Bertelsmann and Napster recognize the importance of working with record labels, songwriters, artists, and music publishers. The involvement of Bertelsmann should encourage this dialogue. Napster insists that it wants to pay artists fairly for the use of their creative efforts. At the same time, it also claims that free service will be continued, although it adds …

> "For a small membership fee, we feel that we can facilitate an enhanced service that you'll find even more valuable and that will allow us to generate revenues to be able to make payments to artists and songwriters for music files that our users share with each other."

Backstage Banter

Napster claims that it has been searching for a system that compensates artists when their music is shared over the Internet. It found an ally in Bertelsmann, the first publisher to market books directly to people in addition to selling them in bookstores. At present, Napster remains independent. Bertelsmann gave the company a loan and was then permitted to buy future shares in the company.

According to John and Shawn Fanning:

> "We will be working with other major labels, music publishers, independent labels, artists, songwriters, and other interested parties to gain acceptance for our membership-based service, and we will be developing a technology that will enable us to evolve in that direction."

One way to co-exist with music companies is to sell a certain amount of shares to record labels and split the advertising, sponsorship, and subscription profits. In any case, as one executive says, "The grassroots emotional response to Napster can't be stopped."

Despite all efforts to repress downloading music from the Web, it seems unlikely that anything can permanently stop it. The same sort of controversy resulted when videos first hit the scene, and companies feared that the consumers' ability to tape shows off their televisions would cut into profits and violate copyright laws. In the end, companies and proponents of Web sites supplying free music will be forced to come to terms and work out an arrangement that is mutually beneficial to them and to the songwriter. It won't be easy, however. As of February 2001, the Ninth Circuit Court of Appeals had ruled against Napster, sabotaging the efforts of John and Shawn Fanning to keep the major labels from shutting it down. Napster insists that its users are not copyright infringers, and says it intends to continue discussions with record labels. Shawn Fanning is developing a Napster service that would offer additional benefits to members of the community and, more important, make payments to artists.

Working the Internet

When I started out on my tentative, cautious Internet journey, I asked myself what career opportunities the Web offered me. At the time, I had written a book, *Titanic Adventure,* based on my wife's experience as the first woman in history to lead a seagoing expedition and bring up artifacts from the legendary ship. Just as someone would promote a song or a musical, I wanted to promote the book; the same principles apply.

In searching the Internet, I discovered hundreds of Web sites devoted to the Titanic. I e-mailed most of these people and developed friendships with them. Our mutual fascination with the Titanic cemented the bonds, and before long my book sales had tripled.

But He's Too Important!

Making cold calls, especially to number one producers or CEOs of major corporations, is tough. But if you write to the same individuals on the Internet, the prospect seems less threatening. You're more philosophical if they don't respond; the rejection isn't as direct or personal.

Through the Internet, I've had the privilege of forming valued relationships with film and television scorer Lee Holdridge and novelist Pat Conroy, among others. After a while on the Internet, you'll begin to feel that everybody is one large family, and most of them can be contacted.

Tonos

Three musical giants have pointed out the incalculable value of the Web with their new songwriter's site, Tonos. Tonos supplies tremendous opportunities to writers. Its purpose is to "seek out undiscovered talent." It defines itself as "a global community of musicians within every style and level of accomplishment."

The towering trio who launched Tonos are Carole Bayer Sager, lyricist for number-one smashes with Marvin Hamlisch, Burt Bacharach, and Leo Sayer; David Foster, one of the best and most successful producers in the history of the music business; and Kenneth "Babyface" Edmonds, who has written 95 hits.

Carole Bayer Sager described to me her vision and overall aspirations for Tonos this way:

> "What David, Kenny, and I are attempting to do is change the way music can be created, and the way people can be discovered. Most important is changing how people can collaborate with each other, because the Internet is tearing down all geographic boundaries.

> "Let's say someone has written a song and has a keyboard, but now he or she wants to find a producer for that song. The person might search through our database to find a vocalist who sounds like Brandy, say, or Stevie Wonder. Whatever this writer is looking for, we have a community that puts up samples of what their work sounds like. The writer can actively search for a project to join, or wait for someone to spot his or her sample and call to offer a project.

> "We have people collaborating from everywhere. We want to give people access to talent that never gets to hear them. If I get a song in the mail, all of us at Tonos can listen to it, and all the hitmakers at Tonos can listen. We can also

collaborate. Carole King and I put up a lyric and thousands of people wrote tunes. One girl wrote a tune that was so good that Kenny is recording it with Faith Hill! We give people an opportunity to collaborate with us, and each other!

"Sometimes we'll put up a song which is half complete, and have people take a shot at it. Sometimes we'll put up a track. Or put up our hits and have people sing to them. So it's constantly allowing people to interact, and giving them the tools. To do that, on the Internet—that's what the Internet is all about. A giant swap meet online. it's very empowering to mentor people, give them advice, so they can either learn keyboard or guitar on the site. A community that's been formed around music.

"I found a girl on Tonos, and I'm writing with her. We're going into the studio, and I'm delighted."

So bring up www.tonos.com and become part of what Carole calls "a place for new voices, new artists, new creators—a new frontier."

Two Tonos projects are ...

➤ **Road to Fame Challenge.** Singers are invited to submit their demos. One talented vocalist will win an all-expenses-paid trip to Los Angeles, and a chance when he or she arrives to do a demo at Capitol Recording and meet an A&R executive at a major record label. This vocalist will also receive round-trip airfare and three nights of hotel accommodations.

➤ **Demo Derby.** A weekly Web site showcase platform of upcoming talent that hasn't been signed to a record label. The Demo Derby features new and developing artists who the Tonos A&R team deems exciting and worthy of inclusion.

As Tonos puts it, "Want to work with one of our hitmakers? Join one of our Hitmaker projects and add your track to one created by some of the biggest names in the music industry."

Record Labels

Every record label has different requirements, and you can study these requirements on the Web. Familiarize yourself with the record labels' needs, their personnel, and the artists on their rosters. *Billboard* at www.billboard.com is the perfect place to begin, but it's only the tip of the iceberg.

Workshops

There are two ways to learn engineering and technology in a studio: You can experiment and feel your way by studying manuals and trying out things until you begin to comprehend the mysteries of your equipment. Or you can study with experts. A multitude of studio engineering and technology programs is available. Surf the Web and evaluate them to see which ones meet your special requirements.

Publishers

You'll want to put together a list of all the best, most active publishers, and the Internet is the ideal place to start. Once you compile your list of names from the Web, your immediate priority will be to separate the ones who only promote full catalogues they've already acquired, such as a catalogue by Rodgers and Hammerstein or The Beatles, from those who are eager to take on new material and new songwriters.

Hirschhorn's Hints

Through the Internet, you have a better chance to understand and market your material than songwriters ever did in the past. Armed with this information, you won't make the kind of mistake I did as a newcomer by sending a Bobby Vinton–type ballad to Atlantic Records—not exactly their type of thing.

The Importance of History

As a songwriter, you want to hear every conceivable kind of music. Just because your preference is R&B or pop doesn't mean you should close your mind to information about other musical harmonies and beats.

Hirschhorn's Hints

Listening is just one way to internalize music. Carefully read all the Web sites that give musical background and history about the giants in each field. Learn what drove them to excel in their chosen areas and what their music means to them. From blues legend Taj Mahal to Jimmy Webb, Savage Garden to Sisqo, biographies of fellow composers and lyricists always prove to be an inspiration. Read about Jewish music, Irish music, jazz, blues, and classical music. Search for stories, interviews, and historical information.

Whenever I'm not working, I'm reading about other writers and identifying with their dreams and aspirations. The Internet makes me feel I'm part of a huge, artistic fraternity, and when I pull up stories about other people in the music field, it stimulates my own creativity, gives me new ideas, and gets me writing.

The Simon Syndrome

Paul Simon was a folk-oriented Jewish boy from Queens, New York. Yet he opened his mind and heart to African rhythms and influences with the groundbreaking *Graceland* album. He didn't simply say, "My specialty is folk rock" and slam the door on awareness of other musical styles. Bob Dylan wasn't playing gospel music when he first appeared in Greenwich Village, but think of the gospel flavor that distinguished "Slow Train Comin'."

Incorporating other styles believably doesn't come only from using your ear; it's a total commitment of mind and emotion as well. You must absorb other worlds both mentally and psychologically in order to recapture their flavor with conviction.

Other Opinions

Look no further than the Web when you want to know what appeals to others and to understand the relative merits of what's being done. Whether it's general music criticism (rec.music.reviews, alt.cd-rom.reviews) or extensive *Billboard* coverage, the Internet fills you in on contemporary music culture.

Lyricists can always benefit by reading and studying the words of others. If you want to practice writing tunes, take words from already existing tunes and write your own melodies. See if you can make the lyrics scan as comfortably as the composers of the original tunes did.

Looking Ahead

When history books refer to the golden age of songwriting, they usually mean the period before 1950. Few will argue that Richard Rodgers, Larry Hart, George Gershwin, Cole Porter, E. Y. Harburg, Harold Arlen, Oscar Hammerstein, and Jerome Kern wrote immortal melodies and lyrics. But golden ages take different forms. If diversity is a definition of a creatively rich time, the twenty-first century is a golden age that offers new, unprecedented opportunities for songwriters.

When I first started out as a Brill Building composer, the avenues for songwriters were sharply divided. Pop writers didn't go to Nashville, and if they did, they were looked upon with suspicion. R&B writers rarely crossed onto the pop charts. Country writers stayed on the country charts; a crossover to the Hot 100 was almost impossible unless the song was redone with a pop star. Today there are no hard-and-fast lines separating songs, artists, or types of material.

Reading the Grammy Tea Leaves

A study of various Grammy categories shows how many areas a songwriter can venture into. For a broad overview of the whole of music, listen to every song on the following lists. It's the best possible way to keep up with a market that's constantly changing, and to identify future trends.

Song of the Year

Song of the Year is a broad category that embraces all genres. The only requirement is quality. A sample list of titles and authors demonstrates how open, all-embracing, and democratic the category is. These songs are not the Grammy nominees; they're my own choices of representative samples of different moods and styles.

> "After Tonight" by Mariah Carey, David Foster, and Diane Warren
>
> "Arms of Jesus" by Clay Crosse and Regie Hamm
>
> "Asi Quiero Vivir" by Rodeundo Lima
>
> "Been There" by Clint Black and Steve Wariner
>
> "Boyz-N-the Hood" by O'Shea Jackson, Eric Wright, and Andre Young
>
> "Friends Never Say Goodbye" by Elton John and Tim Rice
>
> "Our Affair" by Carly Simon

Hirschhorn's Hints

You'll find several sites that provide lyrics for your study and enjoyment. Check out alt.music.lyrics. After you display or print the lyrics, go over them line by line.

The Freelance Writer's Heroine

Diane Warren pulls off miracles, and most of the time she does it without co-writers. In 2000 Warren again demonstrated that a freelance songwriter can dominate without singing or producing. She had the following songs in contention:

> "After Tonight" (with David Foster and Mariah Carey)
>
> "Can I Come Over?"
>
> "Can't Fight the Moonlight"
>
> "Can't Take That Away" (with Mariah Carey)
>
> "Could I Have This Kiss Forever?"
>
> "Give Me You"
>
> "I Learned from the Best"
>
> "I Turn to You"
>
> "I Want You To"
>
> "I'll Be"

Backstage Banter

Winning a Grammy has the same positive effect on songs that Oscars have on movies. Bob Dylan's album, *Time Out of Mind*, shot from 122 to 27 on the charts after it won a Grammy award in 1997.

"Need to Be Next to You"

"Painted on My Heart"

"Please Remember"

"Por Siempre Tu"

"Spanish Guitar"

Best Rock Song

For those who write with a harder, tougher edge, this category contains rock, hard rock, and metal songs such as:

Hirschhorn's Hints

When writing a lyric, make sure that your hero or heroine is in the grip of a powerful emotion. As Diane Warren puts it, "I'm always attracted to songs with strong characters."

"Again" by Lenny Kravitz

"Desperation" by Rick Denzien

"Girl from the Gutter" by Robert Hawes, Sascha Akonietzko, and Tim Skold

"Hell on High Heels" by Mick Mars, Vince Neil, and Nikki Sixx

"Last Resort" by Papa Roach

"Sour Girl" by Dean DeLeo and Scott Weiland

"Where Did You Go?" by Full Devil Jacket and Malcolm Springer

Best R&B Song

The following list features a sampling of the best new R&B:

"Coming Back Home" by Allstar, Joel Campbell, Joe Thomas, and BeBe Winans

"Dance with Me" Richard Adler, Debelah Morgan, Giloh Morgan, and Jerry Ross

"He Wasn't Man Enough" by Lashawn Daniels, Fred Jerkins III, Rodney Jerkins, and Harvey Mason Jr.

"Incomplete" by Anthony Crawford and Montell Jordan

"Side by Side" by Lamont Dozier and Spencer Proffer

"Thank You in Advance" by Shep Crawford

"Try Again" by S. Garrett and T. Mosley

Best Country Song

Give a listen to these hot country sounds:

"Breathe" by Stephanie Bentley and Holly Lamar

"Feels Like Love" by Vince Gill

"I Hope You Dance" by Mark D. Sanders and Tia Sillers

"If I Should Fall Behind" by Bruce Springsteen

"Kiss This" by Philip Douglas, Aaron Tippin, and Thea Tippin

"Prayin' for Daylight" by Steve Bogard and Rick Giles

"She's More" by Rob Crosby and Liz Hengber

"We Danced" by Chris DuBois and Brad Paisley

Trouble Clef

Don't ever say to yourself, "I'm just a country writer, or an R&B writer" or any other kind of writer. You're a songwriter. Bruce Springsteen isn't known as a country composer, yet he wrote "If I Should Fall Behind," which was placed in the Grammy country category.

Best Song Written for a Motion Picture, Television, or Other Visual Media

From Elton John to Bob Dylan, the following movie songs show how diverse motion picture songs are today:

"Don't Say You Love Me" (from *Pokémon: The First Movie*) by Jimmy Bralower, Marit Larsen, Marion Ravn, and Peter Zizzo

"A Fool in Love" (from *Meet the Parents*) by Randy Newman

"Friends Never Say Goodbye" (from Elton John's *The Road to El Dorado*) by Elton John and Tim Rice

"I Need You" (from *Jesus*, the epic mini-series) by Ty Lacy and Dennis Matkosky

"Things Have Changed" (from *Wonder Boys*) by Bob Dylan

"When She Loved Me" (from *Toy Story 2*) by Randy Newman

"Yours Forever" (from *The Perfect Storm*) by George Green, James Horner, and John Mellencamp

Other Categories

The Grammys also honor the best dance recordings, which are albums filled with songs that sweep people out of their chairs and onto the dance floor. Some of the best in 2001, by title and performer: "You Wanna Be a Star" (Alisha), "When I Get Close to You" (Jocelyn Enriquez), "Love Is the Healer" (Donna Summer), and "Jumbo" (Underworld).

You can write for albums whether they're Latin jazz, rock gospel, pop/contemporary gospel, Latin pop, merengue, salsa, blues, contemporary folk, Native American music, world music, instrumentals, or even polka albums!

Grammys 2001

The Grammy winners for 2001 are an exciting rhythmic and melodic mixture, well worth studying:

➤ **Song of the Year:** "Beautiful Day" by U2, sung by U2

➤ **Rock Song:** "With Arms Wide Open" by Scott Stapp and Mark Tremonti, sung by Creed

➤ **R&B Song:** "Say My Name" by LaShawn Daniels, Fred Jerkins III, Rodney Jerkins, Beyonce Knowles, LeToya Luckett, LaTavia Roberson, and Kelendria Rowland; sung by Destiny's Child

➤ **Country Song:** "I Hope You Dance" by Mark D. Sanders and Tia Sillers, sung by Lee Ann Womack

Common Denominators

The exciting array of alternatives is enough to make a songwriter dizzy, but as different as these alternatives appear, they still demand the same rules of craftsmanship:

➤ An unforgettable hook

➤ A memorable title

➤ A dynamite idea

➤ Powerful visual imagery

➤ A vivid beat

➤ An interesting chord progression

The future promises more and more technological innovations, such as thousands of new sounds and additional tracks (the mind boggles at how many tracks studios will eventually offer). But remember: State-of-the-art isn't the same as art! You can have all the technology at your fingertips, but it means little if you can't come up with an infectious tune and a lyric that connects emotionally with your listener.

You can have the biggest star in the country sing your song, but it won't reach the Top 10 unless the song has most of the hit ingredients in the preceding list. I've had superstars sing my songs, and they've languished at Number 50, and I've also seen my other tunes reach number one with newcomers.

There's a truism about motion picture scores: A great score will improve a bad movie, but it won't save it. Never rationalize that great productions, fine arrangements, and brilliant vocals will turn your tune into a hit. When you think of the word *hit,* think of the following words:

H	Hook
I	Idea
T	Title

Say the word "hit" over and over again, and then keep reminding yourself what the letters stand for. Go to sleep repeating, "Hook, idea, title," followed by "hit." Your songwriting will improve dramatically within two weeks. Within four weeks, you'll have commerciality permanently embedded in your psyche.

Funkadelic's George Clinton once proclaimed, "Funk is the future." Then rock critic Jon Landau told the world, "I've seen rock and roll's future, and its name is Bruce Springsteen." But the future isn't any one thing; it's a constant flow of evolution and change. There will always be some new, unexpected future, and that future could be you.

The Least You Need to Know

➤ You can use the Web to promote songs and shows.

➤ You can find publishers, producers, and potential partners on the Internet.

➤ The Web has hundreds of music-oriented sites.

➤ The way to keep on top of the market and gain a broad overview is to listen to Grammy nominees and winners in all genres.

Glossary

a cappella   Singing without instrumental accompaniment.

A&R (artists and repertoire) director   Record company executive who signs new artists and chooses songs for them.

acoustic instrument   An instrument that is neither amplified nor electronic.

administration   Handling of financial and contractual matters relating to songs.

advance   Money paid up front to writers and later deducted from their royalties.

AFM (American Federation of Musicians)   Union for musicians and arrangers.

AFTRA   American Federation of Television and Radio Artists.

AGAC   American Guild of Authors and Composers.

alliteration   Group of words in which the first letter is the same.

alternative music   Music that goes against the mainstream, including grunge, techno, and punk.

analog recording   Recording medium in which the sound is made up of magnetic particles.

arrhythmic   Music without rhythm or rhythmic change.

ASCAP (American Society of Authors, Composers, and Publishers)   One of three societies responsible for collecting royalties from airplay.

atonality   Music without a key or tonal center.

augmented   Raising the tone half a step.

bitonality   Music composed in two separate keys that are played simultaneously, which often produces a dissonant, jarring effect.

blue notes   Flatted thirds, fifths, sixths, or sevenths that project a distinctive blues sound.

BMI (Broadcast Music, Inc.)   Society that collects royalties for airplay.

bridge   Section that follows the hook. Also known as the release.

chord   Three tones or more struck at the same time.

chorus   Repeated section of a song.

CHR   Contemporary hit radio.

chromatic scale   A scale built totally on half steps.

compressor   Device that limits sound and keeps it more consistent and even.

co-publish   Ownership of publishing rights to a song by two or more individuals.

copyist   Individual who copies and often transposes a musical score. This work is also known as music preparation.

copyright   Protecting your work from being stolen by registering it with the U.S. Copyright Office.

cover record   The release of a re-recorded song.

crossover   Airplay garnered for a record in two or more markets.

cue   Musical segment written by composer or orchestrator to back action or dialogue sequences in film, television, or videos.

DAT   Digital audio tape.

digital recording   Recording medium in which the sound source is turned into a numerical value.

diminished   Lower a note a half step.

e-mail   Electronic mail.

engineer   Person skilled at operating studio equipment for record or film sessions.

enharmonic   Two same-sounding notes with different names, for example, F-sharp and G-flat.

fader   Control used to alter sound levels.

flat   Lowering of a note by a half step.

Harry Fox Agency   Organization that specializes in collecting mechanical royalties.

headset   Earphones.

hip-hop   A musical genre that blends R&B, disco, and rap.

hook   A catchy, repetitive section of a song, which is generally required if the song is to become a hit.

house   Dance music incorporating samples from other tunes.

interval   Distance between two tones.

lead sheet   A composer's self-written sheet music that includes the tune, lyrics, and chords.

leader   Blank sections of tape separating one song from another.

limiter   Device that minimizes peaks of sound.

manager   Person who supervises the development of a performer's career.

master   Completed song pressed into a record.

mechanical royalties   Earnings from CD and cassette sales.

mix   Balancing and blending separate tracks into one or two channels and high-lighting the instrumental and vocal parts for dramatic effect.

modulation   Changing from one key to another.

MP3   Small file format designed to store audio files on a computer.

music library   A library of canned music, available to film, television, radio, and commercial producers for use in their shows.

music publisher   Individual or company that specializes in acquiring commercial songs and placing them with artists or on film and television. The publisher collects royalties generated by its catalogue of songs.

NARAS   National Academy of Recording Arts and Sciences.

NAS   National Academy of Songwriters.

new country music   Country with strong rock influences.

octave   Interval between the first and eighth note of the diatonic scale.

overdub   Recording of vocal or instrumental parts onto a basic multi-track recording.

pitch   Presenting your material to a publisher, a producer, or an artist.

polyrhythm   Two rhythmic patterns played at the same time.

producer   Individual who handles all aspects of a project: choosing the artist, finding the material, supervising the recording, and mixing the final product.

professional manager   Staff member of a publishing firm who evaluates and acquires material and then promotes it to producers, artists, and film and television companies.

program director   Person who decides which records will be added to a radio station's playlist.

public domain   Works that are not copyrighted or whose copyrights have lapsed.

residuals   Compensation to singers and musicians for their participation in a television show or a commercial.

rate   Agreed-upon royalty percentage.

RIAA   Recording Industry Association of America.

scale   Minimum union wage.

self-contained artist   One who writes his or her own songs.

SESAC (Society of European Stage Authors and Composers)   Like BMI and ASCAP, a performing rights organization that collects airplay royalties for writers and publishers.

SFX   Sound effects.

SGA   Songwriter's Guild of America.

sharp   Raising of a note by a half step.

SOCAN (Society of Composers, Authors, and Music Publishers of Canada)   Performing rights organization that collects Canadian airplay royalties.

soundtrack   Audio portion of a motion picture or videotape that includes narration and music.

split publishing   Division of publishing that can encompass two, three, or more publishers.

storyboard   Sketches illustrating scenes for film, television, or video.

synchronization   Timing procedure of a musical soundtrack to action on video or film.

synthesizer   Electronic instrument that can emulate any orchestral sound and that contains unusual sounds of its own.

tonic   The first note of a scale.

trade magazines   Publications that deal with the music industry.

up-front payment   Money given before a job is completed.

urban   Dance, rap, and R&B.

verse   First portion of a song, prior to the hook.

Resources

Music Publications of Special Interest

American Songwriter
1009 17th Avenue South
Nashville, TN 37212-2201
1-800-739-8712

Billboard
5505 Wilshire Boulevard
Los Angeles, CA 90036
323-525-2300

Music Connection
4731 Laurel Canyon Boulevard
North Hollywood, CA 91607
818-755-0101

Music Magazine
49 Music Square West
Nashville, TN 37203
615-321-9160

R & R (Radio & Records)
10100 Santa Monica Boulevard
Los Angeles, CA 90067
310-553-4330

Rolling Stone
5750 Wilshire Boulevard
Los Angeles, CA 90036
323-930-3300

Songwriter's Market
F & W Publications
1507 Dana Avenue
Cincinnati, OH 45207
1-800-289-0963

Motion Picture Publications

Daily Variety (New York)
245 West 17th Street
New York, NY 10011
323-965-4476

Daily Variety (Los Angeles)
5700 Wilshire Boulevard, Suite 120
Los Angeles, CA 90036
323-857-6600

The Hollywood Reporter
5055 Wilshire Boulevard
Los Angeles, CA 90036-4396
323-525-2000

The Hollywood Reporter Blu-Book Directory
5055 Wilshire Boulevard
Los Angeles, CA 90036
323-525-2150

Organizations

Academy of Country Music
6255 West Sunset Boulevard #923
Hollywood, CA 90028
323-462-2351

This organization promotes country music, and its membership includes songwriters, producers, recording artists, and other participants in the music industry.

American Federation of Musicians (AFM)
7080 Hollywood Boulevard, Suite 1020
Los Angeles, CA 90028
323-461-3441

This union protects musicians by establishing fair wage scales and working conditions.

American Federation of Television and Radio Artists (AFTRA)
260 Madison Avenue
New York, NY 10016
212-532-0800

This union was established to protect announcers, narrators, and vocalists.

American Society of Composers, Authors and Publishers (ASCAP)
www.ascap.com

Complete contact information for ASCAP is in Chapter 23, "Royalties and Guilds."

Broadcast Music, Inc. (BMI)
www.bmi.com

Complete contact information for BMI is in Chapter 23.

Broadway on Sunset
10800 Hesby, Suite 9
North Hollywood, CA 91601
818-508-9270

This organization offers composers the opportunity to test their musical theater material in front of audiences. Workshops, lectures, interviews with successful writers, and consultation services are included.

The Dramatists Guild, Inc.
1501 Broadway, Suite 701
New York, NY 10036
212-391-8384

This organization protects composers, lyricists, and playwrights.

Gospel Music Association (GMA)
1205 Division Street
Nashville, TN 37203
615-242-0303

This organization is for gospel publishers, writers, and recording or performing artists.

The Harry Fox Agency, Inc.
711 3rd Avenue
New York, NY 10017
212-370-5330

This agency protects publishers by collecting mechanical royalties and auditing record labels.

Nashville Songwriters Association, International (NSAI)
1701 West End Avenue, 3rd Floor
Nashville, TN 37203
615-256-3354

This organization promotes songwriters worldwide.

National Academy of Popular Music (NAPM)
330 West 58th Street, Suite 411
New York, NY 10019-1827
212-957-9230

This organization includes songwriters, producers, publishers, and record executives.

National Academy of Recording Arts and Sciences (NARAS)
3402 Pico Boulevard
Santa Monica, CA 90405
310-392-3777

Everyone involved in making records, including songwriters, producers, singers, musicians, and recording engineers, belongs to this organization.

National Academy of Songwriters (NAS)
6430 Hollywood Boulevard, Suite 705
Hollywood, CA 90028
323-462-1108

This songwriter protection organization offers evaluation of material, a tip sheet for song placement, workshops, and a collaborator network.

National Association of Composers/USA
PO Box 49256
Los Angeles, CA 90049
310-541-8213

This society promotes and publicizes songwriters.

National Association of Music Merchants (NAMM)
5790 Armada Drive
Carlsbad, CA 92008
760-438-8001

This organization promotes the music products industry.

National Association of Recording Merchandisers (NARM)
9 Eves Drive, Suite 120
Marlton, NJ 08053
609-596-2221

This organization specializes in the interests of distributors, software suppliers, and retailers.

National Music Publishers Association (NMPA)
711 3rd Avenue
New York, NY 10017
212-370-5330

This organization offers workshops and newsletters to its publisher members.

Pacific Northwest Songwriters Association
PO Box 98564
Seattle, WA 98198
206-824-1568

This organization offers monthly workshops, a quarterly newsletter, and contact with producers, publishers, recording artists, and labels.

Recording Industry Association of America, Inc. (RIAA)
1330 Connecticut Avenue, NW, Suite 300
Washington, DC 20036
202-775-0101

This nonprofit organization is dedicated to promoting the interests of record labels.

SESAC (Society of European Stage Authors and Composers)
421 West 54th Street
New York, NY 10019
212-586-3450

One of three organizations (along with BMI and ASCAP) that log airplay internationally for writers and publishers.

Songwriter's Guild of America (SGA)
1560 Broadway, Suite 1306
New York, NY 10036
212-768-7902

This organization protects songwriters in their dealings with publishers and offers a fair, up-to-date contract.

Southern Songwriters Guild, Inc.
PO Box 52656
Shreveport, LA 71136-2656
318-798-1122

This organization holds a "Song of the Year" contest, and its goal is to promote the craft of songwriting.

Toronto Musicians' Association
101 Thorncliffe Park Drive
Toronto, Ontario M4H 1M2
Canada
416-421-1020

You must be a Canadian citizen or show proof of immigrant status to join this organization.

Music Publishers

Almo Music Corp.
360 North La Cienega Boulevard
Los Angeles, CA 90048
310-289-3080

Big Fish Music Publishing Group
11927 Magnolia Boulevard, #3
North Hollywood, CA 91607
818-984-0377

BMG Music Publishing
1540 Broadway, 39th Floor
New York, NY 10036-4263
212-930-4000

Chrysalis Music
8500 Melrose Avenue, Suite 207
Los Angeles, CA 90069
310-652-0066

Disney Music Publishing
500 South Buena Vista Street
Burbank, CA 91521-6182
818-569-3228

DreamWorks SKG Music Publishing
9268 West 3rd Street
Beverly Hills, CA 90210
310-234-7700

EMI Music Publishing
1290 Avenue of the Americas,
42nd Floor
New York, NY 10104
212-830-2000

Famous Music Publishing Companies
10635 Santa Monica Boulevard,
Suite 300
Los Angeles, CA 90025
310-441-1300

Fricon Music Company
11 Music Square East, Suite 301
Nashville, TN 37203
615-826-2288

Sellwood Publishing
170 North Maple
Fresno, CA 93702
559-255-1717

Sony Music Publishing
550 Madison Avenue, 18th Floor
New York, NY 10022
212-833-4729

Warner/Chappell Music, Inc.
10585 Santa Monica Boulevard,
3rd Floor
Los Angeles, CA 90025-4950
310-441-8600

Zomba Music Publishing
137-139 West 25th Street
New York, NY 10001
212-824-1744

Online Resources

ASN (All Songwriter's Network)
www.tiac.net/users/asn/index.htm

Billboard On Line
www.billboard.com

Harmony Central
www.harmony-central.com

Jeff Mallett's Songwriter Site
www.lyricist.com

Jeff Jackson Songwriting and Music Business Page
www.mindspring.com/~hitmeister

Lyrical Line
www.lyricalline.com

Seattle Songwriting Workshop
www.knab.com

Steve Schalchlin's Survival Site
www.bonusround.com

Online Thesaurus
www.thesaurus.com

Words in over 400 dictionaries
www.onelook.com

Latin Music

Billboard's International Latin Music Buyer's Guide
Billboard Directories
575 Prospect Street
Lakewood, NJ 08701
1-800-363-7119

ASCAP Miami
209 9th Street
Miami, FL 33139
305-673-3446
Contact: Vanessa Rodriguez

BMI Miami
5201 Blue Lagoon Drive, Suite 310
Miami, FL 33126
305-266-3636
Contact: Diane J. Almodovar

Contests and Competitions

Entering contests seems like a long shot, but writers are often surprised and delighted to find that they've won money as well as recognition. The following are contests that offer both.

American Songwriter Magazine Lyric Contest
American Songwriter Magazine
1009 17th Avenue South
Nashville, TN 37212
615-321-6096

European International Competition for Composers
226 East 2nd Street, Suite 5D
New York, NY 10009
212-387-0111

Great American Song Contest
PMB 135
6327-C SW Capitol Hill Highway
Portland, OR 97201-1937
503-515-9025

The John Lennon Songwriting Contest
459 Columbus Avenue, Box 120
New York, NY 10024
Fax: 212-579-4320

National Songwriter's Network Contests
3870 La Sierra Avenue
PMB #101
Riverside, CA 92505
909-422-3539

Pulitzer Prize in Music
709 Journalism
Columbia University
New York, NY 10027
212-854-3841

Richard Rodgers Awards
American Academy of Arts of Letters
633 West 155th Street
New York, NY 10032
212-368-5900

USA Songwriting Competition
Dept. AW98, Box 15711
Boston, MA 02215
781-397-0256

Words By
332 Eastwood Avenue
Feasterville, PA 19053
215-953-0952

Index

Symbols

12-bar blues, 136

42nd Street, 188

110 in the Shade, 188

20,000 Quips and Quotes, 83

A

a capella, 23

Academy of Country Music, 292

accompanists, gaining training through employment, 7

acting out lyrics, 87-88

adult fairy tales (musicals), 183-184

advertisements (writing jingles), 150-153

  altering existing tunes, 150

  analyzing the objectives, 150

  avoiding obscurity, 150

  budgets, 152

    getting paid, 152

    package deals, 153

    publishing rights, 152

  commonalities among viewers, 149-150

  figuring out needs of the company, 148

  jingles with personality, 151

  keeping the emphasis on the singer, 151

  offering three different versions, 152

  playing with words, 151

  pre-planning everything, 152

  seeking a partner, 153

  thinking of commercials as mini musicals, 151

  typical ad campaign, 148

Afanasieff, Walter (producer), 252

AFM (American Federation of Musicians), 292

AFTRA (American Federation of Television and Radio Artists), 292

agents, singers/ songwriters, 224

  major agencies, 225

  small agencies, 224

Ahern, Brian (producer), 252

AIDS online diary, Steve Schalchlin, 273

Ain't Misbehavin', 185

Alesiss Q20 multieffects processor, 208

All Songwriter's Network. *See* ASN

all-girl groups, history of songwriting, 23

alliteration, 86-87

Almo Music Corp., 294

altering existing tunes, writing advertisements/ commercials, 150

American Federation of Musicians. *See* AFM

American Federation of Television and Radio Artists. *See* AFTRA

American Society of Composers, Authors, and Publishers. *See* ASCAP

American Songwriter Magazine, 291

  Lyric Contest, 297

analog electronics, home-studio equipment, 235

analyzing
  nonvisual lyrics, 74
  objectives, writing advertisements/commercials, 150
angels, theater production backers, 190
animals, as songwriting inspiration, 33
animated musicals, 172
  charm songs, 175
  choosing performers, 176
    bringing out the actor's best qualities, 177
    matching vocal ranges, 177
  dialogue versus music, 173
  keeping up with current styles, 172
    modern voiceover musicals, 173
    television musicals, 172
  making changes, 178-179
  monetary rewards, 179
  nailing the characters, 174
  placing the songs, 174-175
  standing up to the stars of the show, 175

step-out songs, 175
visualizing yourself as a choreographer, 177-178
Annie, 183
apologies, as universal songwriting theme, 31
appearances, singers/songwriters, 227
Applause, 188
approaches to demos, 200-206
  choosing a studio, 205
  choosing the musicians, 202-203
  choosing the singers, 201-203
  combination-voice demos, 201
  enlisting creative support, 205
  figuring costs, 204
    keeping in-studio costs down, 204
    royalties, 204
  guitar-voice demos, 201
  handling studio disasters, 206
  maintaining tempo, 206
  piano-voice demos, 200
  solo singer demos, 201
  staying creatively focused, 206

unisex singer demos, 201
  when you are the artist, 203
Argent, Rod (producer), 252
artists, creating songs for, 39
  as a composer, 39
  as a lyricist, 39-40
ASCAP (American Society of Composers, Authors, and Publishers), 54, 258-260, 292
  locations, 262
  membership, 260
  payment procedure, 261-262
  showcases and awards, 260
ASN (All Songwriter's Network) Web site, 295
assign switches, home-studio equipment, 235
attitude toward deadlines, partnerships, 49-50
audiovisual productions. *See* AV productions
automation systems, 239
AV (audiovisual) productions, children's educational music, 153
avoiding obscurity, writing advertisements/commercials, 150
awards, ASCAP, 260

B

Bacharach, Burt (producer), 252

banishing writer's block, 26

   focus and concentration, 26

   satisfying yourself, 27

Barnum, 187

Bascombe, Dave (producer), 252

Beach Boys, The, 19

Beatles, The, 19-20

Beauty and the Beast, 183

begging titles, 62

Bells Are Ringing, 189

Benson, Howard (producer), 253

Berlin, Irving, 16

Bible adaptations (musicals), 189

Big Fish Music Publishing Group, 294

Big River, 187

Billboard, 291

   International Latin Music Buyer's Guide, 295

   On Line, 295

biographies (musical), 186-187

Blackboard Jungle, The, 18

blackface, history of songwriting, 14

Blake, Tchad (producer), 253

bluegrass (country music genre), 130

blues

   12-bar blues, 136

   as universal songwriting theme, 29

   R&B, 136

      Chicago soul, 140

      controversial gospel music, 137

      disco and dance, 141-142

      doo wop music, 137

      funk movement, 141

      Louis Jordan's Tympany Five, 137

      minstrel songs, 136

      Motown classics, 139-140

      Motown sound, 139

      Robert Johnson influence, 137

      Southern soul, 141

      top hits, 138-139

BMG Music Publishing, 294

BMI (Broadcast Music, Inc.), 54, 258-266, 292

   locations, 266-267

   membership, 263

   payment procedure, 264-266

      bonus rate levels, 265

      cable television, 266

      public television, 266

      radio, 266

   seminars, workshops, and showcases, 263-264

bonus rate levels (BMI payment procedure), 265

book titles, as inspiration for song titles, 64

bouncing tracks, home-studio equipment, 235

boxing in rhymes, 82

Boys from Syracuse, 189

breaking up, as universal songwriting theme, 30

bridges, 87

Brigadoon, 186

Brill Building pop era, 22

Broadcast Music, Inc. *See* BMI

Broadway on Sunset, 292

Brown, James (funk music), 19, 141

bubblegum records, 23

budgets

   advertisements/ commercial jingles, 152

      getting paid, 152

      package deals, 153

      publishing rights, 152

   producing songs, 247

built-in drama, titles, 61-62

business decisions, partnerships, 55

buying home-studio equipment, 237

C

Cabaret, 185

cabaret artists, 230-231

cable television, BMI payment system, 266

Candide, 187

candles, as word in song titles, 66

cassette recording, 10

casting your songs, 212

  creative selling, 220

  finding common denominators in an artist's work, 213

  personal casting, 213-215

  publishers, 215-218

    being your own publisher, 220

    signing with a publisher, 218-220

    what publishers do for you, 216

    with production companies, 216

  researching who needs new material, 212-213

categories of rhyme, 80

Cats, 184

cautions, copyrights, 268

century of songwriting, 15

  Berlin, Irving, 16

  blackface, 14

  Cohan, George M., 15

  Cole, Nat "King," 17

  Crosby, Bing, 17

  Freed, Alan, 17

  Gershwin, George, 16

  Great Depression, 16

  Hammerstein, Oscar, 17

  Hart, Lorenz, 17

  Kern, Jerome, 15

  MTV and VH1, 21

    movies, 21

    videos, 22

  Porter, Cole, 16

  ragtime, 14

  rap revolution, 21

  rock and roll, 18-24

    all-girl groups, 23

    Beach Boys, The, 19

    Beatles, The, 19-20

    Berry Gordy's Motown, 20

    Brill Building pop era, 22

    bubblegum records, 23

    disco era, 23

    doo wop era, 23

    Dylan, Bob, 18

    folk rock era, 23

    gospel era, 23

    hard rock era, 23

    Brown, James 19

    R&B era, 23

    rap/hip-hop era, 23

    rockabilly era, 23

    Rolling Stones, 20

    soft rock era, 23

    soul era, 23

    Springsteen, Bruce, 21

    women's movement, 20

  Rodgers, Richard 17

  Sinatra, Frank 17

  vaudeville, 13

  World War II, 16

chance encounters, generating ideas, 31

characters

  musicals, capturing essence of the character in the songs, 174

  titles, 60-61

Charles, Ray (Southern soul), 141

charm songs, 175

Chicago soul, 140

Chiccarelli, Joe (producer), 253

children's music, 153

  doing the research, 153

  educational productions, 153-154

respecting the minds of children, 154

avoiding preaching, 155

creating real characters, 155

framing your story, 155

freeing your mind, 157

including darker aspects, 156

keeping the song moving, 155

making it modern, 154

matching the songs to the story, 156

chord

patterns, country music, 131-132

progressions, melodies, 102-103

chorus, home-studio equipment, 235

Chorus Line, 184

Chrysalis Music, 294

clichés, bending (country music current), 130

Clivilles, Robert (producer), 253

club blues, 137

Cohan, George M., 15

Cole, David (producer), 253

Cole, Nat "King," 17

collaborators (partnerships), 47-48

attitude toward deadlines, 49-50

business decisions, 55

competition, 50

cover records, 57

egos, 50

expressing reservations, 50

foreign/American, 55-58

importance of the job, 49

part-time, 51

punctuality problems, 49-50

seeking a partner, 52-54

songwriting spouses, 51

sticking to your passion, 51

work habits, 49

colors

as songwriting inspiration, 33

thinking in colors, 78

combination-voice demos, 201

commentators, putting your knowledge to work, 9

commercials (writing jingles), 148-152

altering existing tunes, 150

analyzing the objectives, 150

avoiding obscurity, 150

budgets, 152

getting paid, 152

package deals, 153

publishing rights, 152

commonalities among viewers, 149-150

figuring out needs of the company, 148

jingles with personality, 151

keeping the emphasis on the singer, 151

offering three different versions, 152

playing with words, 151

pre-planning everything, 152

thinking of commercials as mini musicals, 151

typical ad campaign, 148

competition among partners, 50

competitions, 297

Complete Rhyming Dictionary, 83

composers

creating songs for artists, 39

Newman, Randy, 41

compressors, home-studio equipment, 235

computer software, home-studio equipment, 237

contemporary music culture, Internet, 280

contests, 297

Copyright Act of 1976, 270

Copyright Office, 268

copyright, 10
  basics, 267
    cautions, 268
    registration, 268
  Napster, 274
    fund-raising, 275
    future of music downloading, 275-276

costs, figuring for demonstration records, 204
  keeping in-studio costs down, 204
  royalties, 204

counterpoint musical training, 5

country gospel (country music genre), 130

country music
  chord patterns, 131-132
  currents, 127
    bended clichés, 130
    down-home directness, 130
    down-to-earth drama, 127
    dramatic overstatement, 128

honesty, 127

honky-tonk heartache, 128

loose and playful quality, 129

raw reality, 127

simplicity, 129

spirituality, 128

spoken dialogue, 129

universal feelings, 128

visual imagery, 128

genres, 130
  bluegrass, 130
  country gospel, 130
  country pop, 131
  country rock, 131
  folk, 131
  gospel, 131
  hillbilly, 130
  honky-tonk, 130
  old-time country, 131
  outlaw country, 131
  R&B, 131
  rockabilly, 131
  traditional country, 131
  western swing, 130

history, 126-127

Grand Ole Opry, 126

Nashville, 125, 132-133

recommended listening, 133-134

country pop (country music genre), 131

country rock (country music genre), 131

cover records, partnerships, 57

creating
  hooks, 94
  songs for artists, 39
    as a composer, 39
    as a lyricist, 39-40

creed, Songwriter's Guild of America, 269

criticism
  hooks, 96
  partnerships, 50

Crosby, Bing, 17

cross collateralization, 248

cry, as word in song titles, 66

Cubase, 237

cue sheets, 261

currents in country music, 127
  bended clichés, 130
  down-home directness, 130
  down-to-earth drama, 127
  dramatic overstatement, 128
  honesty, 127
  honky-tonk heartache, 128
  loose and playful quality, 129

raw reality, 127

simplicity, 129

spirituality, 128

spoken dialogue, 129

universal feelings, 128

visual imagery, 128

Cuscuna, Michael (producer), 253

cutting the best track, producing songs, 249

D

Daily Variety, 161

    Los Angeles, 291

    New York, 291

dance

    music, 141-142

    titles, 64

David, Hal, 40

Davies, Rhett (producer), 253

days of the week, as songwriting inspiration, 33

deejaying, putting your knowledge to work, 9

delay, home-studio equipment, 235

Dell's Complete Rhyming Dictionary, 83

Demo Derby, Tonos Web site, 278

demonstration records (demos), 199-209

choosing a studio, 205

choosing the musicians, 202-203

choosing the singers, 201-203

enlisting creative support, 205

figuring costs, 204

    keeping in-studio costs down, 204

    royalties, 204

handling studio disasters, 206

home demos, 207

    equipment, 207-208

    playing different mixes, 208

    presentation, 208-209

    upgrading equipment slowly, 207

maintaining tempo, 206

musical approaches, 200

    combination-voice demos, 201

    guitar-voice demos, 201

    piano-voice demos, 200

    solo singer demos, 201

    unisex singer demos, 201

staying creatively focused, 206

when you are the artist, 203

dialogue versus music in musicals, 173

dictionaries

    Dictionary of American Idioms, 83

    Dictionary of American Slang, 83

    Dictionary of Clichés, 83

    Dictionary of Modern Quotations, 83

    Modern Rhyming Dictionary, 83

    New Comprehensive American Rhyming Dictionary, 84

    New Rhyming Dictionary and Poet's Handbook, 83

    rhyming, 83

    Songwriter's Rhyming Dictionary, 83

    Webster's Compact Rhyming Dictionary, 83

digital

    music workstations, home-studio equipment, 238

    systems, home-studio equipment, 236

disco

    era, 23

    music, 141-142

Disney Music Publishing, 294

Do I Hear a Waltz? 188

dobro, 131

doo wop
  era, 23
  music, 137

down-home directness (country music current), 130

down-to-earth drama (country music current), 127

downloading music (Napster), 274
  fund-raising, 275

dramatic overstatement (country music current), 128

Dramatists Guild, Inc., 292

Dreamgirls, 187

DreamWorks SKG Music Publishing, 294

dummy lines, 44

Dylan, Bob, 18

E

earnings, producing songs, 248

Edmonds, Kenneth "Babyface," 277

educational productions, children's music, 153-154

egos, partnerships, 50

elements of a melody, 101
  prosody, 107-108
  reliable rhythms, 103
  singability
    chord progressions, 102-103
    intervals, 102

EMI Music Publishing, 294

emotional connection, hooks, 92

employment, gaining training while employed, 6-7
  accepting offers, 8
  accompanists, 7
  joining an orchestra, 8
  local gigs, 7
  session playing, 7

endings, rhyme, 81

endless love, as universal songwriting theme, 30

enlisting creative support for demos, 205

Entry-Level (E) Bonus Payment rate (BMI), 265

EQ process (equalization process), home-studio equipment, 236

equalization process. *See* EQ process

equipment (home studios), 234-235

analog electronics, 235

assign switches, 235

bouncing tracks, 235

chorus, 235

compressors, 235

computer software, 237

delay, 235

digital music workstations, 238

digital systems, 236

EQ process, 236

frequency, 236

inexpensive approaches, 238-239

input signals, 236

interface, 236

internal sync, 236

levels, 236

limiter devices, 236

memory, 238

MIDI system, 236

mixers, 236

monitor amps, 236

monitors, 236

output signals, 236

patch bay devices, 236

reading the manuals, 235

recommendations, 237-238

samplers, 236

saturation point, 236

sequencer devices, 236

sequencers, 234

signal processors, 236

signals, 236

sync mode, 236

sync track, 236

synchronizers, 236

synthesizers, 236

where to buy, 237

European International Competition for Composers, 297

Evita, 187

experimentation, producing hit songs, 250-252

choosing a voice first, 251

playing with the atmosphere, 251

varying themes, 251

extremes, rap music, 143

F

fairy tales, adult musicals, 183-184

faithlessness, as universal songwriting theme, 30

false rhymes, 80-82

Falsettos, 189

Famous Music Publishing Companies, 294

fantasies (musical), 186

feeding the media, singers/songwriters, 228-229

fees, lawyer, 226

feminine rhymes, 80

figures, 96

figuring costs, demonstration records, 204

keeping in-studio costs down, 204

royalties, 204

first lines, titles, 67-68

Fogerty, John (producer), 253

folk (country music genre), 131

folk rock era, 23

foreign/American partnerships, 55-58

cover records, 57

Fosse, 184

Fostex 16-track, 238

four-minute screenplays, as songwriting inspiration, 34

Freed, Alan, 17

freelancers, Diane Warren, 281

frequency, home studio equipment, 236

Fricon Music Company, 294

Friml, Rudolph, 15

fund-raising, Napster, 275

funk music, 141

future of music downloading, 275-276

G

Garrett, Snuff (producer), 253

generating ideas, 32

animals, 33

banishing writer's block, 26

focus and concentration, 26

satisfying yourself, 27

colors, 33

days of the week, 33

four-minute screenplays, 34

holidays, 34

inner motivation, 35

inspirational characters, 27

loved ones, 28-29

people on the street, 28

your own life, 29

location backgrounds, 33

media, 31

chance encounters, 31

current attitudes, 32

names, 32

questions and answers, 34

religion, 32

universal themes, 29

apologies, 31

blues, 29

breaking up, 30

endless love, 30

faithlessness, 30

nostalgia, 31

307

pride in parents, 30
tragedy, 29-30
genres of country music, 130
 bluegrass, 130
 country gospel, 130
 country pop, 131
 country rock, 131
 folk, 131
 gospel, 131
 hillbilly, 130
 honky-tonk, 130
 old-time country, 131
 outlaw country, 131
 R&B, 131
 rockabilly, 131
 traditional country, 131
 western swing, 130
geographic titles, 65
Gershwin, George, 16
GMA (Gospel Music Association), 292
Gordy, Berry (Motown), 20
gospel
 country music genre, 131
 era, 23
 music, controversy with the blues era, 137
Gospel Music Association. *See* GMA
Grammy Awards, studying the categories, 280-284

Best Country Song, 283
Best R&B, 282
Best Rock Song, 282
Best Song Written for Motion Picture, Television or other Visual Media, 283
Diane Warren songs, 281
Song of the Year, 281
Grand Hotel, 188
Grand Ole Opry, 126
Great American Song Contest, 297
Great Depression, history of songwriting, 16
guilds
 ASCAP, 259-260
 locations, 262
 membership, 260
 payment procedure, 261-262
 showcases and awards, 260
 BMI, 262
 locations, 266-267
 membership, 263
 payment procedure, 264-266
 seminars, workshops, and showcases, 263-264
 copyright basics, 267
 cautions, 268
 registration, 268

SESAC, 267
 locations, 267
Songwriter's Guild of America, 269
 Copyright Act of 1976, 270
 creed, 269
 songwriter's contract, 269
guitar-voice demos, 201
Gypsy, 187

H

Haley, Bill, 18
Hammerstein, Oscar, 17
happenings in songwriting, 271
 Internet, 272
 contemporary music culture, 280
 other miracles, 274
 record label's requirements, 278
 researching publishers, 279
 Steve Schalchlin's miracle, 272-273
 studying other artists, 279-280
 Tonos, 277-278
 working the Internet, 276
 workshops, 278

Napster, 274
> fund-raising, 275
> future of music downloading, 275-276
> rules of craftsman-ship, 284-285
> studying Grammy categories, 280-284
>> Best Country Song, 283
>> Best R&B, 282
>> Best Rock Song, 282
>> Best Song Written for Motion Picture, Television or other Visual Media, 283
>> Diane Warren songs, 281
>> Song of the Year, 281

hard rock era, 23
Harmony Central Web site, 295
Harrison, George, 19
Harry Fox Agency, Inc., 292
Hart, Lorenz, 17
Hawaiin guitar, 131
Hello, Dolly!, 188
hillbilly (country music genre), 130
hip-hop music, 143
historical musicals, 185-186

history
> country music, 126-127
>> *Grand Ole Opry*, 126
> R&B, 136
>> controversial gospel music, 137
>> doo wop music, 137
>> Louis Jordan's Tympany Five, 137
>> minstrel songs, 136
>> Motown sound, 139
>> Robert Johnson's influence, 137
>> top hits, 138-139
> songwriting, 15
>> Berlin, Irving, 16
>> blackface, 14
>> Cohan, George M., 15
>> Cole, Nat "King," 17
>> Crosby, Bing, 17
>> Freed, Alan, 17
>> Gershwin, George, 16
>> Great Depression, 16
>> Hammerstein, Oscar, 17
>> Hart, Lorenz, 17
>> Kern, Jerome, 15
>> MTV and VH1, 21
>> Porter, Cole, 16
>> ragtime, 14
>> rap revolution, 21
>> rock and roll, 18-24

>> Rodgers, Richard, 17
>> Sinatra, Frank, 17
>> vaudeville, 13
>> World War II, 16

holds, 217
holidays, as songwriting inspiration, 34
Hollywood Reporter, 161, 292
Hollywood Reporter Blu-Book Directory, 292
home demos, 207
> equipment, 207-208
> playing different mixes, 208
> presentation, 208-209
> upgrading equipment slowly, 207
home studios, 233
> equipment, 234-235
>> analog electronics, 235
>> assign switches, 235
>> bouncing tracks, 235
>> chorus, 235
>> compressors, 235
>> computer software, 237
>> delay, 235
>> digital music work-stations, 238
>> digital systems, 236
>> EQ process, 236
>> frequency, 236

inexpensive approaches, 238-239

input signals, 236

interface, 236

internal sync, 236

levels, 236

limiter devices, 236

memory, 238

MIDI system, 236

mixers, 236

monitor amps, 236

monitors, 236

output signals, 236

patch bay devices, 236

reading the manuals, 235

recommendations, 237-238

samplers, 236

saturation point, 236

sequencer devices, 236

sequencers, 234

signal processors, 236

signals, 236

sync mode, 236

sync track, 236

synchronizers, 236

synthesizers, 236

where to buy, 237

making music

keeping it short, 240

live versus synthesized music, 239

mixing, 240-241

old versus new arranging, 241

recording sessions, 241-242

honesty (country music current), 127

honky-tonk (country music genre), 130

honky-tonk heartache (country music current), 128

hooks (repetition), 91-92

awareness of what appeals to others, 95

connecting with emotions, 92

consciousness of hooks, 94

creating and testing, 94

criticism, 96

instrumental breaks, 95

re-evaluation, 95

versus verses, 95

hoping titles, 62

hot-blooded titles, 62-63

I

I'm Getting My Act Together and Taking It on the Road, 189

ideas, generating, 32

animals, 33

banishing writer's block, 26-27

colors, 33

days of the week, 33

four-minute screenplays, 34

holidays, 34

inner motivation, 35

inspirational characters, 27-29

loved ones, 28-29

people on the street, 28

your own life, 29

location backgrounds, 33

media, 31-32

names, 32

questions and answers, 34

religion, 32

universal themes, 29-31

apologies, 31

blues, 29

breaking up, 30

endless love, 30

faithlessness, 30

nostalgia, 31

pride in parents, 30

tragedy, 29-30

illusion of reality, creating for stage musicals, 181

   including as many songs as desired, 183

   writing songs with energy and an edge, 182

in-studio costs, demonstration records, 204

industry contacts, seeking a partner, 53

inexpensive approaches, home-studio equipment, 238-239

inner motivation, generating songwriting ideas, 35

inner rhymes, 80-81

input signals, home studio equipment, 236

inspirations

   characters (generating ideas), 27

     loved ones, 28-29

     people on the street, 28

     your own life, 29

   titles, 64

     book titles, 64

     dances, 64

     geographic titles, 65

     one-word titles, 64

Instant Quotation, 83

instrumental breaks, hooks, 95

interface, home-studio equipment, 236

internal sync, home-studio equipment, 236

International Thesaurus of Quotations, The, 83

Internet happenings, 272

   contemporary music culture, 280

   other miracles, 274

   record label's requirements, 278

   researching publishers, 279

   Steve Schalchlin's miracle, 272

     AIDS online diary, 273

   studying other artists, 279

     Simon, Paul, 280

   Tonos, 277-278

     Demo Derby, 278

     Road to Fame Challenge, 278

   working the Internet, 276

   workshops, 278

intervals, melodies, 102

Into the Woods, 189

J

Jeff Jackson Songwriting and Music Business Page (Web site), 295

Jeff Mallett's Songwriter Site (Web site), 295

Jekyll and Hyde, 187

Jerome Robbins' Broadway, 185

jingles with personality, writing advertisements/commercials, 151

John Lennon Songwriting Contest, 297

Johns, Andy (producer), 253

Johnson, Robert, influence on R&B music, 137

Jolson, Al, 14

Jones, Quincy (producer), 253

Joplin, Scott, 14

Jordan, Louis (Tympany Five), 137

K

Kaye, Lenny (producer), 254

Kern, Jerome, 15

kiss, as word in song titles, 67

Kiss Me Kate, 16

Korg's D8 digital recording studio, 208

Kurzweil 2000s, 239

L

labels, signing with a label as a singer/songwriter, 229

  major-league labels, 229-230

  minor labels, 230

landscapes, visual lifestyles, 72-73

Lange, Robert John "Mutt" (producer), 254

Latin music, 295

lawyers' fees, 226

lead sheets

  preparing, 11-12

  versus lyric sheets, submitting songs, 11

leaders, 209

leitmotif musical theme, 186

Lennon, John, 19

Les Misérables, 185

letters, as words in song titles, 66

levels, home-studio equipment, 236

libretto, 15

limiter devices, home-studio equipment, 236

Lion King, 186

Little Shop of Horrors, 186

live music versus synthesized, making music in home studios, 239

live musicals, 172

  charm songs, 175

  choosing performers, 176

    bringing out the actor's best qualities, 177

    matching vocal ranges, 177

  dialogue versus music, 173

  keeping up with current styles, 172

    modern voiceover musicals, 173

    television musicals, 172

  making changes, 178-179

  monetary rewards, 179

  nailing the characters, 174

  placing the songs, 174-175

  standing up to the stars of the show, 175

  step-out songs, 175

  visualizing yourself as a choreographer, 177-178

    meeting with the arranger, 177

location backgrounds, as songwriting inspiration, 33

locations

  ASCAP, 262

  BMI, 266-267

  SESAC, 267

loose and playful quality (country music current), 129

lyric sheets versus lead sheets, submitting songs, 11

Lyrical Line Web site, 295

lyricists

  creating songs for artists, 39-40

  David, Hal, 40

  Rice, Tim, 40

lyrics

  acting out, 87-88

  versus music (what comes first?), 37-43

    attention to titles, 42

    creating songs for artists, 39-40

    defined borders, 42

    feeling your way to creativity, 45

    major songwriters, 40-41

    practicing lyrics and melodies, 41-43

    rhythm in your mind, 41

    rhythmic pulse, 44

M

Mackie 1-402-VLZ pro, 208

Magic Show, 189

major-league labels, singers/songwriters, 229-230

Mame, 188

managers, mutual obsession, 225

manuals, home-studio equipment, 235

masculine rhymes, 80

masters versus demos, 206

Mayfield, Curtis (Chicago soul), 140

McCartney, Paul, 19

mechanical royalty rights, 269

mechanicals, 218

media (generating ideas), 31
  chance encounters, 31
  current attitudes, 32

melodies
  elements, 101
    prosody, 107-108
    reliable rhythms, 103
    singability, 102-103
  figures, 96
  riffs, 96-99

melodists, Richard Rodgers, 40

membership
  ASCAP, 260
  BMI, 263
  SGA, 269

memory, home-studio equipment, 238

message in the music, titles, 62

Mid-Level (M) Bonus Payment rate (BMI), 265

MIDI system (musical instrument digital interface), home-studio equipment, 236

minimalist harmonies, 182

minor labels, singers/songwriters, 230

minstrel songs, 136

Miss Saigon, 185

mixers, home-studio equipment, 236

mixtures of rhyme, 80-81

Modern Arranging Techniques, 164

Modern Rhyming Dictionary, 83

modern voiceover musicals, 173

monetary rewards, writing scores for musicals, 179

monitor amps, home-studio equipment, 236

monitors, home-studio equipment, 236

Most Happy Fella, 188

motion pictures, publications, 291-292

Motown
  classics, 139-140
  Gordy, Berry, 20
  history of songwriting, 20
  sound, R&B history, 139

movie
  adaptations (musicals), 188
  scorers, 159-161
    adjusting to titles, 166
    asking questions and doing the research, 165
    capturing the essence of the movie, 164
    combining formal study with practical experience, 169-170
    following the right leader, 164
    making yourself known and heard, 160
    preparing songs ahead of time, 162
    providing reassurance, 164-165
    respecting the material, 162
    rules, 168-169

spotting notes, 166

studying publications, 161

underscoring, 163-164

working out a strategy, 163

working with music supervisors, 165-166

MTV, history of songwriting, 21

movies, 21

videos, 22

music

bringing up imagery, 78

children's. *See* children's music

country. *See* country music

critics, putting their knowledge to work, 9

Latin, 295

making in home studios

keeping it short, 240

live versus synthesized music, 239

mixing, 240-241

old versus new arranging, 241

recording sessions, 241-242

organizations, 292-294

publications, motion pictures, 291-292

publishers, 294

R&B. *See* R&B

rap. *See* rap music

versus dialogue in musicals, 173

versus lyrics (what comes first?), 37-43

attention to titles, 42

creating songs for artists, 39-40

defined borders, 42

feeling your way to creativity, 45

major songwriters, 40-41

practicing lyrics and melodies, 41-43

rhythm in your mind, 41

rhythmic pulse, 44

Music Arranging and Orchestration, 164

Music Connection, 291

Music Magazine, 291

musical instrument digital interface. *See* MIDI system

musical repetition, 89

hooks, 91-92

awareness of what appeals to others, 95

connecting with emotions, 92

consciousness of hooks, 94

creating and testing, 94

criticism, 96

instrumental breaks, 95

re-evaluation, 95

versus verses, 95

repeat hits, 92

simplicity, 91

tempo, 92

musical training, 3-4

counterpoint, 5

preserving ideas and submitting songs, 9

cassette recording, 10

lead sheets versus lyric sheets, 11

preparing lead sheets, 11-12

prestige versus poverty, 5-6

putting your knowledge to work, 8

deejaying, 9

letting the music keep you going, 9

music critics or commentators, 9

teaching, 8

while employed, 6-7

accepting offers, 8

accompanists, 7

joining an orchestra, 8

local gigs, 7

session playing, 7

musicals

adult fairy tales, 183-184

Bible adaptations, 189

biographies, 186-187

fantasies, 186

historical, 185-186

live and animated, 172

charm songs, 175

choosing performers, 176-177

dialogue versus music, 173

keeping up with current styles, 172-173

making changes, 178-179

monetary rewards, 179

nailing the characters, 174

placing the songs, 174-175

standing up to the stars of the show, 175

step-out songs, 175

visualizing yourself as a choreographer, 177-178

movie adaptations, 188

novel adaptations, 187

offbeat adaptations, 189

original stories, 189

play adaptations, 188

revues, 184-185

Shakespearean plots, 189

stage, creating illusions of reality, 181

writing songs with energy and an edge, 182

getting your musical on stage, 189-194

writing for popular in-person performers, 194

N

names, as songwriting inspiration, 32

NAMM (National Association of Music Merchants), 293

NAPM (National Academy of Popular Music), 293

Napster, 274

fund-raising, 275

future of music downloading, 275-276

NARAS (National Academy of Recording Arts and Sciences), 293

NARM (National Association of Recording Merchandisers), 293

NAS (National Academy of Songwriters), 293

Nashville, country music, 125, 132-133

Nashville Songwriters Association, International. *See* NSAI

National Academy of Popular Music. *See* NAPM

National Academy of Recording Arts and Sciences. *See* NARAS

National Academy of Songwriters. *See* NAS

National Association of Composers/USA, 293

National Association of Music Merchants. *See* NAMM

National Association of Recording Merchandisers. *See* NARM

National Music Publishers Association. *See* NMPA

National Songwriter's Network Contests, 297

new arranging, making music in home studios, 241

New Comprehensive American Rhyming Dictionary, 84

New Rhyming Dictionary and Poet's Handbook, 83

Newman, Randy, 41

Nine, 186

NMPA (National Music Publishers Association), 293

nonprofessional vocalists, 205

nostalgia, as universal songwriting theme, 31

note against note. *See* counterpoint

novel adaptations (musicals), 187

NSAI (Nashville Songwriters Association, International), 293

numbers in song titles, 67

O

offbeat adaptations (musicals), 189

Oklahoma, 17

old arranging, making music in home studios, 241

old-time country (country music genre), 131

one-word titles, 64

online resources, 295

Online Thesaurus Web site, 295

open rhymes, 80

orchestras, gaining training through employment, 8

orchestration. *See* scorers

organizations, 292-294

original stories (musicals), 189

outlaw country (country music genre), 131

output signals, home-studio equipment, 236

outside songs, 39

P

Pacific Northwest Songwriters Association, 293

Pacific Overtures, 186

package deals, advertisement/ commercial jingles, 153

part-time collaborators, 51

partnerships, 47-48
 attitude toward deadlines, 49-50
 competition, 50
 cover records, 57

 egos, 50
 expressing reservations, 50
 foreign/American, 55-58
  cover records, 57
 importance of the job, 49
 part-time collaborators, 51
 punctuality problems, 49-50
 seeking a partner, 52-53
  advertisements, 53
  ASCAP, 54
  BMI, 54
  business decisions, 55
  establishing industry contacts, 53
  local, 52
  long shots, 54
  SESAC, 54
  working with an artist, 54
 songwriting spouses, 51
 sticking to your passion, 51
 work habits, 49

patch bay devices, home-studio equipment, 236

payment procedure
 advertisement/ commercial jingles, 152

ASCAP, 261-262

BMI, 264-266

bonus rate levels, 265

cable television, 266

public television, 266

radio, 266

Penguin Rhyming, 83

perfect rhyme, 80

performers, selecting for musicals, 176

bringing out the actor's best qualities, 177

matching vocal ranges, 177

personal casting, selling your songs, 213-215

Phantom of the Opera, 187

piano-voice demos, 200

Pippin, 189

placement of songs in musicals, 174-175

play adaptations (musicals), 188

pleading titles, 62

Porter, Cole, 16

powerful emotions titles, 63

preparing lead sheets, 11-12

presentation of home demos, 208-209

preserving ideas, supplies, 9

cassette recording, 10

lead sheets versus lyric sheets, 11

preparing lead sheets, 11-12

pride in parents, as universal songwriting theme, 30

process of rewriting, 117

choosing the right environment, 118-119

creating your own time patterns, 118

outlook as a brand new song, 118

pretending someone else wrote the song, 118

telling yourself it's fun, 118

process of songwriting, 37-38

creating songs for artists, 39

as a composer, 39

as a lyricist, 39-40

music versus lyrics, 43

attention to titles, 42

defined borders, 42

feeling your way to creativity, 45

major songwriters, 40-41

practicing lyrics and melodies, 41-43

rhythm in your mind, 41

rhythmic pulse, 44

producers, 252

Afanasieff, Walter, 252

Ahern, Brian, 252

Argent, Rod, 252

Bacharach, Burt, 252

Bascombe, Dave, 252

Benson, Howard, 253

Blake, Tchad, 253

Chiccarelli, Joe, 253

Clivilles, Robert, 253

Cole, David, 253

Cuscuna, Michael, 253

Davies, Rhett, 253

Fogerty, John, 253

Garrett, Snuff, 253

Johns, Andy, 253

Jones, Quincy, 253

Kaye, Lenny, 254

Lange, Robert John "Mutt," 254

Z., David, 253

producing hit songs, 243-245

being a director, 246

choosing how involved you will be, 246

cutting the best track, 249

experimentation, 250-252

choosing a voice first, 251

playing with the atmosphere, 251

varying themes, 251

job of a producer, 245

musical approaches, 249

potent performances, 250

soul power, 249

usable errors, 250

planning a recording date, 246

budgeting, 247

choosing the songs, 246

earnings, 248

rehearsal, 248

trying different studios, 247

working with your engineer, 247

top producers, 252

Afanasieff, Walter, 252

Ahern, Brian, 252

Argent, Rod, 252

Bacharach, Burt, 252

Bascombe, Dave, 252

Benson, Howard, 253

Blake, Tchad, 253

Chiccarelli, Joe, 253

Clivilles, Robert, 253

Cole, David, 253

Cuscuna, Michael, 253

Davies, Rhett, 253

Fogerty, John, 253

Garrett, Snuff, 253

Johns, Andy, 253

Jones, Quincy, 253

Kaye, Lenny, 254

Lange, Robert John "Mutt," 254

Z., David, 253

Promises, Promises, 188

prosody, melodies, 107-108

protagonists, 60

public television, BMI payment system, 266

publications, motion pictures, 291-292

publishers, 294

researching on the Internet, 279

selling your songs, 215-218

being your own publisher, 220

publishers with production companies, 216

signing with a publisher, 218-220

what publishers do for you, 216

publishing rights, advertisement/ commercial jingles, 152

Pulitzer Prize in Music, 298

Q

qualities, singers/ songwriters, 226

appearance, 227

Russ Regan's rules, 227

quantizing, 237

questions and answers, as songwriting inspiration, 34

R

R & R (*Radio & Records*), 291

R&B (Rhythm and Blues)

Chicago soul, 140

country music genre, 131

disco and dance, 141-142

era, 23

funk movement, 141

history, 136

controversial gospel music, 137

doo wop music, 137

Louis Jordan's Tympany Five, 137

minstrel songs, 136

Motown sound, 139

Robert Johnson influence, 137

top hits, 138-139

Motown classics, 139-140

Southern soul, 141

"race" records, Alan Freed, 18, 138

radio, BMI payment system, 266

ragtime, history of songwriting, 14

Ragtime, 187

rap music, 142-143

extremes, 143

hip-hop, 143

recommended listening, 144-145

revolution, history of songwriting, 21

Russ Regan, 143-144

rap/hip-hop era, 23

raw reality (country music current), 127

reading the manuals, home-studio equipment, 235

reasons to resist rewriting, 111-117

best will be thrown away, 112

bridges are not significant, 113

chord progressions similar to hit songs, 113

criticism from partner, 117

desire to finish, 114

ending is satisfactory, 115

first draft is always best, 114

planning to fix in the studio, 114

received a poor judgment, 116

received praise, 116

rhymes are like compromises, 112

rhythm fits the words, 113

second verses are not important, 113

title is strong enough, 114

recitative singing, 186

recommended listening

country music, 133-134

rap music, 144-145

record labels, requirements, Internet research, 278

Recording Industry Association of America, Inc. *See* RIAA

recording sessions, making music in home studios, 241-242

re-evaluation, hooks, 95

Regan, Russ (rap expert), 143-144

Register of Copyrights, 10

registration, copyrights, 268

rehearsals, producing songs, 248

releasing hits, getting your musical on stage, 193-194

reliable rhythms, melodies, 103

religion, as songwriting inspiration, 32

repeat hits, repetition, 92

repetition, 89

hooks, 91-92

awareness of what appeals to others, 95

connecting with emotions, 92

consciousness of hooks, 94

creating and testing, 94

criticism, 96

instrumental breaks, 95

re-evaluation, 95

versus verses, 95

repeat hits, 92

simplicity, 91

tempo, 92

researching children's
music, 153
resources
online, 295
organizations,
292-294
publications, 291
motion pictures,
291-292
revues (musicals),
184-185
rewriting
reasons to resist
rewriting
best will be thrown
away, 112
bridges are not
significant, 113
chord progressions
similar to hit
songs, 113
criticism from
partner, 117
desire to be
finished, 114
ending is satisfac-
tory, 115
first draft is always
best, 114
plan to fix in the
studio, 114
received a poor
judgment, 116
received praise, 116
rhymes are like
compromises, 112
rhythm fits the
words, 113

second verses are
not important,
113
title is strong
enough, 114
starting the process,
117
choosing the right
environment,
118-119
creating your own
time patterns, 118
outlook as a brand-
new song, 118
pretending some-
one else wrote the
song, 118
telling yourself it is
fun, 118
sticking with it, 121
changing your
instruments, 120
critical responses
from business
persons, 119-120
when a record lost
its momentum,
119
rhyming
boxing in, 82
categories, 80
dictionaries, 83
endings, 81
inner, 81
mixtures, 80-81
schemes, 84-85
without reason, 82

Rhythm and Blues. *See*
R&B
rhythmic pulse, 44
rhythms, as element of
melodies, 103
RIAA (Recording
Industry Association of
America, Inc.), 293
Rice, Tim, 40
Richard Rodgers Awards,
298
riffs, 96-99
*Rise and Fall of Popular
Music, The*, 14
Road to Fame
Challenge, Tonos Web
site, 278
rock and roll, history of
songwriting, 18-24
all-girl groups, 23
Beach Boys, The, 19
Beatles, The, 19-20
Berry Gordy's
Motown, 20
Brill Building pop era,
22
Brown, James, 19
bubblegum records,
23
disco era, 23
doo wop era, 23
Dylan, Bob, 18
folk rock era, 23
gospel era, 23
hard rock era, 23
R&B era, 23

rap/hip-hop era, 23

rockabilly era, 23

Rolling Stones, 20

soft rock era, 23

soul era, 23

Springsteen, Bruce, 21

women's movement, 20

rockabilly

country music genre, 131

era, 23

Rodgers, Richard, 17, 40

Roget's International Thesaurus, 83

Rolling Stone, 291

Rolling Stones, 20

Romberg, Sigmund, 15

royalties

ASCAP, 259-260

locations, 262

membership, 260

payment procedure, 261-262

showcases and awards, 260

BMI, 262

locations, 266-267

membership, 263

payment procedure, 264-266

seminars, workshops, and showcases, 263-264

copyright basics, 267

cautions, 268

registration, 268

demonstration records, 204

SESAC, locations, 267

rules

craftsmanship, 284-285

scoring a film, 168-169

S

Sager, Carole Bayer, 277

samplers, home-studio equipment, 236

saturation point, home-studio equipment, 236

Sayer, Leo, 277

Scarlet Pimpernel, 187

Schalchlin, Steve, Internet miracle, AIDS online diary, 272-273

schemes, rhyme, 84-85

scorers (orchestration of a film), 159-170

adjusting to titles, 166

asking questions and doing the research, 165

capturing the essence of the movie, 164

combining formal study with practical experience, 169-170

following the right leader, 164

making yourself known and heard, 160

preparing songs ahead of time, 162

providing reassurances, 164-165

respecting the material, 162

rules, 168-169

spotting notes, 166

studying publications, 161

underscoring, 163-164

working out a strategy, 163

working with music supervisors, 165-166

Scoring for Films, 164

searching colorful rhyme words, dictionaries, 82-83

Seattle Songwriting Workshop Web site, 295

seeking a partner, 52-53

advertisements, 53

ASCAP, 54

BMI, 54

establishing industry contacts, 53

local, 52

long shots, 54

SESAC, 54

working with an artist, 54

selling your songs, 212

creative selling, 220

finding common denominators in an artist's work, 213

personal casting, 213-215

publishers, 215-218

being your own publisher, 220

signing with a publisher, 218-220

what publishers do for you, 216

with production companies, 216

researching who needs new material, 212-213

Sellwood Publishing, 294

seminars, BMI, 263-264

senses, developing visual lifestyle, 76-77

paying attention to how people talk, 77

recording impressions, 77

smell, 76

sound, 76

taste, 76

touch, 76

sequencer devices, home-studio equipment, 236

SESAC (Society of European Stage Authors and Composers), 54, 258-267, 294

sessions, recording, making music in home studios, 241-242

setting the tone, titles, 61

built-in drama, 61-62

hot-blooded, 62-63

message in the music, 62

pleading, hoping, and begging, 62

powerful emotion, 63

Seven Brides for Seven Brothers, 183

SGA (Songwriter's Guild of America), 294

Copyright Act of 1976, 270

creed, 269

membership, 269

songwriter's contract, 269

Shakespearean plots (musicals), 189

Showboat, 15

showcases

ASCAP, 260

BMI, 263-264

signal processors, home-studio equipment, 236

signing

labels

major-league labels, 229-230

minor labels, 230

publisher, 218-220

simple and straightforward titles, 59-60

simplicity (country music current), 129

Sinatra, Frank, 17

singability, melodies

chord progressions, 102-103

intervals, 102

singers/songwriters

agents, 224

major agencies, 225

small agencies, 224

cabaret artists, 230-231

contracts, Songwriter's Guild of America, 269

feeding the media, 228-229

lawyers' fees, 226

personal managers, mutual obsession, 225

qualities, 226

appearances, 227

Russ Regan's rules, 227

signing with a label, 229

major-league labels, 229-230

minor labels, 230

Slang! 83

smell, attention to use in lyrics, 76

Smokey Joe's Café, 185

Society of European Stage Authors and Composers. *See* SESAC

soft rock era, 23

solo singer demos, 201

songs

charm, 175

placement in musicals, 174-175

producing, 243-245

being a director, 246

budgeting, 247

choosing how involved you will be, 246

cutting the best track, 249

earnings, 248

experimentation, 250-252

job of a producer, 245

musical approaches, 249-250

planning a recording date, 246-247

rehearsals, 248

top producers, 252-254

working with your engineer, 247

step-out songs, 175

submitting, 9

cassette recording, 10

lead sheets versus lyric sheets, 11

preparing lead sheets, 11-12

Songwriter's Guild of America. *See* SGA

Songwriter's Market, 291

Songwriter's Rhyming, 83

Songwriter's Rhyming Dictionary, 83

Sony Music Publishing, 294

Sophisticated Ladies, 185

soul era, 23

sound, attention to use in lyrics, 76

Sound of Music, 17

South Pacific, 17

Southern Songwriters Guild, Inc., 294

Southern soul, 141

spirituality (country music current), 128

spoken dialogue (country music current), 129

spotting notes, scorers, 166

spouses as partners, 51

Springsteen, Bruce, 21

stage musicals

creating illusions of reality, 181

including as many songs as desired, 183

writing songs with energy and an edge, 182

getting your musical on stage, 189

angels, 190

cutting a CD, 192

finding a theater, 192

local productions, 190-191

organizing a workshop, 191-192

producer's viewpoint, 193

releasing hits from the show, 193-194

taking it on the road, 192

talent scouting, 191

writing for popular in-person performers, 194

Starlight Express, 186

step-out songs, 175

Steve Schalchlin's Survival Site (Web site), 295

structure, 85-86
    bridges, 87
studios
    choosing for record-
      ing demos, 205
    home. *See* home
      studios
studying Grammy cate-
    gories, 280-284
    Best Country Song,
      283
    Best R&B, 282
    Best Rock Song, 282
    Best Song Written for
      Motion Picture,
      Television or other
      Visual Media, 283
    Diane Warren songs,
      281
    Song of the Year, 281
submitting songs,
    supplies, 9
    cassette recording, 10
    lead sheets versus
      lyric sheets, 11
    preparing lead sheets,
      11-12
Sunset Boulevard, 188
Super (S) Bonus
    Payment rate (BMI),
    265
supervisors, music,
    scorers association
    with, 165-166
supplies, preserving
    ideas and submitting
    songs, 9

cassette recording, 10
lead sheets versus
    lyric sheets, 11
preparing lead sheets,
    11-12
Sweeney Todd, 188
sync mode, home-studio
    equipment, 236
sync track, home-studio
    equipment, 236
synchronizers, home-
    studio equipment, 236
synethesia, 78
synthesized music versus
    live, making music in
    home studios, 239
synthesizers, home-
    studio equipment, 236

T

talent scouting, getting
    your musical on stage,
    191
taste, attention to use in
    lyrics, 76
*Techniques of
    Orchestration*, 164
television musicals, 172
temp tracks, 166
tempo
    maintaining for
      demos, 206
    repetition, 92
testing hooks, 94
Theater Directory, 192
theaters, locating for
    your stage musical, 192

thinking in colors, 78
through-sung, 186
Titanic, 185
titles, 59
    characters, 60-61
    first lines, 67-68
    inspirations, 64
      book titles, 64
      dance songs, 64
      geographic titles, 65
      one-word titles, 64
    setting the tone, 61
      built-in drama,
        61-62
      hot-blooded, 62-63
      message in the
        music, 62
      pleading, hoping,
        and begging, 62
      powerful emotion,
        63
    simple and straight-
      forward, 59-60
    storing, 65
    words that work, 65
      candles, 66
      cry and tears, 66
      kiss, 67
      letters, 66
      numbers, 67
      only, 67
      sweet, 66

Tonos (songwriter's Web site), 277-278
  Demo Derby, 278
  Road to Fame Challenge, 278
top producers, 252
  Afanasieff, Walter, 252
  Ahern, Brian, 252
  Argent, Rod, 252
  Bacharach, Burt, 252
  Bascombe, Dave, 252
  Benson, Howard, 253
  Blake, Tchad, 253
  Chiccarelli, Joe, 253
  Clivilles, Robert, 253
  Cole, David, 253
  Cuscuna, Michael, 253
  Davies, Rhett, 253
  Fogerty, John, 253
  Garrett, Snuff, 253
  Johns, Andy, 253
  Jones, Quincy, 253
  Kaye, Lenny, 254
  Lange, Robert John "Mutt," 254
  Z., David, 253
Toronto Musicians' Association, 294
touch, attention to use in lyrics, 76
traditional country (country music genre), 131

tragedy, as universal songwriting theme, 29-30
training (musical), 3-4
  counterpoint, 5
  preserving ideas and submitting songs, 9
    cassette recording, 10
    lead sheets versus lyric sheets, 11
    preparing lead sheets, 11-12
  prestige versus poverty, 5-6
  putting your knowledge to work, 8
    deejaying, 9
    letting the music keep you going, 9
    music critics or commentators, 9
    teaching, 8
  while employed, 6-7
    accepting offers, 8
    accompanists, 7
    joining an orchestra, 8
    local gigs, 7
    session playing, 7
transposing, 205
Tucker, Sophie, 14
Two Gentlemen from Verona, 189
Tympany Five, Louis Jordan, 137

U

U.S. Government Copyright Office, 10
underscoring, 160-164
union of words and music. *See* prosody
unisex singer demos, 201
universal feelings (country music current), 128
universal themes (generating ideas), 29
  apologies, 31
  blues, 29
  breaking up, 30
  endless love, 30
  faithlessness, 30
  nostalgia, 31
  pride in parents, 30
  tragedy, 29-30
Unsinkable Molly Brown, 183
Upper-Level (U) Bonus Payment rate (BMI), 265
USA Songwriting Competition, 298

V

vaudeville, history of songwriting, 13
verses versus hooks, 95

VH1, history of songwriting, 21
movies, 21
videos, 22
videos, history of songwriting, 22
visual imagery (country music current), 128
visual songwriters, 71
attention to senses, 76-77
paying attention to how people talk, 77
recording impressions, 77
smell, 76
sound, 76
taste, 76
touch, 76
listening to music, 78
thinking in colors, 78
visual lifestyles, 72
analyzing nonvisual lyrics, 74
avoiding verbose, 76
concentrating on ordinary activities, 75
landscapes, 72-73
noting drama in details, 73-74
read incessantly, 73
starting with cereal, 72
studying consistently visual writers, 74
voiceover musicals, 173
vowels, 87

W

Warner/Chappell Music, Inc., 295
Warren, Diane, 281
Web sites
ASCAP (American Society of Composers, Authors and Publishers), 292
ASN (All Songwriter's Network), 295
Billboard On Line, 295
BMI (Broadcast Music, Inc.), 292
Harmony Central, 295
Jeff Jackson Songwriting and Music Business Page, 295
Jeff Mallett's Songwriter Site, 295
Lyrical Line, 295
Online Thesaurus, 295
Seattle Songwriting Workshop, 295
Steve Schalchlin's Survival Site, 295
Words in over 400 dictionaries, 295

Webster's Compact Rhyming Dictionary, 83
western swing (country music genre), 130
Will Rogers Follies, 187
women's movement, history of songwriting, 20
Words By (contest), 298
Words in over 400 dictionaries Web site, 295
words that work (song titles), 65
candles, 66
cry and tears, 66
kiss, 67
letters, 66
numbers, 67
only, 67
sweet, 66
Words to Rhyme With, 84
work habits, partnerships, 49
working styles (songwriting process), 37-43
attention to titles, 42
creating songs for artists, 39
as a composer, 39
as a lyricist, 39-40
defined borders, 42
feeling your way to creativity, 45
major songwriters, 40-41
David, Hal, 40
Newman, Randy, 41

Rice, Tim, 40

Rodgers, Richard, 40

practicing lyrics and melodies, 41-43

rhythm in your mind, 41

rhythmic pulse, 44

working the Internet, 276

workshops

BMI, 263-264

Internet, 278

workstation, digital music, home-studio equipment, 238

World War II, history of songwriting, 16

writer's block, banishing, 26

focus and concentration, 26

satisfying yourself, 27

Writer's Rhyming, 83

X–Y–Z

Yamaha EX5, 208

Your Own Thing, 189

Z., David (producer), 253

Ziegfeld, Florenz (vaudeville), 13

Zomba Music Publishing, 295